Hands-On Neural Network Programming with C#

Add powerful neural network capabilities to your C# enterprise applications

Matt R. Cole

BIRMINGHAM - MUMBAI

Hands-On Neural Network Programming with C#

Commissioning Editor: Pravin Dhandre
Acquisition Editor: Divya Poojari
Content Development Editor: Unnati Guha
Technical Editor: Dinesh Chaudhary
Copy Editor: Safis Editing
Project Coordinator: Manthan Patel
Proofreader: Safis Editing
Indexer: Rekha Nair
Graphics: Jisha Chirayil
Production Coordinator: Nilesh Mohite

First published: September 2018

Production reference: 1270918

Published by Packt Publishing Ltd.
Livery Place
35 Livery Street
Birmingham
B3 2PB, UK.

ISBN 978-1-78961-201-1

www.packtpub.com

This book is dedicated to my always supportive and loving wife, Nedda.
I also want to thank the hard-working and professional team at Packt
for their hard work and dedication to bringing all my books to market.

`mapt.io`

Mapt is an online digital library that gives you full access to over 5,000 books and videos, as well as industry leading tools to help you plan your personal development and advance your career. For more information, please visit our website.

Why subscribe?

- Spend less time learning and more time coding with practical eBooks and Videos from over 4,000 industry professionals

- Improve your learning with Skill Plans built especially for you

- Get a free eBook or video every month

- Mapt is fully searchable

- Copy and paste, print, and bookmark content

Packt.com

Did you know that Packt offers eBook versions of every book published, with PDF and ePub files available? You can upgrade to the eBook version at `www.packt.com` and as a print book customer, you are entitled to a discount on the eBook copy. Get in touch with us at `customercare@packtpub.com` for more details.

At `www.packt.com`, you can also read a collection of free technical articles, sign up for a range of free newsletters, and receive exclusive discounts and offers on Packt books and eBooks.

Contributors

About the author

Matt R. Cole is a developer and author with 30 years' experience. Matt is the owner of Evolved AI Solutions, a provider of advanced Machine Learning/Bio-AI, Microservice and Swarm technologies. Matt is recognized as a leader in Microservice and Artificial Intelligence development and design. As an early pioneer of VOIP, Matt developed the VOIP system for NASA for the International Space Station and Space Shuttle. Matt also developed the first Bio Artificial Intelligence framework which completely integrates mirror and canonical neurons. In his spare time Matt authors books, and continues his education taking every available course in advanced mathematics, AI/ML/DL, Quantum Mechanics/Physics, String Theory and Computational Neuroscience.

About the reviewers

Gaurav Aroraa has an M.Phil in computer science. He is a Microsoft MVP, certified as a scrum trainer/coach, XEN for ITIL-F, and APMG for PRINCE-F and PRINCE-P. Gaurav serves as a mentor at IndiaMentor and webmaster at dotnetspider, and he cofounded Innatus Curo Software LLC. Over more than 19 years of his career, he has mentored over a thousand students and professionals in the industry. You can reach Gaurav via Twitter @g_arora.

Rich Pizzo has many years of experience in the design and development of software and systems. He was a senior architect and project lead, especially in the realm of financial engineering and trading systems. He was the chief technologist at two companies. His knowledge and expertise in digital electronics left its mark in the software domain, as well in providing heterogeneous solutions to tough optimization problems. He has come up with many unique solutions for maximizing computing performance, utilizing Altera FPGAs and the Quartus development environment and test suite.

Packt is searching for authors like you

If you're interested in becoming an author for Packt, please visit `authors.packtpub.com` and apply today. We have worked with thousands of developers and tech professionals, just like you, to help them share their insight with the global tech community. You can make a general application, apply for a specific hot topic that we are recruiting an author for, or submit your own idea.

Table of Contents

Preface

This book will help users learn how to develop and program neural networks in C#, as well as how to add this exciting and powerful technology to their own applications. Using many open source packages as well as custom software, we will work our way from simple concepts and theory to powerful technology that everyone can use.

Who this book is for

This book is for the C# .NET developer looking to learn how to add neural network technology and techniques to their applications.

What this book covers

Chapter 1, *A Quick Refresher*, give you a basic refresher on neural networks.

Chapter 2, Building our First Neural Network Together, shows what activations are, what their purpose is, and how they appear visually. We will also present a small C# application to visualize each using open source packages such as Encog, Aforge, and Accord.

Chapter 3, Decision Trees and Random Forests, helps you to understand what decision trees and random forests are and how they can be used.

Chapter 4, *Face and Motion Detection*, will have you use the Accord.Net machine learning framework to connect to your local video recording device and capture real-time images of whatever is within the camera's field of view. Any face in the field of view will be then tracked.

Chapter 5, *Training CNNs Using ConvNetSharp*, will focus on how to train CNNs with the open source package ConvNetSharp. Examples will be used to illustrate the concepts for the user.

Chapter 6, *Training Autoencoders Using RNNSharp*, will have you use the autoencoders of the open source package RNNSharp to parse and handle various corpuses of text.

Chapter 7, *Replacing Back Propagation with PSO*, presents how particle swarm optimization can replace neural network training methods such as back propagation for training a neural network.

Chapter 8, *Function Optimizations: How and Why*, introduces you to function optimization, which is an integral part of every neural network.

Chapter 9, *Finding Optimal Parameters*, will show you how to easily find the most optimal parameters for your neural network functions using Numeric and Heuristic Optimization techniques.

Chapter 10, *Object Detection with TensorFlowSharp*, will expose the reader to the open source package TensorFlowSharp.

Chapter 11, *Time Series Prediction and LSTM Using CNTK*, will see you using the Microsoft Cognitive Toolkit, formerly known as CNTK, as well as long short-term memory (LSTM), to accomplish time series prediction.

Chapter 12, *GRUs Compared to LSTMs, RNNs, and Feedforward Networks*, deals with Gated Recurrent Units (GRUs), including how they compare to other types of neural network.

Appendix A, *Activation Function Timings*, shows different activation functions and their respective plots.

Appendix B, *Function Optimization Reference*, includes different optimization functions.

To get the most out of this book

In this book, we assume the reader has a basic knowledge and familiarity with C# .NET software development and knows their way around Microsoft Visual Studio.

Download the example code files

You can download the example code files for this book from your account at www.packt.com. If you purchased this book elsewhere, you can visit www.packt.com/support and register to have the files emailed directly to you.

You can download the code files by following these steps:

1. Log in or register at www.packt.com.
2. Select the **SUPPORT** tab.

3. Click on **Code Downloads & Errata**.
4. Enter the name of the book in the **Search** box and follow the onscreen instructions.

Once the file is downloaded, please make sure that you unzip or extract the folder using the latest version of:

- WinRAR/7-Zip for Windows
- Zipeg/iZip/UnRarX for Mac
- 7-Zip/PeaZip for Linux

The code bundle for the book is also hosted on GitHub at `https://github.com/PacktPublishing/Hands-On-Neural-Network-Programming-with-CSharp`. In case there's an update to the code, it will be updated on the existing GitHub repository.

We also have other code bundles from our rich catalog of books and videos available at `https://github.com/PacktPublishing/`. Check them out!

Download the color images

We also provide a PDF file that has color images of the screenshots/diagrams used in this book. You can download it here: `http://www.packtpub.com/sites/default/files/downloads/9781789612011_ColorImages.pdf`.

Code in Action

Visit the following link to check out videos of the code being run: `http://bit.ly/2DlRfgO`.

Conventions used

There are a number of text conventions used throughout this book.

`CodeInText`: Indicates code words in text, database table names, folder names, filenames, file extensions, pathnames, dummy URLs, user input, and Twitter handles. Here is an example: "Mount the downloaded `WebStorm-10*.dmg` disk image file as another disk in your system."

A block of code is set as follows:

```
m_va.Copy(vtmp, m_bestVectors[i])
m_va.Sub(vtmp, particlePosition);
m_va.MulRand(vtmp, m_c1);
m_va.Add(m_velocities[i], vtmp);
```

When we wish to draw your attention to a particular part of a code block, the relevant lines or items are set in bold:

```
BasicNetworknetwork = EncogUtility.SimpleFeedForward(2, 2, 0, 1, false);
///Create a scoring/fitness object
ICalculateScore score = new TrainingSetScore(trainingSet);
```

Bold: Indicates a new term, an important word, or words that you see onscreen. For example, words in menus or dialog boxes appear in the text like this. Here is an example: "Select **System info** from the **Administration** panel."

Warnings or important notes appear like this.

Tips and tricks appear like this.

Get in touch

Feedback from our readers is always welcome.

General feedback: If you have questions about any aspect of this book, mention the book title in the subject of your message and email us at customercare@packtpub.com.

Errata: Although we have taken every care to ensure the accuracy of our content, mistakes do happen. If you have found a mistake in this book, we would be grateful if you would report this to us. Please visit www.packt.com/submit-errata, selecting your book, clicking on the Errata Submission Form link, and entering the details.

Piracy: If you come across any illegal copies of our works in any form on the Internet, we would be grateful if you would provide us with the location address or website name. Please contact us at copyright@packt.com with a link to the material.

If you are interested in becoming an author: If there is a topic that you have expertise in and you are interested in either writing or contributing to a book, please visit authors.packtpub.com.

Reviews

Please leave a review. Once you have read and used this book, why not leave a review on the site that you purchased it from? Potential readers can then see and use your unbiased opinion to make purchase decisions, we at Packt can understand what you think about our products, and our authors can see your feedback on their book. Thank you!

For more information about Packt, please visit packt.com.

A Quick Refresher 1

Welcome to *Hands-On Neural Network Development Using C#*. I want to thank you for purchasing this book and for taking this journey with us. It seems as if, everywhere you turn, everywhere you go, all you hear and read about is machine learning, artificial intelligence, deep learning, neuron this, artificial that, and on and on. And, to add to all that excitement, everyone you talk to has a slightly different idea about the meaning of each of those terms.

In this chapter, we are going to go over some very basic neural network terminology to set the stage for future chapters. We need to be speaking the same language, just to make sure that everything we do in later chapters is crystal clear.

I should also let you know that the goal of the book is to get you, a C# developer, up and running as fast as possible. To do this, we will use as many open source libraries as possible. We must do a few custom applications, but we've provided the source code for these as well. In all cases, we want you to be able to add this functionality to your applications with maximal speed and minimal effort.

OK, let's begin.

Neural networks have been around for very many years but have made a resurgence over the past few years and are now a hot topic. And that, my friends, is why this book is being written. The goal here is to help you get through the weeds and into the open so you can navigate your neural path to success. There is a specific focus in this book on C# .NET developers. I wanted to make sure that the C# developers out there had handy resources that could be of some help in their projects, rather than the Python, R, and MATLAB code we more commonly see. If you have Visual Studio installed and a strong desire to learn, you are ready to begin your journey.

First, let's make sure we're clear on a couple of things. In writing this book, the assumption was made that you, the reader, had limited exposure to neural networks. If you do have some exposure, that is great; you may feel free to jump to the sections that interest you the most. I also assumed that you are an experienced C# developer, and have built applications using C#, .NET, and Visual Studio, although I made no assumptions as to which versions of each you may have used. The goal is not about C# syntax, the .NET framework, or Visual Studio itself. Once again, the purpose is to get as many valuable resources into the hands of developers, so they can embellish their code and create world-class applications.

Now that we've gotten that out of the way, I know you're excited to jump right in and start coding, but to make you productive, we first must spend some time going over some basics. A little bit of theory, some fascinating insights into the whys and wherefores, and we're going to throw in a few visuals along the way to help with the rough-and-tough dry stuff. Don't worry; we won't go too deep on the theory, and, in a few pages from here, you'll be writing and going through source code!

Also, keep in mind that research in this area is rapidly evolving. What is the latest and greatest today is old news next month. Therefore, consider this book an overview of different research and opinions. It is not the be-all-and-end-all bible of everything neural network-related, nor should it be perceived to be. You are very likely to encounter someone else with different opinions from that of the writer. You're going to find people who will write apps and functions differently. That's great—gather all the information that you can, and make informed choices on your own. Only doing by that will you increase your knowledge base.

This chapter will include the following topics:

- Neural network overview
- The role of neural networks in today's enterprises
- Types of learning
- Understanding perceptions
- Understanding activation functions
- Understanding back propagation

Technical requirements

Basic knowledge of C# is a must to understand the applications that we will develop in this book. Also, Microsoft Visual Studio (Any version) is a preferred software to develop applications.

Neural network overview

Let's start by defining exactly what we are going to call a neural network. Let me first note that you may also hear a neural network called an **Artificial Neural Network (ANN)**. Although personally I do not like the term *artificial*, we'll use those terms interchangeably throughout this book.

> *"Let's state that a neural network, in its simplest form, is a system comprising several simple but highly interconnected elements; each processes information based upon their response to external inputs."*

Did you know that neural networks are more commonly, but loosely, modeled after the cerebral cortex of a mammalian brain? Why didn't I say that they were modeled after humans? Because there are many instances where biological and computational studies are used from brains from rats, monkeys, and, yes, humans. A large neural network may have hundreds or maybe even thousands of processing units, where as a mammalian brain has billions. It's the neurons that do the magic, and we could in fact write an entire book on that topic alone.

Here's why I say they do all the magic: If I showed you a picture of Halle Berry, you would recognize her right away. You wouldn't have time to analyze things; you would know based upon a lifetime of collected knowledge. Similarly, if I said the word *pizza* to you, you would have an immediate mental image and possibly even start to get hungry. How did all that happen just like that? Neurons! Even though the neural networks of today continue to gain in power and speed, they pale in comparison to the ultimate neural network of all time, the human brain. There is so much we do not yet know or understand about this neural network; just wait and see what neural networks will become once we do!

Neural networks are organized into *layers* made up of what are called **nodes** or **neurons**. These nodes are the neurons themselves and are interconnected (throughout this book we use the terms *nodes* and *neurons* interchangeably). Information is presented to the input layer, processed by one or more *hidden* layers, then given to the *output* layer for final (or continued further) processing—lather, rinse, repeat!

But what is a neuron, you ask? Using the following diagram, let's state this:

> *"A neuron is the basic unit of computation in a neural network"*

As I mentioned earlier, a neuron is sometimes also referred to as a node or a unit. It receives input from other nodes or external sources and computes an output. Each input has an associated **weight (w1 and w2 below)**, which is assigned based on its relative importance to the other inputs. The node applies a function f (an activation function, which we will learn more about later on) to the weighted sum of its inputs. Although that is an extreme oversimplification of what a neuron is and what it can do, that's basically it.

Let's look visually at the progression from a single neuron into a very deep learning network. Here is what a single neuron looks like visually based on our description:

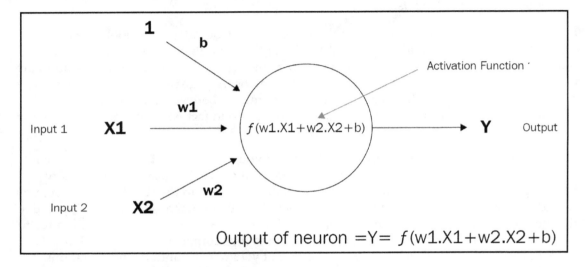

Next, the following diagram shows a very simple neural network comprised of several neurons:

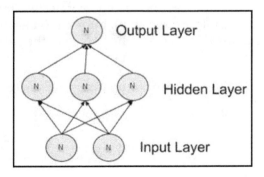

Here is a somewhat more complicated, or deeper, network:

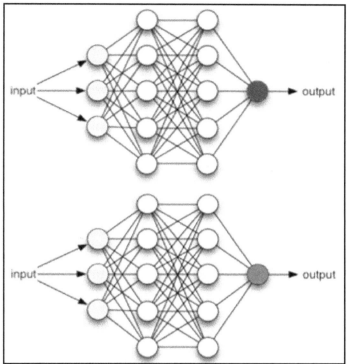

Neural network training

Now that we know what a neural network and neurons are, we should talk about what they do and how they do it. How does a neural network learn? Those of you with children already know the answer to this one. If you want your child to learn what a cat is, what do you do? You show them cats (pictures or real). You want your child to learn what a dog is? Show them dogs. A neural network is conceptually no different. It has a form of **learning rule** that will modify the incoming weights from the input layer, process them through the hidden layers, put them through an activation function, and hopefully will be able to identify, in our case, cats and dogs. And, if done correctly, the cat does not become a dog!

One of the most common learning rules with neural networks is what is known as the **delta rule**. This is a *supervised* rule that is invoked each time the network is presented with another learning pattern. Each time this happens it is called a **cycle** or **epoch**. The invocation of the rule will happen each time that input pattern goes through one or more *forward* propagation layers, and then through one or more *backward* propagation layers.

More simply put, when a neural network is presented with an image it tries to determine what the answer might be. The difference between the correct answer and our guess is the **error** or **error rate**. Our objective is that the error rate gets either minimized or maximized. In the case of minimization, we need the error rate to be as close to 0 as possible for each guess. The closer we are to 0, the closer we are to success.

As we progress, we undertake what is termed a **gradient descent**, meaning we continue along toward what is called the **global minimum**, our lowest possible error, which hopefully is paramount to *success*. We descend toward the global minimum.

Once the network itself is trained, and you are happy, the training cycle can be put to bed and you can move on to the testing cycle. During the testing cycle, only the forward propagation layer is used. The output of this process results in the *model* that will be used for further analysis. Again, no back propagation occurs during testing.

A visual guide to neural networks

In this section, I could type thousands of words trying to describe all of the combinations of neural networks and what they look like. However, no amount of words would do any better than the diagram that follows:

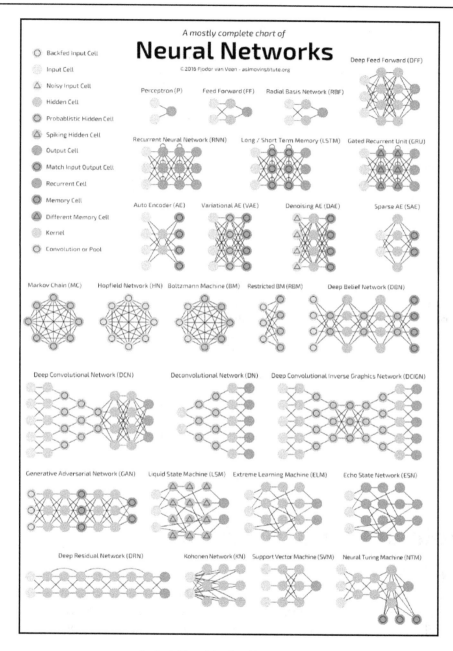

Let's talk about a few of the more common networks from the previous diagram:

- **Perceptron:** This is the simplest feed-forward neural network available, and, as you can see, it does not contain any hidden layers:

- **Feed-forward network:** This network is perhaps the simplest type of artificial neural network devised. It contains multiple neurons (nodes) arranged in **layers**. Nodes from adjacent layers have **connections** or **edges** between them. Each connection has **weights** associated with them:

- **Recurrent neural network (RNN):** RNNs are called *recurrent* because they perform the same task for every element of a sequence, with the output depending on the previous computations. They are also able to look back at previous steps, which form a sort of **short-term memory**:

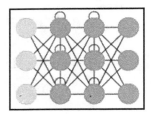

The role of neural networks in today's enterprises

As developers, our main concern is how can we apply what we are learning to real world scenarios. More concretely, in an enterprise environment, what are the opportunities for using a neural network? Here are just a few ideas (out of many) for applications of a neural network:

- In a scenario where relationships between variables are not understood

- In a scenario where relationships are difficult to describe
- In a scenario where the goal is to discover irregular patterns in data
- Classify data to recognize patterns such as animals, vehicles, and so on
- Signal processing
- Image recognition (emotion, sentiment, age, gender, and so on)
- Text translation
- Handwriting recognition
- Autonomous vehicles
- And tons more!

Types of learning

Since we talked about our neural network learning, let's briefly touch on the three different types of learning you should be aware of. They are **supervised**, **unsupervised**, and **reinforcement**.

Supervised learning

If you have a large test dataset that matches up with known results, then supervised learning might be a good choice for you. The neural network will process a dataset; compare its output against the known result, adjust, and repeat. Pretty simple, huh?

Unsupervised learning

If you don't have any test data, and it is possible to somehow derive a cost function from the behavior of the data, then unsupervised learning might be a good choice for you. The neural network will process a dataset, use the `cost` function to tell how much the error rate is, adjust the parameters, then repeat. All this while working in real time!

Reinforcement learning

Our final type of learning is **reinforcement** learning, better known in some circles as **carrot-and-stick**. The neural network will process a dataset, learn from the data, and if our error rate decreases, we get the carrot. If the error rate increases, we get the stick. Enough said, right?

Understanding perceptrons

The most basic element that we will deal with is called the neuron. If we were to take the most basic form of an activation function that a neuron would use, we would have a function that has only two possible results, 1 and 0. Visually, such a function would be represented like this:

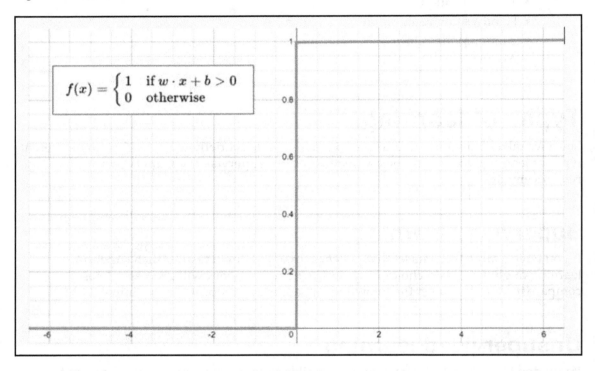

This function returns 1 if the input is positive or 0, otherwise it returns 0. A neuron whose activation function is like this is called a **perceptron**. It is the simplest form of neural network we could develop. Visually, it looks like the following:

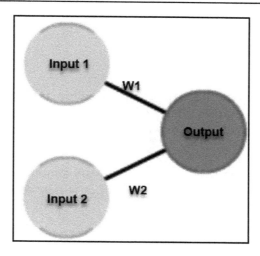

The perceptron follows the feed-forward model, meaning inputs are sent into the neuron, processed, and then produce output. Inputs come in, and output goes out. Let's use an example.

Let's suppose that we have a single perceptron with two inputs as shown previously. For the purposes of this example, input 0 will be x1 and input 1 will be x2. If we assign those two variable values, they will look something like this:

Input 0: x1 = 12
Input 1: x2 = 4

Each of those inputs must be **weighted**, that is, multiplied by some value, which is often a number between -1 and 1. When we create our perceptron, we begin by assigning them random weights. As an example, Input 0 (**x1**) will have a weight we'll label **w1**, and input 1, **x2** will have a weight we'll label **w2**. Given this, here's how our weights look for this perceptron:

Weight 0: 0.5
Weight 1: -1

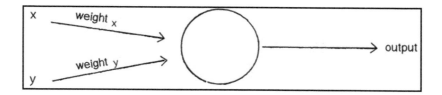

Once the inputs are *weighted*, they now need to be summed. Using the previous example, we would have this:

6 + -4 = 2

That sum would then be passed through an activation function, which we will cover in much more detail in a later chapter. This would generate the output of the perceptron. The activation function is what will ultimately tell the perceptron whether it is *OK to fire*, that is, to activate.

Now, for our activation function we will just use a very simple one. If the sum is positive, the output will be 1. If the sum is negative, the output will be -1. It can't get any simpler than that, right?

So, in pseudo code, our algorithm for our single perceptron looks like the following:

- For every input, multiply that input by its weight
- Sum all the weighted inputs
- Compute the output of the perceptron based on that sum passed through an activation function (the sign of the sum)

Is this useful?

Yes, in fact it is, and let's show you how. Consider an input vector as the coordinates of a point. For a vector with n elements, the point would like it's in a n-dimensional space. Take a sheet of paper, and on this paper, draw a set of points. Now separate those two points by a single straight line. Your piece of paper should now look something like the following:

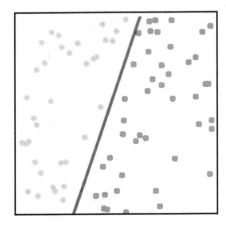

As you can see, the points are now divided into two sets, one set on each side of the line. If we can take a single line and clearly separate all the points, then those two sets are what is known as linearly separable.

Our single perceptron, believe it or not, will be able to learn where this line is, and when your program is complete, the perceptron will also be able to tell whether a single point is above or below the line (or to the left or the right of it, depending upon how the line was drawn).

Let's quickly code a `Perceptron` class, just so it becomes clearer for those of you who love to read code more than words (like me!). The goal will be to create a simple perceptron that can determine which side of the line a point should be on, just like the previous diagram:

```
class Perceptron {

float[] weights;
```

The constructor could receive an argument indicating the number of inputs (in this case three: *x*, *y*, and a bias) and size the array accordingly:

```
Perceptron(int n) {
    weights = new float[n];
    for (int i = 0; i<weights.length; i++) {
```

The `weights` are picked randomly to start with:

```
        weights[i] = random(-1,1);
    }
}
```

Next, we'll need a function for the perceptron to receive its information, which will be the same length as the array of weights, and then return the output value to us. We'll call this `feedforward`:

```
int feedforward(float[] inputs) {
    float sum = 0;
    for (int i = 0; i<weights.length; i++) {
      sum += inputs[i]*weights[i];
    }
```

The result is the sign of the sum, which will be either -1 or +1. In this case, the perceptron is attempting to guess which side of the line the output should be on:

```
    return activate(sum);
}
```

Thus far, we have a minimally functional perceptron that should be able to make an educated guess as to where our point will lie.

Create the `Perceptron`:

```
Perceptron p = new Perceptron(3);
```

The input is 3 values: *x, y,* and bias:

```
float[] point = {5,-2,19};
```

Obtain the answer:

```
int result = p.feedforward(point);
```

The only thing left that will make our perceptron more valuable is the ability to train it rather than have it make educated guesses. We do that by creating a `train` function such as this:

1. We will introduce a new variable to control the learning rate:

    ```
    float c = 0.01;
    ```

2. We will also provide the inputs and the known answer:

    ```
    void train(float[] inputs, int desired) {
    ```

3. And we will make an educated guess according to the inputs provided:

    ```
    int guess = feedforward(inputs);
    ```

4. We will compute the `error`, which is the difference between the answer and our `guess`:

    ```
    float error = desired - guess;
    ```

5. And, finally, we will adjust all the weights according to the error and learning constant:

    ```
    for (int i = 0; i<weights.length; i++) {
        weights[i] += c * error * inputs[i];
    ```

So, now that you know and see what a perceptron is, let's add **activation functions** into the mix and take it to the next level!

Understanding activation functions

An activation function is added to the output end of a neural network to determine the output. It usually will map the resultant values somewhere in the range of -1 to 1, depending upon the function. It is ultimately used to determine whether a neuron will *fire* or *activate*, as in a light bulb going on or off.

The activation function is the last piece of the network before the output and could be considered the supplier of the output value. There are many kinds of activation function that can be used, and this diagram highlights just a very small subset of these:

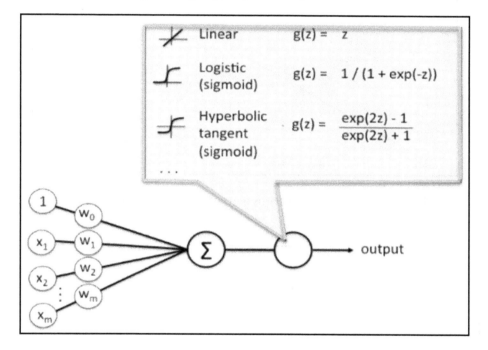

There are two types of activation function—linear and non-linear:

- **Linear**: A linear function is that which is on, or nearly on, a straight line, as depicted here:

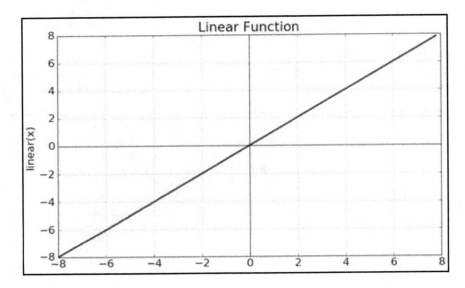

- **Non-linear**: A non-linear function is that which is not on a straight line, as depicted here:

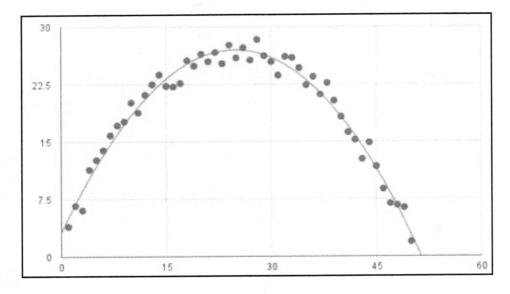

Visual activation function plotting

When dealing with activation functions, it is important that you visually understand what an activation function looks like before you use it. We are going to plot, and then benchmark, several activation functions for you to see:

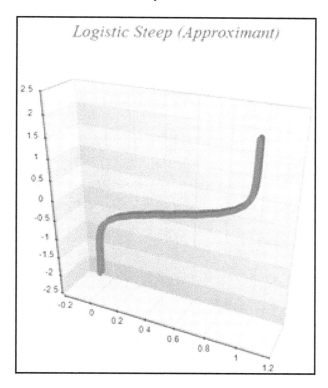

This is what the logistic steep approximation and Swish activation function look like when they are plotted individually. As there are many types of activation function, the following shows what all our activation functions are going to look like when they are plotted together:

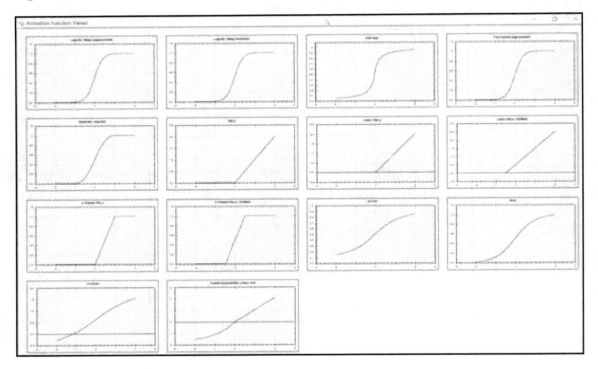

 Note: You can download the program that produces the previous output from the SharpNeat project on GitHub `https://github.com/colgreen/sharpneat`.

At this point, you may be wondering why we even care what the plots look like—great point. We care because you are going to be using these quite a bit once you progress to hands-on experience, as you dive deeper into neural networks. It's very handy to be able to know whether your activation function will place the value of your neuron in the on or off state, and what range it will keep or need the values in. You will no doubt encounter and/or use activation functions in your career as a machine-learning developer, and knowing the difference between a Tanh and a LeakyRelu activation function is very important.

Function plotting

For this example, we are going to use the open source package **SharpNeat**. It is one of the most powerful machine- learning platforms anywhere, and it has a special activation function plotter included with it. You can find the latest version of SharpNeat at `https://github.com/colgreen/sharpneat`. For this example, we will use the **ActivationFunctionViewer** project included as shown:

ActivationFnBenchmarks	ActivationFnBenchmarks project upgraded to new format.
ActivationFunctionViewer	Multiple plots in a grid arrangement. Submission from Matt Cole, with...
Box2dTestHarness	Updated assembly versions to 2.4.0.0.
EfficacySampler	ActivationFnBenchmarks project upgraded to new format.
SharpNeatConsole	Updated assembly versions to 2.4.0.0.
SharpNeatDomains	Re-instated RbfFnRegressionExperiment. Addresses #29.
SharpNeatDomainsExtra	Redzen nuget update 7.2.2 -> 7.2.3
SharpNeatGUI	Redzen nuget update 7.2.2 -> 7.2.3
SharpNeatLib	Applied volatile modifier to run state variables that are accessed by...
SharpNeatViewLib	Genome view rendering tweaks:
Settings.StyleCop	fixed untracked files
SharpNeat.sln	Solution file version number bumper from VisualStudioVersion 14.0.254...
clean_up.bat	fixed untracked files

Once you have that project open, search for the `PlotAllFunctions` function. It is this function that handles the plotting of all the activation functions as previously shown. Let's go over this function in detail:

```
private void PlotAllFunctions()
{
    Clear everything out.
    MasterPane master = zed.MasterPane;
    master.PaneList.Clear();
    master.Title.IsVisible = true;
    master.Margin.All = 10;

    Here is the section that will plot each individual function.
    PlotOnMasterPane(Functions.LogisticApproximantSteep, "Logistic
```

```
Steep (Approximant)");

PlotOnMasterPane(Functions.LogisticFunctionSteep, "Logistic Steep
(Function)");

PlotOnMasterPane(Functions.SoftSign, "Soft Sign");

PlotOnMasterPane(Functions.PolynomialApproximant, "Polynomial
Approximant");

PlotOnMasterPane(Functions.QuadraticSigmoid, "Quadratic Sigmoid");

PlotOnMasterPane(Functions.ReLU, "ReLU");

PlotOnMasterPane(Functions.LeakyReLU, "Leaky ReLU");

PlotOnMasterPane(Functions.LeakyReLUShifted, "Leaky ReLU
(Shifted)");

PlotOnMasterPane(Functions.SReLU, "S-Shaped ReLU");

PlotOnMasterPane(Functions.SReLUShifted, "S-Shaped ReLU
(Shifted)");

PlotOnMasterPane(Functions.ArcTan, "ArcTan");

PlotOnMasterPane(Functions.TanH, "TanH");

PlotOnMasterPane(Functions.ArcSinH, "ArcSinH");

PlotOnMasterPane(Functions.ScaledELU, "Scaled Exponential Linear
Unit");

Reconfigure the Axis
zed.AxisChange();

Layout the graph panes using a default layout
using (Graphics g = this.CreateGraphics())
{
    master.SetLayout(g, PaneLayout.SquareColPreferred);
}
```

MainPlot Function

Behind the scenes, the 'Plot' function is what is responsible for
executing   and plotting each function.

```
private void Plot(Func<double, double> fn, string fnName, Color
```

```
graphColor, GraphPane gpane = null)
{
    const double xmin = -2.0;
    const double xmax = 2.0;
    const int resolution = 2000;
    zed.IsShowPointValues = true;
    zed.PointValueFormat = "e";

    var pane = gpane ?? zed.GraphPane;
    pane.XAxis.MajorGrid.IsVisible = true;
    pane.YAxis.MajorGrid.IsVisible = true;
    pane.Title.Text = fnName;
    pane.YAxis.Title.Text = string.Empty;
    pane.XAxis.Title.Text = string.Empty;
    double[] xarr = new double[resolution];
    double[] yarr = new double[resolution];
    double incr = (xmax - xmin) / resolution;
    doublex = xmin;

    for(int i=0; i<resolution; i++, x += incr)
    {
        xarr[i] = x;
        yarr[i] = fn(x);
    }

    PointPairList list1 = new PointPairList(xarr, yarr);
    LineItem li = pane.AddCurve(string.Empty, list1, graphColor,
    SymbolType.None);
    li.Symbol.Fill = new Fill(Color.White);
    pane.Chart.Fill = new Fill(Color.White,
    Color.LightGoldenrodYellow, 45.0F);
}
```

The main point of interest from the earlier code is highlighted in yellow. This is where the activation function that we passed in gets executed and its value used for the y axis plot value. The famous **ZedGraph** open source plotting package is used for all graph plotting. Once each function is executed, the respective plot will be made.

Understanding back propagation

Back propagation, which is short for **the backward propagation of errors**, is an algorithm for supervised learning of neural networks using gradient descent. This calculates what is known as **the gradient of the error** function, with respect to the network's weights. It is a generalized form of the delta rule for perceptrons all the way to multi-layer feed-forward neural networks.

Unlike forward propagation, back-prop calculates the gradients by moving backwards through the network. The gradient of the final layer of weights is calculated first, and the gradient of the first layer is hence calculated last. With the recent popularity in deep learning for image and speech recognition, back-prop has once again taken the spotlight. It is, for all intents and purposes, an efficient algorithm, and today's version utilizes GPUs to further improve performance.

Lastly, because the computations for back-prop are dependent upon the activations and outputs from the forward phase (non-error term for all layers, including hidden), all of these values must be computed prior to the backwards phase beginning. It is therefore a requirement that the forward phase precede the backward phase for every iteration of gradient descent.

Forward and back propagation differences

Let's take a moment to clarify the difference between feed forward and back propagation. Once you understand this, you can visualize and understand much better how the entire neural network flows.

In neural networks, you forward-propagate data to get the output and then compare it with the real intended value to get the error, which is the difference between what the data is suppose to be versus what your machine-learning algorithm actually thinks it is. To minimize that error, you now must *propagate* backward by finding the derivative of error, with respect to each weight, and then subtract this value from the weight itself.

The basic learning that is being done in a neural network is training neurons *when* to get activated, when to fire, and when to be *on* or *off*. Each neuron should activate only for certain types of inputs, not all of them. Therefore, by propagating forward, you see how well your neural network is behaving and find the error(s). After you find out what your network error rate is, you back-propagate and use a form of gradient descent to update new values of the weights. Once again, you will forward-propagate your data to see how well those weights are performing, and then backward-propagate the data to update the weights. This will go on until you reach some minima for error value (hopefully the global minimum and not the local). Again, lather, rinse, repeat!

Summary

In this chapter, we took a brief overview of various neural network terminologies. We reviewed perceptrons, neurons, and back propagation, among other things. In our next chapter, we are going to dive right into coding a complete neural network!

We will cover such topics as neural network training, terminology, synapses, neurons, forward propagation, back propagation, sigmoid function, back propagation, and error calculations.

So, hold onto your hats; the code is coming!

References

- @EVOLVE deep-learning shared information neural network framework, copyright 2016 Matt R Cole, `www.evolvedaisolutions.com`.
- SharpNeat Activation Functions/Viewer: SharpNeat (`https://github.com/colgreen/sharpneat`).

2
Building Our First Neural Network Together

Now that we've had a quick refresher on Neural Networks, I thought that perhaps a good starting point, code-wise, would be for us to write a very simple neural network. We're not going to go crazy; we'll just lay the basic framework for a few functions so that you can get a good idea of what is behind the scenes of many of the APIs that you'll use. From start to finish, we'll develop this network application so that you are familiar with all the basic components that are contained in a neural network. This implementation is not perfect or all-encompassing, nor is it meant to be. As I mentioned, this will merely provide a framework for us to use in the rest of the book. This is a very basic neural network with the added functionality of being able to save and load networks and data. In any event, you will have a foundation from which to write your own neural network and change the world, should you so desire.

In this chapter, we are going to cover the following topics:

- Neural network training
- Terminology
- Synapses
- Neurons
- Forward propagation
- Sigmoid function
- Back propagation
- Error calculations

Technical requirements

You would need to have Microsoft Visual Studio installed on the system.

Check out the following video to see Code in Action: `http://bit.ly/2NYJa5G`.

Our neural network

Let's begin by showing you an of what a simple neural network would look like, visually. It consists of an input layer with 2 inputs, a Hidden Layer with 3 neurons (sometimes called **nodes**), and a final output layer consisting of a single neuron. Of course, neural networks can consist of many more layers (and neurons per layer), and once you get into deep learning you will see much more of this, but for now this will suffice. Remember, each node, which is labeled as follows with an **N**, is an individual neuron – its own little processing brain, if you will:

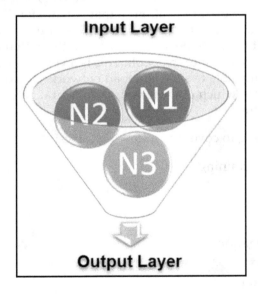

Let's break down the neural network into its three basic parts; inputs, Hidden Layers and outputs:

Inputs: This is the initial data for our network. Each input is a whose output to the Hidden Layer is the initial input value.

Hidden Layers: These are the heart and soul of our network, and all the magic happens. Neurons in this layer are assigned weights for each of their inputs. These weights start off randomized, and are adjusted as the network is trained so that the neuron's output is closer to the expected result (if we are lucky).

Outputs: These are the output our network arrives at after it performs its calculations. The output in our simple case will be either true or false, on or off. The neurons are assigned a weight for each of their inputs, which comes from the previous Hidden Layer. Although it is typically common for there to be only a single output neuron, there's absolutely nothing preventing you from having more, should you need or want more than one.

Neural network training

How do we train a neural network? Basically, we will provide the with a set of input data as well as the results we expect to see, which correspond to those inputs. That data is then run through the network until the network understands what we are looking for. We will train, test, train, test, train, test, on and on until our network understands our data (or doesn't, but that's a whole other conversation). We continue to do this until some designated stop condition is satisfied, such as an error rate threshold. Let's quickly cover some of the terminology we will use while training neural networks.

Back propagation: After our data is run through the network, we to validate that data what we expect to be the correct output. We do this by propagating *backward* (hence backprop or back propagation) through each of the Hidden Layers of our network. The end result is that this adjusts the weights assigned to each of the neuron's inputs in the Hidden Layers as well as our error rate.

Each back propagation layer should, in a perfect world, make our network output closer to what we are expecting, and our error rate will get closer and closer to 0. We may never get to an exact error rate of 0, so even though it may seem not much of a difference, an error rate of 0.0000001 could be more than acceptable to us.

Biases: Biases allow us to modify our function so that we can generate better output for each neuron in our network. In short, a bias allows us to shift the activation function value to the left or the right. Changing the weight changes the steepness or vertical aspect of the Sigmoid.

Momentum: Momentum simply adds a fraction of the previous weight update to the current one. Momentum is used to prevent the system from converging on a local minimum rather than the global minimum. High momentum can be used to help increase the speed of convergence of the system; however, you must be careful as setting this parameter too high can create a risk of overshooting the minimum, which will result in an unstable system. On the other hand, a momentum that is too low cannot reliably avoid local minima, and it can also really slow down the training of the system. So, getting this value correct is paramount for success and something you will spend a considerable amount of time doing.

Sigmoid function: An activation function defines what each neuron's output will be. A Sigmoid function is perhaps the most commonly used activation function. It converts the input into a value which lies between 0 and 1. This function is used to generate our initial weights. A typical Sigmoid function will be able to accept an input value and, from that value, provide both an output value and a derivative.

Learning rate: The learning rate will change the overall learning speed of the system by controlling the size of the weight and bias changes made to the network during the learning phase.

Now that we have this terminology behind us, let's start digging into the code. You should have downloaded the solution from the accompanying software provided for the book, and have it opened in Visual Studio. We use the Community Edition of Visual studio, but you may use whichever version you have.

Feel free to download the software, experiment with it, and embellish it if you need or want to. In your world, your neural network can be anything you like or need it to be, so make it happen. You have the source. Just because you see something one way doesn't make it gospel or written in stone! Learn from what these great open source contributors have provided for us! Remember, this neural network is meant only to give you some idea of the many things that you could do writing your own, as well as teach you some of the basics when it comes to a neural network.

Let's start off by looking at some brief code snippets that will set the stage for the rest of the chapter. We'll start first with a little thing called a **synapse**, which connects one neuron to another. Next, we'll start coding exactly what an individual neuron is, and finally move into discussing forward and backward propagation and what that means to us. We'll show everything in the form of code snippets to make it easier to understand.

Synapses

What is a synapse, you might ask? Simply put, it connects one neuron to another, as well as being a container to hold weight and weight delta values, depicted as follows:

```
public class Synapse
{
    public Guid Id{ get; set; }
    public Neuron InputNeuron{ get; set; }
    public Neuron OutputNeuron{ get; set; }
    public double Weight{ get; set; }
    public double WeightDelta{ get; set; }
}
```

Neurons

We've already discussed what a neuron is, now it's time to express it in code so developers like us can make more sense of it! As you can see, we have both our input and output synapses, our `Bias` and the `Bias Delta`, the `Gradient`, and the actual value of the neuron. The neuron calculates the weighted sum of its inputs, adds a bias, and then decides if the output should `'fire'` – `'be on'`- or not:

```
public class Neuron
{
  public Guid Id{ get; set; }

The synapse that connects to our input side
  public List<Synapse> InputSynapses{ get; set; }

The synapse that connects to our output side
  public List<Synapse> OutputSynapses{ get; set; }
  public double Bias{ get; set; }

Our bias values
  public double BiasDelta{ get; set; }
  public double Gradient{ get; set; }
```

```
The input value to the neuron
  public double Value{ get; set; }

Is the neuron a mirror neuron
public bool IsMirror{ get; set; }

Is the neuron a canonical neuron
public bool IsCanonical{ get; set; }


}
```

Forward propagation

The following is our code for a basic forward propagation process:

```
private void ForwardPropagate(params double[] inputs)
{
  var i = 0;
  InputLayer?.ForEach(a =>a.Value = inputs[i++]);
  HiddenLayers?.ForEach(a =>a.ForEach(b =>b.CalculateValue()));
  OutputLayer?.ForEach(a =>a.CalculateValue());
}
```

To do `ForwardPropagation`, we basically sum all the inputs from each synapse and run the result through our Sigmoid function to get an output. The `CalculateValue` function does this for us.

Sigmoid function

The Sigmoid function is an activation function and, as we previously, perhaps one of the most widely used today. Here's what a Sigmoid function looks like (you do remember our section on activation functions, right?) Its sole purpose (very abstractly) is to bring in the values from the outside edges closer to 0 and 1 without having to worry about values larger than this. This will prevent those values along the edge from running away on us:

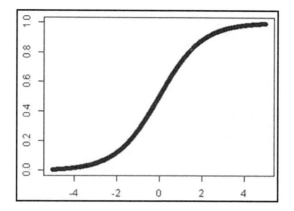

What does a `Sigmoid` function look like in C# code, you might ask? Just like the following:

```
public static class Sigmoid
{
  public static double Output(double x)
  {
    return x < -45.0 ?0.0 : x > 45.0 ? 1.0 : 1.0 / (1.0 + Math.Exp(-x));
  }

  public static double Derivative(double x)
  {
    return x * (1 - x);
  }
}
```

Our `Sigmoid` class will produce the output and the Derivative.

Backward propagation

For back propagation (backprop), we will first calculate the gradient from the output layers, put those values through our Hidden Layer (reversing the direction we took in forward propagation), update the weights, and finally put the value through our output layers, as follows:

```
private void BackPropagate(params double[] targets)
{
  var i = 0;
  OutputLayer?.ForEach(a =>a.CalculateGradient(targets[i++]));
  HiddenLayers?.Reverse();
  HiddenLayers?.ForEach(a =>a.ForEach(b =>b.CalculateGradient()));
  HiddenLayers?.ForEach(a =>a.ForEach(b =>b.UpdateWeights(LearningRate,
```

```
Momentum))));
  HiddenLayers?.Reverse();
  OutputLayer?.ForEach(a =>a.UpdateWeights(LearningRate, Momentum));
}
```

Calculating errors

To calculate our error, we take our actual value and subtract it from our expected value. The closer we are to 0, the better we will be. Note that the following is very little chance that we will ever hit 0, although it could conceivably happen:

```
public double CalculateError(double target)
{
  return target - Value;
}
```

Calculating a gradient

The gradient is calculated by considering the Derivative of the `Sigmoid` function:

```
public double CalculateGradient(double? target = null)
{
  if (target == null)
    return Gradient = OutputSynapses.Sum(a =>a.OutputNeuron.Gradient *
    a.Weight) * Sigmoid.Derivative(Value);

  return Gradient = CalculateError(target.Value) *
Sigmoid.Derivative(Value);
}
```

Updating weights

We update the weights by multiplying the learning rate times our gradient, and then adding in momentum and multiplying by the previous delta. This is then run through each input synapse to calculate the final value:

```
public void UpdateWeights(double learnRate, double momentum)
{
  var prevDelta = BiasDelta;
  BiasDelta = learnRate * Gradient;
  Bias += BiasDelta + momentum * prevDelta;

  foreach (var synapse in InputSynapses)
```

```
  {
    prevDelta = synapse.WeightDelta;
    synapse.WeightDelta = learnRate * Gradient * synapse.InputNeuron.Value;
        synapse.Weight += synapse.WeightDelta + momentum * prevDelta;
  }
}
```

Calculating values

To calculate values, we take the output from our `Sigmoid` function and add to it the bias term:

```
public virtual double CalculateValue()
{
  return Value = Sigmoid.Output(InputSynapses.Sum(a =>a.Weight *
  a.InputNeuron.Value) + Bias);
}
```

Neural network functions

The following basic list contains the functions we are going to develop n order to lay down our neural network foundation:

- Creating a new network
- Importing a network
- Manually entering user data
- Importing a dataset
- Training our network
- Testing our network

With that behind us, let's start coding!

Creating a new network

This menu option will allow us to create a new network from scratch:

```
public NNManager SetupNetwork()
{
    _numInputParameters = 2;

    int[] hidden = new int[2];
    hidden[0] = 3;
    hidden[1] = 1;
    _numHiddenLayers = 1;
    _hiddenNeurons = hidden;
    _numOutputParameters = 1;
    _network = new Network(_numInputParameters, _hiddenNeurons,
    _numOutputParameters);
    return this;
}
```

Notice our return value in this function. This is a fluent interface, meaning that various functions can be chained together into a single statement. Many people prefer this type of interface over the conventional one, but you can feel free to modify the code any way you like. The following is an example of what a fluent interface looks like. Believe it or not, this is a complete neural network:

```
NNManagermgr = new NNManager();
Mgr
.SetupNetwork()
.GetTrainingDataFromUser()
.TrainNetworkToMinimum()
.TestNetwork();
```

Importing an existing network

This function will allow us to import a previously saved network. Again, note the return value that makes this a fluent interface:

```
public static Network ImportNetwork()
{
```

Get the filename of the previously saved network. Once opened, deserialize it into a network structure that we will deal with. (If it didn't work for some reason, abort!):

```
var dn = GetHelperNetwork();
if (dn == null)
return null;
```

Create a `new Network` and a list of neurons to populate:

```
var network = new Network();
  var allNeurons = new List<Neuron>();
```

Copy over the learning rate and the momentum that was previously saved:

```
network.LearningRate = dn.LearningRate;
  network.Momentum = dn.Momentum;
```

Create input layers from our imported network data:

```
foreach (var n in dn.InputLayer)
  {
    var neuron = new Neuron
    {
      Id = n.Id,
      Bias = n.Bias,
      BiasDelta = n.BiasDelta,
      Gradient = n.Gradient,
      Value = n.Value
    };

    network.InputLayer?.Add(neuron);
    allNeurons.Add(neuron);
  }
```

Create our Hidden Layers from our imported network data:

```
foreach (var layer in dn.HiddenLayers)
  {
    var neurons = new List<Neuron>();
    foreach (var n in layer)
    {
      var neuron = new Neuron
      {
        Id = n.Id,
        Bias = n.Bias,
        BiasDelta = n.BiasDelta,
        Gradient = n.Gradient,
        Value = n.Value
      };

      neurons.Add(neuron);
      allNeurons.Add(neuron);
    }
    network.HiddenLayers?.Add(neurons);
  }
```

Create the `OutputLayer` neurons from our imported data:

```
foreach (var n in dn.OutputLayer)
  {
    var neuron = new Neuron
    {
      Id = n.Id,
      Bias = n.Bias,
      BiasDelta = n.BiasDelta,
      Gradient = n.Gradient,
      Value = n.Value
    };

    network.OutputLayer?.Add(neuron);
    allNeurons.Add(neuron);
  }
```

Finally, create the synapses that tie everything together:

```
    foreach (var syn in dn.Synapses)
    {
      var synapse = new Synapse{ Id = syn.Id };
      var inputNeuron = allNeurons.First(x =>x.Id==syn.InputNeuronId);
      var outputNeuron = allNeurons.First(x =>x.Id==syn.OutputNeuronId);
      synapse.InputNeuron = inputNeuron;
      synapse.OutputNeuron = outputNeuron;
      synapse.Weight = syn.Weight;
      synapse.WeightDelta = syn.WeightDelta;

      inputNeuron?.OutputSynapses?.Add(synapse);
      outputNeuron?.InputSynapses?.Add(synapse);
    }
    return network;
  }
```

The following is where we manually enter the data to be used by the network:

```
public NNManager GetTrainingDataFromUser()
{
var numDataSets = GetInput("\tHow many datasets are you going to enter? ",
1, int.MaxValue);

  var newDatasets = new List<NNDataSet>();
  for (var i = 0; i<numDataSets; i++)
  {
    var values = GetInputData($"\tData Set {i + 1}: ");
    if (values == null)
    {
```

```
      return this;
    }

    var expectedResult = GetExpectedResult($"\tExpected Result for Data
    Set {i + 1}: ");
    if (expectedResult == null)
    {
      return this;
    }

    newDatasets.Add(newNNDataSet(values, expectedResult));
  }

  _dataSets = newDatasets;
  return this;
}
```

Importing datasets

The following is how we our datasets:

```
public static List<DataSet>ImportDatasets()
{
  var dialog = new OpenFileDialog
  {
    Multiselect = false,
    Title = "Open Dataset File",
    Filter = "Text File|*.txt;"
  };

  using (dialog)
  {
    if (dialog.ShowDialog() != DialogResult.OK)
    return null;

    using (var file = File.OpenText(dialog.FileName))
    {
```

Deserialize the data and return it:

```
        return
JsonConvert.DeserializeObject<List<DataSet>>(file.ReadToEnd());
    }
  }
}
```

Testing the network

In order to test the network, we to do a simple forward and backward propagation, depicted as follows:

```
public double[] Compute(params double[] inputs)
{
```

Perform forward propagation, as follows:

```
ForwardPropagate(inputs);
```

Return the data, as follows:

```
return OutputLayer.Select(a =>a.Value).ToArray();
}
```

Exporting the network

Export the current network information, as follows:

```
public NNManager ExportNetwork()
{
  Console.WriteLine("\tExporting Network...");
  ExportHelper.ExportNetwork(_network);
  Console.WriteLine("\t**Exporting Complete!**", Color.Green);
  return this;
}
```

Training the network

There are two ways of training the network. One is to a minimum error value, the other is to a maximum error value. Both functions have defaults, although you may wish to make the threshold different for your training, as follows:

```
public NNManager TrainNetworkToMinimum()
{
var minError = GetDouble("\tMinimum Error: ", 0.000000001, 1.0);
Console.WriteLine("\tTraining...");
_network.Train(_dataSets, minError);
Console.WriteLine("\t**Training Complete**", Color.Green);
return this;
}

public NNManager TrainNetworkToMaximum()
{
varmaxEpoch = GetInput("\tMax Epoch: ", 1, int.MaxValue);
if(!maxEpoch.HasValue)
        {
   return this;
        }

Console.WriteLine("\tTraining...");
_network.Train(_dataSets, maxEpoch.Value);
Console.WriteLine("\t**Training Complete**", Color.Green);
return this;
}
```

In both of the preceding function definitions, the neural network `Train` function is called to perform the actual training. This function in turn calls the forward and backward propagation functions for each dataset from within each iteration of the training loop, as follows:

```
public void Train(List<DataSet>dataSets, int numEpochs)
{
  for (var i = 0; i<numEpochs; i++)
  {
    foreach (var dataSet in dataSets)
    {
      ForwardPropagate(dataSet.Values);
      BackPropagate(dataSet.Targets);
    }
  }
}
```

Testing the network

This function allows us to test our network. Again, notice the return value, which makes this a fluent interface. For the most commonly used functions at a higher, more abstract layer, I tried to make the fluent interface available where it would be most beneficial, as follows:

```
public NNManager TestNetwork()
{
Console.WriteLine("\tTesting Network", Color.Yellow);
  while (true)
  {
```

Get the input data from the user, as follows:

```
var values = GetInputData($"\tType{_numInputParameters} inputs: ");
if (values == null)
{
   return this;
}
```

Do the computations, as follows:

```
var results = _network?.Compute(values);
```

Print out the results, as follows:

```
foreach (var result in results)
{
Console.WriteLine("\tOutput: " +
DoubleConverter.ToExactString(result), Color.Aqua);
}

return this;
  }
}
```

Computing forward propagation

This function is where we Compute the forward propagation value based upon the values provided, as follows:

```
public double[] Compute(params double[] inputs)
{
  ForwardPropagate(inputs);
  return OutputLayer.Select(a =>a.Value).ToArray();
}
```

Exporting the network

This function is where we export our network. To us, exporting means serializing the data into a JSON human-readable format, as follows:

```
public NNManager ExportNetwork()
{
  Console.WriteLine("\tExporting Network...");
  ExportHelper.ExportNetwork(_network);
  Console.WriteLine("\t**Exporting Complete!**", Color.Green);
  return this;
}
```

Exporting a dataset

This function is where we export our dataset information. As with exporting the network, this will be done in JSON human readable format:

```
public NNManager ExportDatasets()
{
    Console.WriteLine("\tExporting Datasets...");
    ExportHelper.ExportDatasets(_dataSets);
    Console.WriteLine("\t**Exporting Complete!**", Color.Green);
    return this;
}
```

The neural network

With many of the ancillary, but important, functions coded, we now turn our attention to the meat of the neural network, the network itself. Within a neural network, the network part is an all-encompassing universe. Everything resides within it. Within this structure we will need to store the input, output, and Hidden Layers of neurons, as well as the learning rate and Momentum, as follows:

```
public class Network
{
    public double LearningRate{ get; set; }
    public double Momentum{ get; set; }
    public List<Neuron>InputLayer{ get; set; }
    public List<List<Neuron>>HiddenLayers{ get; set; }
    public List<Neuron>OutputLayer{ get; set; }
    public List<Neuron>MirrorLayer {get; set; }
    public List<Neuron>CanonicalLayer{ get; set; }
```

Neuron connection

Every neuron must be connected to other neurons, and our neuron constructor will handle connecting all the input neurons with the synapses, as follows:

```
public Neuron(IEnumerable<Neuron> inputNeurons) : this()
{
Ensure.That(inputNeurons).IsNotNull();

  foreach (var inputNeuron in inputNeurons)
  {
    var synapse = new Synapse(inputNeuron, this);
    inputNeuron?.OutputSynapses?.Add(synapse);
    InputSynapses?.Add(synapse);
  }
}
```

Examples

Now that we have our code created, let's use a few examples to see how it can be used.

Training to a minimum

In this example, we will use the code we wrote to train a network to a minimum value or threshold. For each step, the network prompts you for the correct data, saving us the process of cluttering up our example code with this. In production, you would probably want to pass in the parameters without any user intervention, in case this is run as a service or microservice:

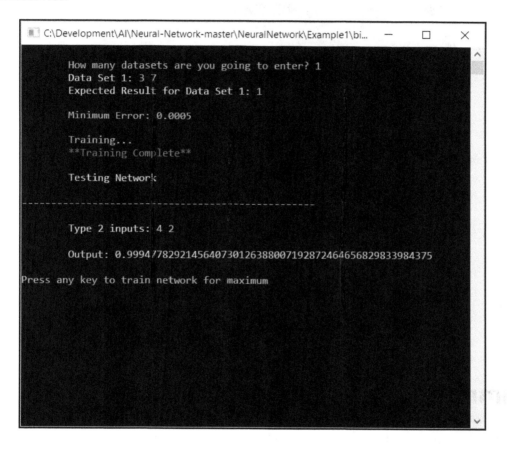

Training to a maximum

In this example, we are going to train the network to reach a maximum value, rather than the minimum, as depicted. We manually enter the data we wish to work with, as well as the expected result. We then allow training to complete. Once completed, we type in our testing input and test the network:

```
            Testing Network
--------------------------------------------------

            Type 2 inputs: 4 2

            Output: 0.99949151467807961779499237309210002422332763671875

Press any key to train network for maximum

            How many datasets are you going to enter? 1
            Data Set 1: 3 7
            Expected Result for Data Set 1: 1

            Max Epoch: 5

            Training...
            **Training Complete**

            Testing Network
--------------------------------------------------

            Type 2 inputs: 4 2

            Output: 0.76503580176199081908094967729994095861911773681640625

Press any key to exit
```

Summary

In this chapter, we saw how to write a complete neural network from scratch. Although the following is a lot we've left out, it does the basics, and we've gotten to see it as pure C# code! We should now have a much better understanding of what a neural network is and what it comprises than when we first started.

In the next chapter, we will begin our journey into more complicated network structures such as recurrent and convolutional neural networks. There's a lot to cover, so hold on to your coding hats!

Decision Trees and Random Forests

3

Decision trees and random forests are powerful techniques that you can use to add power to your applications. Let's walk through some concepts and some code and hopefully have you up and running in no time.

In this chapter, we are going to learn about decision trees and random forests. We will:

- Work through a lot of code samples to show you how you can add this powerful functionality to your applications
- Discuss decision trees
- Discuss random forests

Technical requirements

You will be required to have Microsoft Visual Studio installed in your system. You may also need to refer to open source SharpLearning framework's GitHub repository at `https://github.com/mdabros/SharpLearning`.

Check out the following video to see Code in Action: `http://bit.ly/2O1Lbhr`.

Decision trees

Decision trees can be used for both classification and regression. Decision trees answer sequential questions with a yes/no, true/false response. Based upon those responses, the tree follows predetermined paths to reach its goal. Trees are more formally a version of what is known as a directed acyclic graph. Finally, a decision tree is built using the entire dataset and all features.

Here is an example of a decision tree. You may not know it as a decision tree, but for sure you know the process. Anyone for a doughnut?

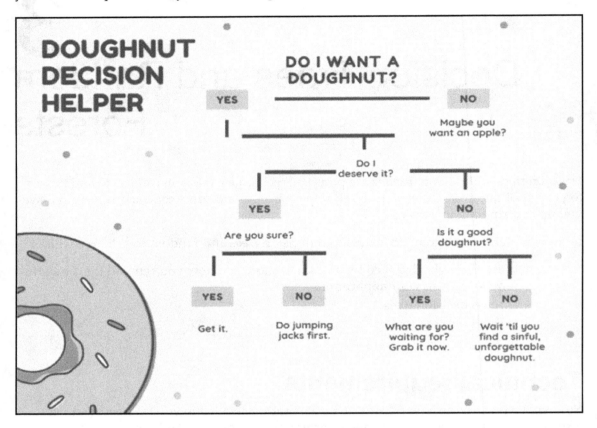

As you can see, the flow of a decision tree starts at the top and works its way downward until a specific result is achieved. The root of the tree is the first decision that splits the dataset. The tree recursively splits the dataset according to what is known as the **splitting metric** at each node. Two of the most popular metrics are **Gini Impurity** and **Information Gain**.

Here is another depiction of a decision tree, albeit without the great donuts!

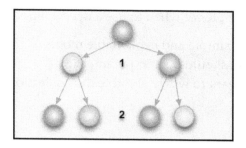

The *depth* of a decision tree represents how many questions have been asked so far. This is the deepest that the tree can go (the total number of questions that may be asked), even if some results can be achieved using fewer questions. For instance, using the preceding diagram, some results can be obtained after 1 question, some after 2. Therefore, the *depth* of that decision tree would be 2.

Decision tree advantages

The following are some advantages from using decision trees:

- Easy interpretation.
- Straightforward, self-explanatory visualizations.
- Can be easily reproduced.
- Can handle both numeric and categorical data.
- Perform well on very large datasets.
- Normally are very fast.
- Depth-wise, the location of the tree allows easy visualization of which features are important. The importance is denoted by the depth of the tree.

Decision tree disadvantages

The following are some disadvantages to using decision trees:

- At each node, the algorithm needs to determine the correct choice. The best choice at one node may not necessarily be the best choice for the entire tree.
- If a tree is deep, it can be prone to what is known as overfitting.
- Decision trees can memorize the training set.

When should we use a decision tree?

The following are some examples of when to use a decision tree:

- When you want a simple and explainable model
- When your model should be non-parametric
- When you don't want to worry about feature selection

Random forests

We have talked about decision trees, and now it's time to discuss random forests. Very basically, a random forest is a collection of decision trees. In random forests, a fraction of the number of total rows and features are selected at random to train on. A decision tree is then built upon this subset. This collection will then have the results aggregated into a single result.

Random forests can also reduce bias and variance. How do they do this? By training on different data samples, or by using a random subset of features. Let's take an example. Let's say we have 30 features. A random forest might only use 10 of these features. That leaves 20 features unused, but some of those 20 features might be important. Remember that a random forest is a collection of decision trees. Therefore, in each tree, if we utilize 10 features, over time most if not all of our features would have been included anyway simply because of the law of averages. So, it is this inclusion that helps limit our error due to bias and variance.

For large datasets, the number of trees can grow quite large, sometimes into the tens of thousands and more, depending on the number of features you are using, so you need to be careful regarding performance.

Here is a diagram of what a random forest might look like:

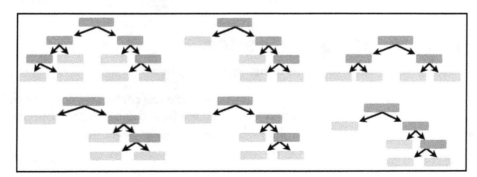

Random forest advantages

The following are some advantages from using random forests:

- More robust than just a single decision tree
- Random forests contain many decision trees and are therefore able to limit overfitting and error
- Depth-wise, the location shows which features contribute to the classification or regression as well as their relative importance
- Can be used for both regression and classification
- Default parameters can be sufficient
- Fast to train

Random forest disadvantages

The following are some disadvantages to using random forests:

- Random forests need to be done in parallel in order to increase speed
- Predictions can be slow to create once trained
- More accuracy requires more trees, and this can result in a slower model

When should we use a random forest?

The following are some examples of when to use random forests:

- When model interpretation is not the most important criterion. Interpretation will not be as easy as a single tree.
- When model accuracy is most important.
- When you want robust classification, regression, and feature selection analysis.
- To prevent overfitting.
- Image classification.
- Recommendation engines.

SharpLearning

Let's now turn our attention to an incredible open source package, SharpLearning. **SharpLearning** is an excellent machine learning framework for individuals to learn about many aspects of machine learning, including decision trees and random forests as we described in the preceding sections. Let's spend a few minutes getting familiar with a few things before we dive into some code samples and example applications.

Terminology

Throughout this chapter you are going to see the following terms used. Here is the context for what each of them means:

- **Learner**: This refers to a machine learning algorithm.
- **Model**: This refers to a machine learning model.
- **Hyper-parameters**: These are the parameters used to adjust and regulate (hopefully) the machine learning model.
- **Targets**: These are more commonly referred to as a dependent variable. In most notations, this will be y. These are the values that we are attempting to model.
- **Observations**: These are the feature matrix, which contains all the information we currently have about the targets. In most notations, this will be x.

Throughout most of our examples we will be focusing on two namespaces within SharpLearning. They are:

- `SharpLearning.DecisionTrees`
- `SharpLearning.RandomForest`

With that behind us, let's start digging into SharpLearning and show you a few concepts relative to how it works.

Loading and saving models

SharpLearning makes it very easy to load and save models to disk. This is a very important part of a machine learning library and SharpLearning is among the easiest to implement.

All models in SharpLearning have a `Save` and a `Load` method. These methods do the heavy lifting of saving and loading a model for us.

As an example, here we will save a model that we learned to disk:

```
model.Save(() => StreamWriter(@"C:\randomforest.xml"));
```

If we want to load this model back in, we simply use the `Load` method:

```
varloadedModel = RegressionForestModel.Load(() =>
newStreamReader(@"C:\randomforest.xml"));
```

Yep, it's that easy and simple to load and save your data models. It is also possible for you to save models using serialization. This will allow us to choose between XML and a Binary format. Another very nice design feature of SharpLearning is that serializing models allows us to serialize to the `IPredictorModel` interface. This makes replacing your models much easier, if each conforms to that interface. Here's how we would do that:

```
varxmlSerializer = new GenericXmlDataContractSerializer();
xmlSerializer.Serialize<IPredictorModel<double>>(model,
 () => new StreamWriter(@"C:\randomforest.xml"));
var loadedModelXml = xmlSerializer
.Deserialize<IPredictorModel<double>>(() => new
StreamReader(@"C:\randomforest.xml"));
```

Algorithm	Train Error	Test Error
RegressionDecisionTreeLearner(default)	0.0518	0.4037

And there you have it, instant training and testing errors.

 When reporting the performance of your model, you should always use the test error even if the training error is lower, since that is an estimate of how well the model generalizes to new data.

Now, let's talk for a second about **hyperparameters**. Hyperparameters are parameters that affect the learning process of the machine learning algorithm. You can adjust them to tune the process and improve performance and reliability. At the same time, you can also incorrectly adjust parameters and have something that does not work as intended. Let's look at a few things that can happen with an incorrectly tuned hyperparameter:

- If the model is too complex, you can end up with what is known as high variance, or **Overfitting**
- If the model ends up being too simple, you will end up with what is known as high bias, or **Underfitting**

For those who have not done so, manually tuning hyperparameters, a process that happens in almost every use case, can take a considerable amount of your time. As the number of hyperparameters increases with the model, the tuning time and effort increase as well. The best way around this is to use an optimizer and let the work happen for you. To this end, SharpLearning can be a huge help to us due to the numerous optimizers that are available for it. Here is a list of just some of them:

- Grid search
- Random search
- Particle swarm (which we will talk about in Chapter 7, *Replacing Back Propagation with PSO*)
- Bayesian optimization
- Globalized bounded nelder mead

Let's start with an example.

Let's create a learner and use the default parameters, which, more than likely, will be good enough. Once we find our parameters and create the learner, we need to create the model. We then will predict the training and test set. Once all of that is complete, we will measure the error on the test set and record it:

```
// create learner with default parameters
var learner = new RegressionSquareLossGradientBoostLearner(runParallel:
false);
// learn model with found parameters
var model = learner.Learn(trainSet.Observations, trainSet.Targets);
// predict the training and test set
var trainPredictions = model.Predict(trainSet.Observations);
var testPredictions = model.Predict(testSet.Observations);
// since this is a regression problem we are using square error as metric
// for evaluating how well the model performs.
var metric = new MeanSquaredErrorRegressionMetric();
// measure the error on the test set.
var testError = metric.Error(testSet.Targets, testPredictions);
```

And here is our test set error

Algorithm	Test Error
RegressionSquareLossGradientBoostLearner (default)	0.4984

With that part complete, we now have our baseline established. Let's use a
`RandomSearchOptimizer` to tune the hyperparameters to see if we can get any better
results. To do this we need to establish the bounds of the hyperparameters, so our
optimizer knows how to tune. Let's look at how we do this:

```
var parameters = new ParameterBounds[]
{
 new ParameterBounds(min: 80, max: 300,
 transform: Transform.Linear, parameterType: ParameterType.Discrete),
 new ParameterBounds(min: 0.02, max: 0.2,
 transform: Transform.Logarithmic, parameterType:
ParameterType.Continuous),
 new ParameterBounds(min: 8, max: 15,
 transform: Transform.Linear, parameterType: ParameterType.Discrete),
 new ParameterBounds(min: 0.5, max: 0.9,
 transform: Transform.Linear, parameterType: ParameterType.Continuous),
 new ParameterBounds(min: 1, max: numberOfFeatures,
 transform: Transform.Linear, parameterType: ParameterType.Discrete),
};
```

Did you notice that we used a Logarithmic transform for the learning rate? Do you know
why we did this? The answer is: to ensure that we had a more even distribution across the
entire range of values. We have a large range difference between our minimum and
maximum values (0.02 -> 0.2), so the logarithmic transform will be best.

We now need a *validation set* to help us measure how well the model generalizes to unseen
data during our optimization. To do this, we will need to further split the training data. To
do this, we are going to leave our current test set out of the optimization process. If we
don't, we risk getting a positive bias on our final error estimate, and that will not be what
we want:

```
var validationSplit = new
RandomTrainingTestIndexSplitter<double>(trainingPercentage: 0.7, seed: 24)
.SplitSet(trainSet.Observations, trainSet.Targets);
```

One more thing that the optimizer will need is an objective function. The function will take
a double array as input (containing the set of hyperparameters) and return an
`OptimizerResult` that contains the validation error and the corresponding set of
hyperparameters:

```
Func<double[], OptimizerResult> minimize = p =>
 {
 var candidateLearner = new RegressionSquareLossGradientBoostLearner(
 iterations: (int)p[0],
learningRate: p[1],
maximumTreeDepth: (int)p[2],
```

```
subSampleRatio: p[3],
featuresPrSplit: (int)p[4],
runParallel: false);
 var candidateModel =
candidateLearner.Learn(validationSplit.TrainingSet.Observations,
validationSplit.TrainingSet.Targets);
 var validationPredictions =
candidateModel.Predict(validationSplit.TestSet.Observations);
 var candidateError = metric.Error(validationSplit.TestSet.Targets,
validationPredictions);
 return new OptimizerResult(p, candidateError);
};
```

Once this `objective` function has been defined, we can now create and run the optimizer to find the best set of parameters. Let's start out by running our optimizer for 30 iterations and trying out 30 different sets of hyperparameters:

```
// create our optimizer
var optimizer = new RandomSearchOptimizer(parameters, iterations: 30,
runParallel: true);
// find the best hyperparameters for use
var result = optimizer.OptimizeBest(minimize);
var best = result.ParameterSet;
```

Once we run this, our optimizer should find the best set of hyperparameters. Let's see what it finds:

- `Trees:` 277
- `learningRate:` 0.035
- `maximumTreeDepth:` 15
- `subSampleRatio:` 0.838
- `featuresPrSplit:` 4

Progress. Now that we have a set of best hyperparameters, which were measured on our validation set, we can create a learner with these parameters and learn a new model using the entire dataset:

```
var learner = new RegressionSquareLossGradientBoostLearner(
  iterations: (int)best[0],
learningRate: best[1],
maximumTreeDepth: (int)best[2],
subSampleRatio: best[3],
featuresPrSplit: (int)best[4],
runParallel: false);
var model = learner.Learn(trainSet.Observations, trainSet.Targets);
```

With our final set of hyperparameters now intact, we pass these to our learner and are able to reduce the test error significantly. For us to do that manually would have taken us an eternity and beyond!

Algorithm	Test Error
RegressionSquareLossGradientBoostLearner (default)	0.4984
RegressionSquareLossGradientBoostLearner (Optimizer)	0.3852

Example code and applications

In the next few sections, we are going to look at some code samples without all the verbosity. This will be pure C# code so it should be something easily understood by all.

Let's take a quick look at how we can use SharpLearning to predict observations. I'll show you an entire code sample without the verbosity:

```
var parser = new CsvParser(() =>new StringReader(Resources.AptitudeData));
var observations = parser.EnumerateRows(v => v != "Pass").ToF64Matrix();
var targets = parser.EnumerateRows("Pass").ToF64Vector();
var rows = targets.Length;
var learner = new ClassificationDecisionTreeLearner(100, 1, 2, 0.001, 42);
varsut = learner.Learn(observations, targets);
var predictions = sut.Predict(observations);
var evaluator = new TotalErrorClassificationMetric<double>();
var error = evaluator.Error(targets, predictions);
Assert.AreEqual(0.038461538461538464, error, 0.0000001);
```

Saving a model

Here is a code sample that will show you how easy it is to save a model:

```
var parser = new CsvParser(() =>new StringReader(Resources.AptitudeData));
var observations = parser.EnumerateRows(v => v != "Pass").ToF64Matrix();
var targets = parser.EnumerateRows("Pass").ToF64Vector();
var learner = new ClassificationDecisionTreeLearner(2);
var sut = learner.Learn(observations, targets);
var writer = new StringWriter();
sut.Save(() => writer);
```

Mean squared error regression metric

Mean squared error (**MSE**) is a metric that measures the average of the squares of the errors. More concretely, it measures the average distance between the estimated values and what is estimated. A mean squared error is always non-negative, and values that are closer to zero are considered more acceptable. SharpLearning makes it incredibly easy to calculate this error metric, as depicted in the following code:

```
var targets = new double[] { 1.0, 2.3, 3.1, 4.4, 5.8 };
var predictions = new double[] { 1.0, 2.0, 3.0, 4.0, 5.0 };
var sut = new MeanSquaredErrorRegressionMetric();
var actual = sut.Error(targets, predictions);
```

F1 score

To talk about an f1 score we must first talk about *Precision* and *Recall*.

Precision is the ratio of correctly predicted positive observations divided by the total predicted positive observations. Less formally, of all the people that said they were coming, how many came?

Recall (sensitivity) is the ratio of correctly predicted positive observations to all observations in total.

F1 score is then the weighted average of Precision and Recall.

Here's how we calculate an f1 score using SharpLearning:

```
var targets = new double[] { 0, 1, 1 };
var predictions = new double[] { 0, 1, 1 };
var sut = new F1ScoreMetric<double>(1);
var actual = sut.Error(targets, predictions);
Assert.AreEqual(0.0, actual);
```

Optimizations

The following is how you can use the *Particle Swarm Optimizer* to return the result that best minimizes the provided function:

```
var parameters = new ParameterBounds[]
{
new ParameterBounds(-10.0, 10.0, Transform.Linear),
new ParameterBounds(-10.0, 10.0, Transform.Linear),
```

```
new ParameterBounds(-10.0, 10.0, Transform.Linear),
};
var sut = new ParticleSwarmOptimizer(parameters, 100);
var actual = sut.OptimizeBest(Minimize);
```

The following is how you can use the *Grid Search Optimizer* to optimize by trying all combinations of the provided parameters:

```
var parameters = new double[][] { new double[]{ 10.0, 20.0, 30.0, 35.0,
37.5, 40.0, 50.0, 60.0 } };
var sut = new GridSearchOptimizer(parameters);
var actual = sut.OptimizeBest(Minimize);
```

The following is how you can use the *Random Search Optimizer* to initialize random parameters between the min and max provided. The result that best minimizes the provided function will be returned:

```
var parameters = new ParameterBounds[]
{
new ParameterBounds(0.0, 100.0, Transform.Linear)
};
var sut = new RandomSearchOptimizer(parameters, 100);
var actual = sut.OptimizeBest(Minimize);
```

Sample application 1

With all this knowledge under our belt, let's go ahead and write our first sample program. The program itself is very simple and meant to show how easy it is to implement such techniques in your applications with a minimal amount of code. To show you exactly what I mean, here is what the output of the program looks like:

The code

Here is the code that implements our sample program and produces the previous output. As you can see, the code is very simple and everything in here (save the shuffling of indices) is code we have already walked through before. We'll keep the verbosity to a minimum so that you can concentrate on the code itself. This sample will read in our data, parse it into observations and target samples, and then create a learner using 1,000 trees. From there we will use the learner to learn and create our model. Once this is complete we will calculate our mean squared error metric and display it on the screen:

```
var parser = new CsvParser(() =>new StringReader(Resources.Glass));
var observations = parser.EnumerateRows(v => v != "Target").ToF64Matrix();
var targets = parser.EnumerateRows("Target").ToF64Vector();
int trees = 1000;
var sut = new RegressionExtremelyRandomizedTreesLearner(trees, 1, 100, 1,
0.0001, 1.0, 42, false);
var indices = Enumerable.Range(0, targets.Length).ToArray();
indices.Shuffle(new Random(42));
indices = indices.Take((int)(targets.Length * 0.7)).ToArray();
var model = sut.Learn(observations, targets, indices);
var predictions = model.Predict(observations);
var evaluator = new MeanSquaredErrorRegressionMetric();
var error = evaluator.Error(targets, predictions);
Console.WriteLine("Error: " + error);
```

Sample application 2 – wine quality

In our next application, we are going to use our knowledge to determine the most important features for wine based upon the model that is created. Here is what our output will look like when we complete it:

```
C:\Development\AI\machinelearning\SharpLearning-master\SharpLearning.Examples-master\WhiteWineTesting\bin\Debug\WhiteW...
Train error: 0.0518 - Test error: 0.4037
FeatureName     Importance
alcohol 100.00
density 53.52
chlorides       31.37
volatile acidity        25.55
free sulfur dioxide     18.13
total sulfur dioxide    13.76
citric acid     11.16
residual sugar  5.93
pH      4.98
fixed acidity   3.58
sulphates       2.49
```

The code

Here is the code for our application. As always, we first load and parse our data into observations and target sample sets. Since this is a regression sample, we'll use a 70/30 split of our data sample: 70% for training, 30% for testing. From there, we create our random forest learner and create our model. After this, we calculate our training and test errors and print out the feature importance in order of importance, as found by our model:

```
var parser = new CsvParser(() =>new StreamReader(Application.StartupPath +
"\\winequality-white.csv"));
var targetName = "quality";
// read in our feature matrix
var observations = parser.EnumerateRows(c => c !=
targetName).ToF64Matrix();
// read in our regression targets
var targets = parser.EnumerateRows(targetName).ToF64Vector();
// Since this is a regression problem, we use the random training/test set
splitter. 30 % of the data is used for the test set.
var splitter = new
RandomTrainingTestIndexSplitter<double>(trainingPercentage: 0.7, seed: 24);
var trainingTestSplit = splitter.SplitSet(observations, targets);
var trainSet = trainingTestSplit.TrainingSet;
var testSet = trainingTestSplit.TestSet;
var learner = new RegressionRandomForestLearner(trees: 100);
var model = learner.Learn(trainSet.Observations, trainSet.Targets);
var trainPredictions = model.Predict(trainSet.Observations);
var testPredictions = model.Predict(testSet.Observations);
// since this is a regression problem we are using squared error as the
metric
// for evaluating how well the model performs.
var metric = new MeanSquaredErrorRegressionMetric();
var trainError = metric.Error(trainSet.Targets, trainPredictions);
var testError = metric.Error(testSet.Targets, testPredictions);
Trace.WriteLine($"Train error: {trainError:0.0000} - Test error:
{testError:0.0000}");
System.Console.WriteLine($"Train error: {trainError:0.0000} - Test error:
{testError:0.0000}");

// the variable importance requires the featureNameToIndex from the
dataset.
// This mapping describes the relation from the column name to the
associated
// index in the feature matrix.
var featureNameToIndex = parser.EnumerateRows(c => c !=
targetName).First().ColumnNameToIndex;

var importances = model.GetVariableImportance(featureNameToIndex);
```

```
var importanceCsv = new StringBuilder();
importanceCsv.Append("FeatureName;Importance");
System.Console.WriteLine("FeatureName\tImportance");
foreach (var feature in importances)
{
importanceCsv.AppendLine();
importanceCsv.Append($"{feature.Key};{feature.Value:0.00}");
System.Console.WriteLine($"{feature.Key}\t{feature.Value:0.00}");
}
Trace.WriteLine(importanceCsv);
```

Summary

In this chapter, we learned about decision trees and random forests. We also learned how to use the open source framework, SharpLearn, to add these powerful features to our applications. In the next chapter, we are going to learn about facial and motion detection and show you how you can enable your application with this exciting technology! You'll meet Frenchie, my pet French Bulldog, who will demonstrate most of the samples we will show. Also, we have a guest poser you will just have to see!

References

- https://github.com/mdabros/SharpLearning

4
Face and Motion Detection

Now it is time for us to get into a really neat application. We'll start off by using the open source package `http://www.aforgenet.com/` to build a face and motion detection application. To do this, you'll need to have a camera installed in your system to see live streaming video. From there, we will use that camera to detect faces as well as motion. In this chapter, we are going to show two separate examples: one for facial detection, the other for motion detection. We'll show you exactly what goes on, and just how fast you can add these capabilities into your application.

In this chapter, we will cover such topics as:

- Facial detection
- Motion detection
- How to use the local video-integrated camera
- Image filtering/algorithms

Let's start out with facial detection. In our example, I'm going to use my friendly little French bulldog to pose for us. Before I do that, please re-read the chapter title. No matter how many times you read it, you'll probably miss the key point here. Notice it says face *DETECTION* and not face *RECOGNITION*. This is so very important I wanted to stop and re-stress it. We are not trying to identify Joe, Bob, or Sally. We are trying to verify that, out of everything we see via our camera, we can *detect* that there is a face there. We are not concerned with whose face it is, just the fact that it is a face! It is so important that we understand this before moving on, otherwise your expectations will be so incorrectly biased that you are going to make yourself confused and upset, and we don't want that!

Facial detection, as I will stress again later, is the first part of facial recognition, a much more complicated beast. If you can't identify, out of all the things that are on the screen, one or more faces, then you'll never be able to recognize whose face it is!

Technical requirements

As a prerequisite, you will need Microsoft Visual Studio(any version) installed on your system. You will also need to access the open source accord framework at `https://github.com/accord-net/framework`.

Check out the following video to see Code in Action: `http://bit.ly/2xH0thh`.

Facial detection

Now, let's take a quick look at our application. You should have the sample solution loaded into Microsoft Visual Studio:

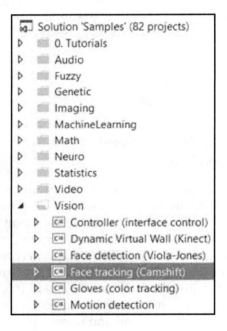

And here's a look at our sample application running. Say Hi to Frenchie everyone!

As you can see, we have a very simple screen that is dedicated to our video capture device. In this case, the laptop camera is our video capture device. Frenchie is kindly posing in front of the camera for us, and as soon as we enable facial tracking, look what happens:

The facial features of Frenchie are now being tracked. What you see surrounding Frenchie are the tracking containers (white boxes), and our angle detector (red line) displayed. As we move Frenchie around, the tracking container and angle detector will track him. That's all well and good, but what happens if we enable facial tracking on a real human face? As you can see in the following screenshot, the tracking containers and angles are tracking the face of our guest poser, just like it did for Frenchie:

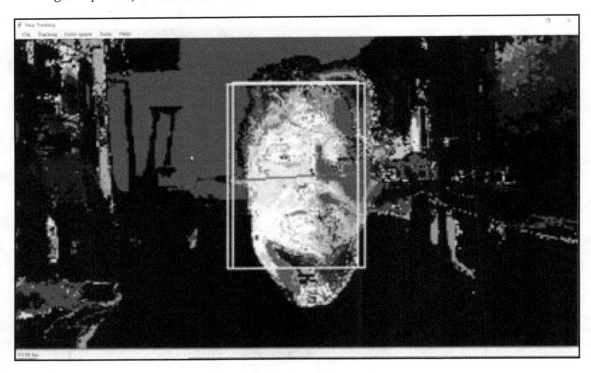

As our poser moves his head from side to side, the camera tracks this, and you can see the angle detectors adjusting to what it recognizes as the angle of the face. In this case you will notice that the color space is in black and white and not color. This is a histogram back projection and is an option that you can change:

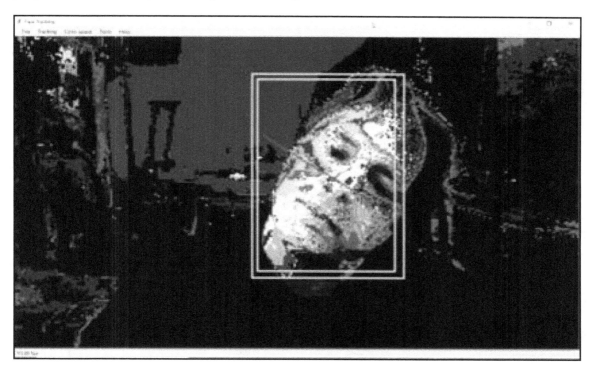

Even as we move farther away from the camera where other objects come into view, the facial detector can keep track of our face among the noise. This is exactly how the facial recognition systems you see in movies work, albeit more simplistic, and within minutes you can be up and running with your own facial recognition application too!:

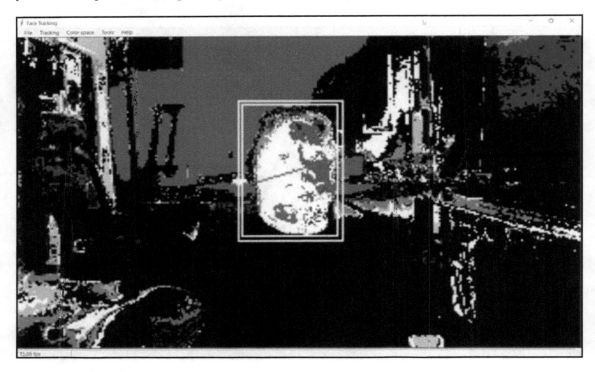

Now that we've seen the outside, let's look under the hood at what is going on.

We need to ask ourselves exactly what the problem is that we are trying to solve here. Well, we are trying to detect (notice I did not say recognize) facial images. While easy for a human, a computer needs very detailed instruction sets to accomplish this feat. Luckily for us there is a very famous algorithm called the Viola-Jones algorithm that will do the heavy lifting for us. Why did we pick this algorithm?:

- Very high detection rates and very low false positives.
- Very good at real-time processing.
- Very good at detecting faces from non-faces. Detecting faces is the first step in facial recognition.

This algorithm requires that the camera has a full-frontal upright view of the face. To be detected, the face will need to be pointing straight towards the camera, not tilted, not looking up or down. Remember, for the moment, we are just interested in facial detection.

To delve into the technical side of things, our algorithm will require four stages to accomplish its job. They are:

- Haar feature selection
- Creating an integral image
- Adaboost training
- Cascading classifiers

We must start by stating that all human faces share some similar properties, such as the eye being darker than the upper cheeks, the nose bridge being brighter than the eyes, your forehead may be lighter than the rest of your face, and so on. Our algorithm matches these up by using what is known as **Haar Features**. We can come up with matchable facial features by looking at the location and size of the eyes, mouth, and bridge of the nose, and so forth. However, here's our problem.

In a 24x24 pixel window, there are a total of 162,336 possible features. Obviously, to try and evaluate them all would be prohibitively expensive, if it would work at all. So, we are going to work with a technique known as **adaptive boosting**, or more commonly, **AdaBoost**. It's another one for your buzzword list, you've heard it everywhere and perhaps even read about it. Our learning algorithm will use AdaBoost to select the best features and train classifiers to use them. Let's stop and talk about it for a moment.

AdaBoost can be used with many types of learning algorithm and is considered the best out-of-the-box algorithm for many tasks. You usually won't notice how good and fast it is until you switch to another algorithm and time it. I have done this countless times, and I can tell you the difference is very noticeable.

Boosting takes the output from other weak-learning algorithms and combines them with a weighted sum that is the final output of the boosted classifier. The adaptive part of AdaBoost comes from the fact that subsequent learners are tweaked in favor of those instances that have been misclassified by previous classifiers. We must be careful with our data preparation though, as AdaBoost is sensitive to noisy data and outliers (remember how we stressed those in Chapter 1, *A Quick Refresher*). The algorithm tends to overfit the data more than other algorithms, which is why in our earlier chapters we stressed data preparation for missing data and outliers. In the end, if *weak* learning algorithms are better than random guessing, AdaBoost can be a valuable addition to our process.

With that brief description behind us, let's look under the covers at what's happening. For this example, we will again use the Accord framework and we will work with the Vision Face Tracking sample. You can download the latest version of this framework from its GitHub location: `https://github.com/accord-net/framework`.

We start by creating a `FaceHaarCascade` object. This object holds a collection of Haar-like features' weak classification stages, or stages. There will be many stages provided, each containing a set of classifier trees that will be used in the decision-making process. We are now technically working with a decision tree. The beauty of the Accord framework is that `FaceHaarCascade` automatically creates all these stages and trees for us without exposing us to the details.

Let's take a look at what a particular stage might look like:

```
List<HaarCascadeStage> stages = new List<HaarCascadeStage>();
List<HaarFeatureNode[]> nodes;
HaarCascadeStage stage;
stage = new HaarCascadeStage(0.822689414024353); nodes = new
List<HaarFeatureNode[]>();
nodes.Add(new[] { new HaarFeatureNode(0.004014195874333382,
0.0337941907346249, 0.8378106951713562, new int[] { 3, 7, 14, 4, -1 }, new
int[] { 3, 9, 14, 2, 2 }) });
nodes.Add(new[] { new HaarFeatureNode(0.0151513395830989,
0.1514132022857666, 0.7488812208175659, new int[] { 1, 2, 18, 4, -1 }, new
int[] { 7, 2, 6, 4, 3 }) });
nodes.Add(new[] { new HaarFeatureNode(0.004210993181914091,
0.0900492817163467, 0.6374819874763489, new int[] { 1, 7, 15, 9, -1 }, new
int[] { 1, 10, 15, 3, 3 }) });
stage.Trees = nodes.ToArray(); stages.Add(stage);
```

As you can see, we are building a decision tree underneath the hood by providing the nodes for each stage with the numeric values for each feature.

Once created, we can use our cascade object to create our `HaarObjectDetector`, which is what we will use for detection. It takes:

- Our facial cascade objects
- The minimum window size to use when searching for objects
- Our search mode—in our case, we are searching for only a single object
- The re-scaling factor to use when re-scaling our search window during the search

```
HaarCascade cascade = new FaceHaarCascade();
detector = new HaarObjectDetector(cascade, 25,
ObjectDetectorSearchMode.Single, 1.2f,
ObjectDetectorScalingMode.GreaterToSmaller);
```

Once created, we are ready to tackle the topic of our video collection source. In our examples, we will simply use the local camera to capture all images. However, the Accord.Net framework makes it easy to use other sources for image capture, such as `.avi` files, animated `.jpg` files, and so forth.

We connect to the camera, select the resolution, and are ready to go:

```
foreach (var cap in device?.VideoCapabilities)
  {
if (cap.FrameSize.Height == 240)
return cap;
if (cap.FrameSize.Width == 320)
return cap;
  }
return device?.VideoCapabilities.Last();
```

With the application now running and our video source selected, our application will look like the following. Once again, enter Frenchie the bulldog! Please excuse the mess, Frenchie is not the tidiest of pets!:

For this demonstration, you will notice that Frenchie is facing the camera, and in the background, we have 2 x 55" monitors, as well as many other items my wife likes to refer to as *junk* (we'll be proper and call it *noise*)! This is done to show how the face detection algorithm can distinguish Frenchie's face amongst everything else! If our detector cannot handle this, it is going to get lost in the noise and will be of little use to us.

With our video source now coming in, we need to be notified when a new frame is received so that we can process it, apply our markers, and so on. We do this by attaching to the `NewFrameReceived` event handler of the video source player, as follows. .NET developers should be very familiar with this:

```
this.videoSourcePlayer.NewFrameReceived += new
Accord.Video.NewFrameEventHandler(this.videoSourcePlayer_NewFrame);
```

Let's look at what happens each time we are notified that a new video frame is available.

The first thing that we need to do is downsample the image to make it easier to work with:

```
ResizeNearestNeighbor resize = new ResizeNearestNeighbor(160, 120);
UnmanagedImagedownsample = resize.Apply(im);
```

With the image in a more manageable size, we will process the frame. If we have not found a facial region, we will stay in tracking mode waiting for a frame that has a detectable face. If we have found a facial region, we will reset our tracker, locate the face, reduce its size in order to flush away any background noise, initialize the tracker, and apply the marker window to the image. All of this is accomplished with the following code:

```
if (regions != null&&regions.Length>0)
  {
tracker?.Reset();
// Will track the first face found
Rectangle face = regions[0];
// Reduce the face size to avoid tracking background
Rectangle window = new Rectangle((int)((regions[0].X + regions[0].Width /
2f) * xscale),
  (int)((regions[0].Y + regions[0].Height / 2f) * yscale), 1, 1);
window.Inflate((int)(0.2f * regions[0].Width * xscale), (int)(0.4f *
regions[0].Height * yscale));
if (tracker != null)
  {
tracker.SearchWindow = window;
tracker.ProcessFrame(im);
  }
marker = new RectanglesMarker(window);
marker.ApplyInPlace(im);
args.Frame = im.ToManagedImage();
tracking = true;
  }
else
  {
detecting = true;
  }
```

If a face was detected, our image frame now looks like the following:

If Frenchie tilts his head to the side, our image frame now looks like the following:

Motion detection

We will now make our focus a bit more wide-scale and detect any motion at all, not just faces. Again, we'll use Accord.Net for this and use the `Motion detection` sample. As with facial recognition, you will see just how simple it is to add this capability to your applications and instantly become a hero at work! Let's make sure you have the correct project loaded into Microsoft Visual Studio:

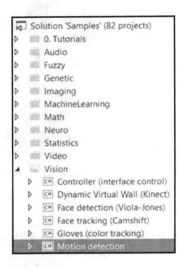

With motion detection, anything that moves on the screen we will highlighted in red, so using the following screenshot you can see that the fingers are moving but everything else remains motionless:

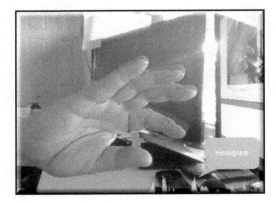

In the following screenshot, you can see more movement, denoted by the red blocks along this anonymous hand:

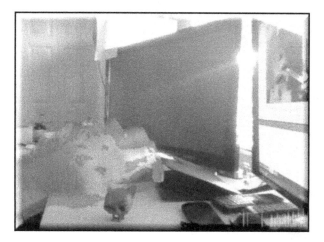

In the following screenshot, you can see that the entire hand is moving:

If we do not wish to process the entire screen area for motion, we can define *motion regions*, where motion detection will occur only in those regions. In the following screenshot, you can see that I defined a motion region. You will notice in upcoming screenshots that this is the only area that motion will be processed from:

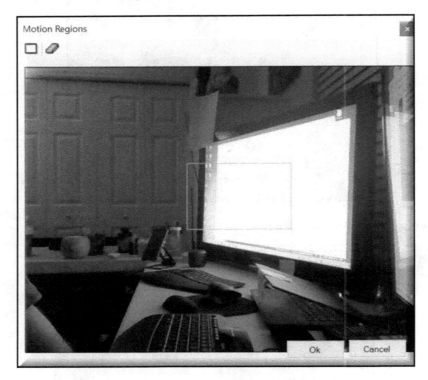

Now, if we create some motion for the camera, you will see that only motion from our defined region is being processed, as follows:

You can also see that, with a motion region defined and Peter the meditating Gnome in front of the region, we are still able to detect motion behind him, but his face is not part of the recognition. You could of course, combine both processes to have the best of both worlds, as follows:

Another option that we can use is Grid Motion Highlighting. This highlights the motion detected region in red squares based upon a defined grid. Basically, the motion area is now a red box, as you can see:

Code

The following snippet shows a simple example of all you need to do to add video recognition to your application. As you can see, it couldn't be any easier:

```
// create motion detector
MotionDetector detector = new MotionDetector(
 new SimpleBackgroundModelingDetector( ),
 new MotionAreaHighlighting( ) );
// continuously feed video frames to motion detector
while ( ... )
{
 // process new video frame and check motion level
 if ( detector.ProcessFrame( videoFrame ) > 0.02 )
 {
 // ring alarm or do something else
 }
}
```

We now open our video source:

```
videoSourcePlayer.VideoSource = new AsyncVideoSource(source);
```

When we receive a new video frame, that's when all the magic happens. The following are all the code it takes to make processing a new video frame a success:

```
private void videoSourcePlayer_NewFrame(object sender,
NewFrameEventArgsargs)
 {
lock (this)
 {
if (detector != null)
 {
floatmotionLevel = detector.ProcessFrame(args.Frame);
if (motionLevel > motionAlarmLevel)
 {
// flash for 2 seconds
flash = (int)(2 * (1000 / alarmTimer.Interval));
 }
// check objects' count
if (detector.MotionProcessingAlgorithm is BlobCountingObjectsProcessing)
 {
BlobCountingObjectsProcessing countingDetector =
(BlobCountingObjectsProcessing)detector.MotionProcessingAlgorithm;
detectedObjectsCount = countingDetector.ObjectsCount;
 }
else
 {
detectedObjectsCount = -1;
 }
// accumulate history
motionHistory.Add(motionLevel);
if (motionHistory.Count> 300)
                {
motionHistory.RemoveAt(0);
                }

if (showMotionHistoryToolStripMenuItem.Checked)
DrawMotionHistory(args.Frame);
             }
         }
```

The key here is detecting the amount of motion that is happening in the frame, which is done with the following code. For this example, we are using a motion alarm level of 0.2, but you can use whatever you like. Once this threshold has been passed, you can do whatever logic you like such as send an email alert, text, start a video capture operation, and so forth:

```
float motionLevel = detector.ProcessFrame(args.Frame);
if (motionLevel > motionAlarmLevel)
{
// flash for 2 seconds
flash = (int)(2 * (1000 / alarmTimer.Interval));
}
```

Summary

In this chapter, we learned about image and motion detection (not recognition!). We used Accord.Net as an example of what open-source tools provide us with when we want to add power to our applications.

In the next chapter, we remain with the image theme, but work on training Convolutional Neural Networks with the open-source package ConvNetSharp.

5
Training CNNs Using ConvNetSharp

In this chapter, we are going to use the phenomenal open source package **ConvNetSharp**, by Cédric Bovar, to demonstrate how to train our **Convolutional Neural Networks (CNNs)**. In this chapter, we will look at the following topics:

- Common neural network modules
- The various terms and concepts related to CNNs
- Convolutional networks that process images

Technical requirements

You will need Microsoft Visual Studio and ConvNetSharp framework for this chapter.

Getting acquainted

Before we begin diving into code, let's cover some basic terminology so that we are all on the same page when referring to things. This terminology applies to CNNs as well as the **ConvNetSharp** framework.

Convolution: In mathematics, a *convolution* is an operation performed on two functions. This operation produces a third function, which is an expression of how the shape of one is modified by the other. This is represented visually in the following diagram:

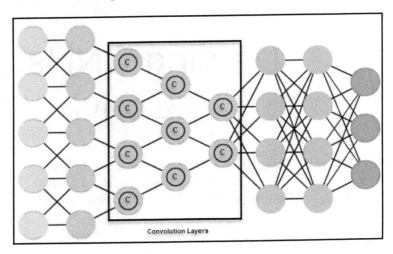

Convolution Layers

It is important to note that the convolutional layer itself is the building block of a CNN. This layer's parameters consist of a set of learnable filters (sometimes called **kernels**). These kernels have a small receptive field, which is a smaller view into the total image, and this view extends through the full depth of the input volume. During the forward propagation phase, each filter is **convolved** across the width and the height of the entire input volume. It is this convolution that computes the dot product between the filter and the input. This then produces a two-dimensional map (sometimes called an **activation map**) of the filter. This helps the network learn which filters should activate when they detect a feature at that respective input position.

Dot product computation: The following diagram is a visualization of what we mean when we say dot product computation:

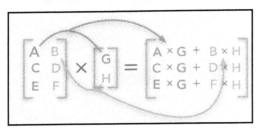

- **Vol class**: In ConvNetSharp, the `Vol` class is simply a wrapper around a one-dimensional list of numbers, their gradients, and dimensions (that is, width, depth, and height).

- **Net class**: In ConvNetSharp, `Net` is a very simple class that contains a list of layers. When a `Vol` is passed through the `Net` class, `Net` iterates through all its layers, forward-propagates each one by calling the `forward()` function, and returns the result of the last layer. During back propagation, `Net` calls the `backward()` function of each layer to compute the gradient.

- **Layers**: As we know, every neural network is just a linear list of layers, and ours is no different. For a neural network, the first layer must be an input layer, and our last layer must be an output layer. Every layer takes an input `Vol` and produces a new output `Vol`.

- **Fully-connected layer**: The fully-connected layer is perhaps the most important layer and is definitely the most interesting in terms of what it does. It houses a layer of neurons that perform weighted addition of all the inputs. These are then passed through a non-linear activation function such as a ReLU.

- **Loss layers** and **classifier layers**: These layers are helpful when we need to predict a set of discrete classes for our data. You can use softmax, SVM, and many other types of layers. As always, you should experiment with your particular problem to see which one works best.

- **Loss layers** and the **L2 regression layer**: This layer takes a list of targets and backward-propagates the L2 loss through them.

- **Convolution layer**: This layer is almost a mirror of the fully-connected layer. The difference here is that neurons are only connected locally to a few neurons in the layer rather than being connected to all of them. They also share parameters.

- **Trainers**: The `Trainer` class takes a network and a set of parameters. It passes this through the network, sees the predictions, and adjusts the network weights to make the provided labels more accurate for that particular input. Over time, the process will transform the network and map all the inputs to the correct outputs.

With that behind us, let's now talk a bit about CNNs themselves. A CNN consists of an input and an output layer; there's no big surprise there. There will be one or more hidden layers which consist of convolutional layers, pooling layers, fully-connected layers, or normalization layers. It is in these hidden layers that the magic happens. Convolutional layers apply a **convolution** operation to the input and pass the result to the next layer. We'll talk more about that in a moment.

As we progress, the activation maps will be stacked for all of the filters that run along the depth dimension. This, in turn, will form the full output volume of the layer itself. Each neuron on that layer processes data only for its own receptive field (the data view it can see). This information is shared with other neurons.

The thing that we have to always keep in mind with a CNN is the input size, which can require an extremely high number of neurons to process, depending on the resolution of the image. This could become architecturally inconvenient, and even intractable, because each pixel is a variable that needs to be processed.

Let's take a look at an example. If we have an image of 100 x 100 pixels, we would all agree that this is a small image. However, this image has 10,000 pixels in total (100 x 100), all of which are weights for each neuron in the second layer. Convolution is key to addressing this issue, as it reduces the number of parameters and allows the network to go deeper with fewer parameters. With 10,000 learnable parameters, the solution may be totally intractable; however, if we reduce that image to a 5 x 5 area, for example, we now have 25 different neurons to handle instead of 10,000, which is much more feasible. This will also help us to eliminate, or at least greatly reduce, the vanishing or exploding gradient problem we sometimes encounter when we train multi-layer networks.

Let's now take a quick look at how this works visually. As shown in the following diagram, we will use the number 6 and run it through a CNN to see if our network can detect the number we are trying to draw. The image at the bottom of the following screenshot is what we will draw. By the time we convolve things all the way up to the top, we should be able to light up the single neuron that denotes the number 6, as follows:

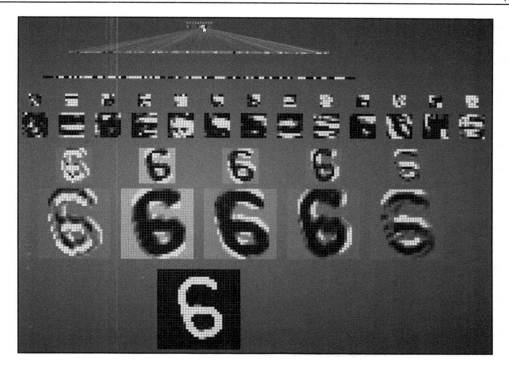

In the preceding screenshot, we can see an input layer (our single number 6), convolutional layers, down-sampling layers, and an output layer. Our progression is as follows: we start with a 32 x 32 image, which leaves us with 1,024 neurons. We then go down to 120 neurons, then to 100 neurons, and finally to 10 neurons in our output layer – that's one neuron for each of the 10 numerical digits. You can see that as we progress towards our output layer, the dimension of the image decreases. As we can see, we have 32 x 32 in our first convolutional layer, 10 x 10 in our second, and 5 x 5 in our second pooling layer.

It's also worth noting that each neuron in the output layer is fully connected to all 100 nodes in the fully-connected layer preceding it; hence, the term fully-connected layer.

If we make a three-dimensional drawing of this network and flip it around, we can better see how convolution occurs. The following diagram depicts just that, as the activated neurons are brighter in color. The layers continue to convolve until a decision is made as to which digit we have drawn, shown as follows:

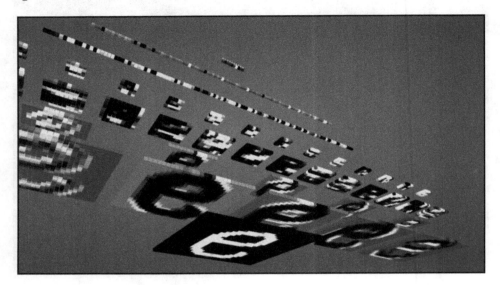

Filters

One of the other unique features of a CNN is that many neurons can share the same vector of weights and biases, or more formally, the same **filter**. Why is that important? Because each neuron computes an output value by applying a function to the input values of the previous layer. Incremental adjustments to these weights and biases are what helps the network to learn. If the same filter can be re-used, then the required memory footprint will be greatly reduced. This becomes very important, especially as the image or receptive field gets larger.

CNNs have the following distinguishing features:

- **Three-dimensional volumes of neurons**: The layers of a CNN have neurons arranged in three dimensions: width, height, and depth. The neurons inside each layer are connected to a small region of the layer before it called their receptive field. Different types of connected layers are stacked to form the actual convolutional architecture, as shown in the following diagram:

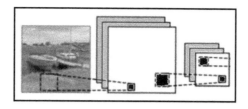

Convolving

- **Shared weights**: In a convolutional neural network, each receptive field (filter) is replicated across the entire visual field, as the preceding image shows. These filters share the same weight vector and bias parameters, and form what is commonly referred to as a **feature map**. This means that all the neurons in a given convolutional layer respond to the same feature within their specific field. Replicating units in this way allows for features to be detected regardless of their position in the visual field. The following diagram is a simple example of what this means:

This is a sample

This is a sample

This is a sample

This is a sample

Creating a network

Using the ConvNetSharp framework, there are three ways in which to create a neural network. First, we can use the `Core.Layers` or `Flow.Layers` objects to create a convolutional network (with or without a computational graph), as shown in the following diagram:

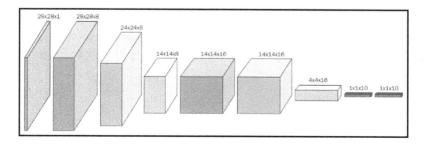

Alternatively, we can create a computational graph like the following:

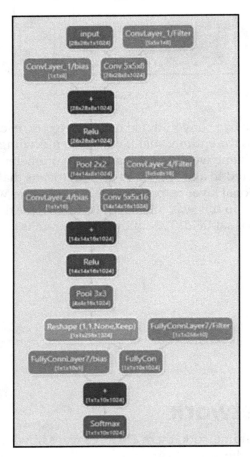

Example 1 – a simple example

Let's take a look at our first example. This is a minimal example in which we will define a **two-layer neural network** and train it on a single data point. We are intentionally making this example verbose so that we can walk through each step together to improve our understanding:

```
var net = new Net<double>();
```

The `InputLayer` variable declares size of input. As shown in the preceding code, we use two-dimensional data. Three-dimensional volumes (width, height, and depth) are required, but if you're not dealing with images then we can leave the first two dimensions (width and height) at a size of 1, as we have done in the following example:

```
net.AddLayer(new InputLayer(1, 1, 2));
```

Declare a fully-connected layer comprising 20 neurons, as follows:

```
net.AddLayer(new FullyConnLayer(20));
```

Next, we need to declare a Rectified Linear Unit non-linearity (ReLU) layer, as follows:

```
net.AddLayer(new ReluLayer());
```

Then, declare a fully-connected layer that will be used by the `SoftmaxLayer` with the following code:

```
net.AddLayer(new FullyConnLayer(10));
```

Declare the linear classifier on top of the previous hidden layer, as follows:

```
net.AddLayer(new SoftmaxLayer(10));
var x = BuilderInstance.Volume.From(new[] { 0.3, -0.5 }, new Shape(2));
```

We then need to move forward with a random data point through the network, as follows:

```
var prob = net.Forward(x);
```

`prob` is a volume. Volumes have property weights that store the raw data, and weight gradients that store gradients. The following code prints approximately 0.50101, as follows:

```
Console.WriteLine("probability that x is class 0: " + prob.Get(0));
```

Next, we need to train the network, specifying that x is class zero and using a stochastic gradient descent trainer, shown as follows:

```
var trainer = new SgdTrainer(net)
{
LearningRate = 0.01, L2Decay = 0.001
};
trainer.Train(x,BuilderInstance.Volume.From(new[]{ 1.0, 0.0, 0.0, 0.0, 0.0,
0.0, 0.0, 0.0, 0.0, 0.0 }, new Shape(1, 1, 10, 1)));
var prob2 = net.Forward(x);
Console.WriteLine("probability that x is class 0: " + prob2.Get(0));
```

The output should now be 0.50374, which is slightly higher than the previous value of 0.50101. This is because the network weights have been adjusted by the `trainer` to give a higher probability to the class we trained the network with (which was zero).

Example 2 – another simple example

As in the previous section, the following example also solves a simple problem, while demonstrating how to save and load a graph as well:

```
var cns = new ConvNetSharp<float>();
```

To create a graph, input the following code:

```
Op<float> cost;
Op<float> fun;
if (File.Exists("test.graphml"))
{
Console.WriteLine("Loading graph from disk.");
var ops = SerializationExtensions.Load<float>("test", true);
fun = ops[0];
cost = ops[1];
}
else
{
var x = cns.PlaceHolder("x");
var y = cns.PlaceHolder("y");
var W = cns.Variable(1.0f, "W", true);
var b = cns.Variable(2.0f, "b", true);
fun = x * W + b;
cost = (fun - y) * (fun - y);
}
var optimizer = new AdamOptimizer<float>(cns, 0.01f, 0.9f, 0.999f, 1e-08f);
using (var session = new Session<float>())
{
```

Next, to compute the dCost/dW at every node of the graph, we use the following code:

```
session.Differentiate(cost);
float currentCost;
do
{
 var dico = new Dictionary<string, Volume<float>> { { "x", -2.0f }, { "y",
1.0f } };
currentCost = session.Run(cost, dico);
Console.WriteLine($"cost: {currentCost}");
var result = session.Run(fun, dico);
```

```
session.Run(optimizer, dico);
}
while (currentCost > 1e-5);
float finalW = session.GetVariableByName(fun, "W").Result;
float finalb = session.GetVariableByName(fun, "b").Result;
Console.WriteLine($"fun = x * {finalW} + {finalb}");
fun.Save("test", cost);
```

To display the graph, input the following code:

```
var vm = new ViewModel<float>(cost);
var app = new Application();
app.Run(new GraphControl { DataContext = vm });
}
```

Example 3 – our final simple example

The following example does a simple calculation and displays the resultant computational graph. The code needed is as follows:

```
var cns = new ConvNetSharp<float>();
```

To create a graph, use the following code:

```
var x = cns.PlaceHolder("x");
var fun = 2.0f * x;
using (var session = new Session<float>())
{
```

Next, to compute the dCost/dW at every node of the graph, we use the following code:

```
session.Differentiate(fun);
```

Finally, to display the graph, input the following code:

```
var vm = new ViewModel<float>(x.Derivate);
var app = new Application();
app.Run(new GraphControl { DataContext = vm });
}
```

Using the Fluent API

For those of you who have the bug for Fluent APIs, ConvNetSharp has done a job of providing one for you.

Just look at the following example to see how easy it is to use the Fluent DSL when adding layers:

```
varnet=FluentNet<double>.Create(24, 24, 1)
.Conv(5, 5, 8).Stride(1).Pad(2)
.Relu()
.Pool(2, 2).Stride(2)
.Conv(5, 5, 16).Stride(1).Pad(2)
.Relu()
.Pool(3, 3).Stride(3)
.FullyConn(10)
.Softmax(10)
.Build();
```

GPU

In order to use GPU capability in your software using ConvNetSharp, you must have CUDA Version 8 and Cudnn Version 6.0 (April 27, 2017) installed. The `Cudnn bin path` should also be referenced in the **PATH** environment variable.

Fluent training with the MNIST database

In the following example, we will train our CNN against the `MNIST` database of images.

To declare a function, use the following code:

```
private void MnistDemo()
{
```

Next, download the training and testing `datasets` with the following command:

```
var datasets = new DataSets();
```

Load `100` validation sets with the following command:

```
if (!datasets.Load(100))
{
return;
}
```

Now it's time to create the neural network using the Fluent API, as follows:

```
this._net = FluentNet<double>.Create(24, 24, 1)
.Conv(5, 5, 8).Stride(1).Pad(2)
.Relu()
.Pool(2, 2).Stride(2)
.Conv(5, 5, 16).Stride(1).Pad(2)
.Relu()
.Pool(3, 3).Stride(3)
.FullyConn(10)
.Softmax(10)
.Build();
```

Create the stochastic gradient descent trainer from the network with the following command:

```
this._trainer = new SgdTrainer<double>(this._net)
{
LearningRate = 0.01,
BatchSize = 20,
L2Decay = 0.001,
Momentum = 0.9
};
do
{
```

Next, get the NextBatch of data with the following code:

```
var trainSample = datasets.Train.NextBatch(this._trainer.BatchSize);
```

Train the data received with the following command:

```
Train(trainSample.Item1, trainSample.Item2, trainSample.Item3);
```

It's now time to get the NextBatch of data; to do so, use the following command:

```
var testSample = datasets.Test.NextBatch(this._trainer.BatchSize);
```

The code can be tested with the following command:

```
Test(testSample.Item1, testSample.Item3, this._testAccWindow);
```

To report the accuracy, input the following command:

```
Console.WriteLine("Loss: {0} Train accuracy: {1}% Test accuracy: {2}%",
this._trainer.Loss, Math.Round(this._trainAccWindow.Items.Average() *
100.0, 2),
Math.Round(this._testAccWindow.Items.Average() * 100.0, 2));
} while (!Console.KeyAvailable);
```

Training the network

To train the convolutional network, we must perform both forward- and backward-propagation, as shown in the following example:

```
public virtual void Train(Volume<T> x, Volume<T> y)
{
Forward(x);
Backward(y);
}
```

The following screenshot illustrates our training in progress:

```
 C:\Development\AI\machinelearning\ConvNetSharp-master\Co...    —    □    ×
Example seen: 720 Fwd: 22.39ms Bckw: 89.85ms
Loss: 1.92352624078333 Train accuracy: 53% Test accuracy: 58%
Example seen: 740 Fwd: 21.85ms Bckw: 90.06ms
Loss: 1.41950561221303 Train accuracy: 56% Test accuracy: 56%
Example seen: 760 Fwd: 21.82ms Bckw: 90.15ms
Loss: 1.87681523159929 Train accuracy: 48% Test accuracy: 54%
Example seen: 780 Fwd: 23.42ms Bckw: 89.7ms
Loss: 1.67777663957109 Train accuracy: 45% Test accuracy: 51%
Example seen: 800 Fwd: 22ms Bckw: 89.47ms
Loss: 1.70291622757551 Train accuracy: 40% Test accuracy: 47%
Example seen: 820 Fwd: 22.01ms Bckw: 89.59ms
Loss: 1.50512485033825 Train accuracy: 43% Test accuracy: 54%
Example seen: 840 Fwd: 24.49ms Bckw: 91.27ms
Loss: 1.47737906037866 Train accuracy: 40% Test accuracy: 56%
Example seen: 860 Fwd: 22.03ms Bckw: 91.29ms
Loss: 1.28981352810234 Train accuracy: 50% Test accuracy: 60%
Example seen: 880 Fwd: 23.46ms Bckw: 90.91ms
Loss: 1.20406880951785 Train accuracy: 55% Test accuracy: 66%
Example seen: 900 Fwd: 22.04ms Bckw: 91.05ms
Loss: 1.18954053517371 Train accuracy: 66% Test accuracy: 69%
Example seen: 920 Fwd: 22.19ms Bckw: 90.5ms
Loss: 1.22823050848969 Train accuracy: 68% Test accuracy: 69%
Example seen: 940 Fwd: 21.96ms Bckw: 90.33ms
Loss: 0.815247982569938 Train accuracy: 75% Test accuracy: 69%
Example seen: 960 Fwd: 21.68ms Bckw: 89.72ms
Loss: 1.19716597057811 Train accuracy: 70% Test accuracy: 67%
Example seen: 980 Fwd: 22.06ms Bckw: 90.12ms
Loss: 1.54102802385204 Train accuracy: 66% Test accuracy: 69%
Example seen: 1000 Fwd: 23.76ms Bckw: 89.9ms
```

Testing the data

This section details the `Test` function, which will show us how to test the data we have trained. We get the network prediction and track the accuracy for each label that we have with the following command:

```
private void Test(Volume x, int[] labels, CircularBuffer<double> accuracy,
bool forward = true)
{
if (forward)
{
```

`Forward` momentum can be found with the following code:

```
this._net.Forward(x);
}
var prediction = this._net.GetPrediction();
for (var i = 0; i < labels.Length; i++)
{
```

To track the `accuracy`, input the following code:

```
accuracy.Add(labels[i] == prediction[i] ? 1.0 : 0.0);
}
}
```

Predicting data

Predicting data in this instance means predicting the `argmax` value. To do this, we assume that the last layer of the network is a `SoftmaxLayer`. Prediction occurs when we call the `GetPrediction()` function, as follows:

```
public int[] GetPrediction()
{
var softmaxLayer = this._lastLayer as SoftmaxLayer<T>;
if (softmaxLayer == null)
{
throw new Exception("Function assumes softmax as last layer of the net!");
}
var activation = softmaxLayer.OutputActivation;
var N = activation.Shape.Dimensions[3];
var C = activation.Shape.Dimensions[2];
var result = new int[N];
for (varn = 0; n < N; n++)
{
```

```
varmaxv = activation.Get(0, 0, 0, n);
varmaxi = 0;
for (vari = 1; i < C; i++)
{
var output = activation.Get(0, 0, i, n);
if (Ops<T>.GreaterThan(output, maxv))
{
maxv = output;
maxi = i;
}
}
result[n] = maxi;
}
return result;
}
```

Computational graphs

The following screenshots two computational graphs that we created based on our example applications:

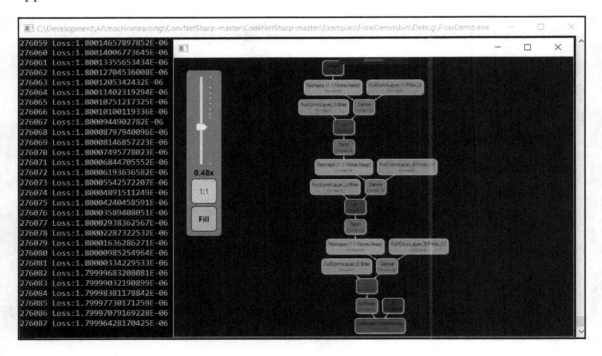

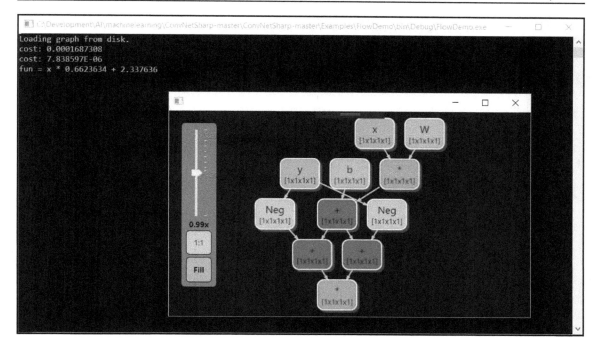

Summary

In this chapter, we used the open source package ConvNetSharp to explain CNNs. We looked at how to test and train these networks and also learned why they are convolutional. We worked with several example applications to explain how ConvNetSharp functions and operates. In the next chapter, we will look at autoencoders and RNNSharp, exposing you further to recurrent neural networks.

References

- ConvNetSharp Copyright (c) 2018 Cédric Bovar. Used with permission granted.
- The mostly complete chart of neural networks, explained, Asimov Institute, used with permission granted.
- http://scs.ryerson.ca/~aharley/vis/conv/flat.html

Training Autoencoders Using RNNSharp

In this chapter, we will be discussing **autoencoders** and their usage. We will talk about what an autoencoder is, the different types of autoencoder, and present different samples to help you better understand how to use this technology in your applications. By the end of this chapter, you will know how to design your own autoencoder, load and save it from disk, and train and test it.

The following topics are covered in this chapter:

- What is an autoencoder?
- Different types of autoencoder
- Creating your own autoencoder

Technical requirements

You will require Microsoft Visual Studio.

What is an autoencoder?

An autoencoder is an unsupervised learning algorithm that applies back propagation and sets target values equal to the inputs. An autoencoder learns to compress data from the input layer into shorter code, and then it uncompresses that code into something that closely matches the original data. This is better known as **dimensionality reduction**.

The following is a depiction of an autoencoder. The original images are encoded, and then decoded to reconstruct the original:

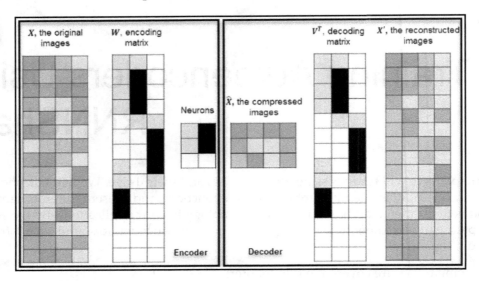

Different types of autoencoder

The following are different types of autoencoder:

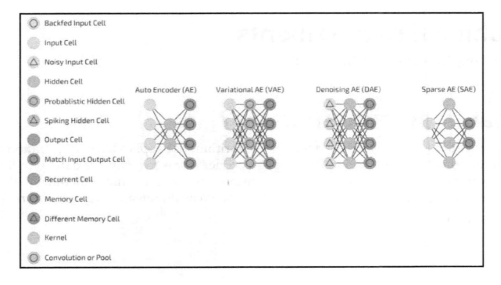

Let's briefly discuss autoencoders and the variants we have just seen. Please note that there are other variants out there; these are just probably the most common that I thought you should at least be familiar with.

Standard autoencoder

An autoencoder learns to compress data from the input layer into smaller code, and then uncompress that code into something that (hopefully) matches the original data. The basic idea behind a standard autoencoder is to encode information automatically, hence the name. The entire network always resembles an hourglass, in terms of its shape, with fewer hidden layers than input and output layers. Everything up to the middle layer is called the encoding part, everything after the middle layer is called the decoding part, and the middle layer itself is called, as you have probably guessed, the code. You can train autoencoders by feeding input data and setting the error status as the difference between the input and what came out. Autoencoders can be built so that encoding weights are the same as decoding weights.

Variational autoencoders

Variational autoencoders have the same architecture as autoencoders but are taught something else: an approximated probability distribution of the input samples. This is because they are a bit more closely related to Boltzmann and Restricted Boltzmann Machines. They do however rely on Bayesian mathematics as well as a re-parametrization trick to achieve this different representation. The basics come down to this: taking influence into account. If one thing happens in one place, and something else happens somewhere else, they are not necessarily related. If they are not related, then error propagation should consider that. This is a useful approach, because neural networks are large graphs (in a way), so it helps to be able to rule out the influence some nodes have on other nodes as you dive into deeper layers.

De-noising autoencoders

De-noising autoencoders reconstruct the input from a corrupted version of themselves. This does two things. First, it tries to encode the input while preserving as much information as possible. Second, it tries to undo the effect of the corruption process. The input is reconstructed after a percentage of the data has been randomly removed, which forces the network to learn robust features that tend to generalize better. De-noising autoencoders are autoencoders where we feed the input data with noise (such as making an image grainier). We compute the error the same way, so the output of the network is compared to the original input without noise. This encourages the network to learn not details but broader features, which are usually more accurate, as they are not affected by constantly changing noise.

Sparse autoencoders

Sparse autoencoders are, in a way, the opposite of autoencoders. Instead of teaching a network to represent information in less space or fewer nodes, we try to encode information in more space. Instead of the network converging in the middle and then expanding back to the input size, we blow up the middle. These types of network can be used to extract many small features from a dataset. If you were to train a sparse autoencoder the same way as an autoencoder, you would in almost all cases end up with a pretty useless identity network (as in, what comes in is what comes out, without any transformation or decomposition). To prevent this, we feed back the input, plus what is known as a **sparsity driver**. This can take the form of a threshold filter, where only a certain error is passed back and trained. The other error will be irrelevant for that pass and will be set to zero. In a way, this resembles spiking neural networks, where not all neurons fire all the time.

Creating your own autoencoder

Now that you are an expert on autoencoders, let's move on to less theory and more practice. Let's take a bit of a different route on this one. Instead of using an open-source package and showing you how to use it, let's write our own autoencoder framework that you can enhance to make your own. We'll discuss and implement the basic pieces needed, and then write some sample code showing how to use it. We will make this chapter unique in that we won't finish the usage sample; we'll do just enough to get you started along your own path to autoencoder creation. With that in mind, let's begin.

Let's start off by thinking about what an autoencoder is and what things we would want to include. First off, we're going to need to keep track of the number of layers that we have. These layers will be Restricted Boltzmann Machines for sure. Just so you know, we'll also refer to **Restricted Boltzmann Machines** as **RBMs** from time to time, where brevity is required.

So, we know we'll need to track the number of layers that our autoencoder has. We're also going to need to monitor the weights we'll need to use: learning rate, recognition weights, and generative weights. Training data is important, of course, as are errors. I think for now that should be it. Let's block out a class to do just this.

Let's start with an `interface`, which we will use to calculate errors. We will only need one method, which will calculate the error for us. The RBM will be responsible for doing this, but we'll get to that later:

```
public interface IErrorObserver
{
void CalculateError(double PError);
}
```

Before we define our RBM class, we'll need to look at the layers that it will use. To best represent this, we'll create an `abstract` class. We'll need to track the state of the layer, the bias used, the amount of bias change, the activity itself, and how many neurons it will have. Rather than distinguish between mirror and canonical neurons, we'll simply represent all neuron types as one single object. We also will need to have multiple types of RBM layer. Gaussian and binary are two that come to mind, so the following will be the base class for those layers:

```
public abstract class RestrictedBoltzmannMachineLayer
{
protected double[] state;
protected double[] bias;
protected double[] biasChange;
protected double[] activity;
protected int numNeurons = 0;
}
```

We must keep in mind that our RBM will need to track its weights. Since weights are applied through layers with a thing called a **synapse**, we'll create a class to represent all we want to do with weights. Since we'll need to track the weights, their changes, and the pre- and post-size, let's just create a class that encapsulates all of that:

```
public class RestrictedBoltzmannMachineWeightSet
{
private int preSize;
```

```
private int postSize;
private double[][] weights;
private double[][] weightChanges;
}
```

Next, as our learning rate encompasses features such as weights, biases, and momentum, we will be best served if we create a separate class to represent all of this:

```
public struct RestrictedBoltzmannMachineLearningRate
{
internal double weights;
internal double biases;
internal double momentumWeights;
internal double momentumBiases;
}
```

Finally, let's create a class that encompasses our training data:

```
public struct TrainingData
{
public double[] posVisible;
public double[] posHidden;
public double[] negVisible;
public double[] negHidden;
}
```

With all of this now defined, let's go ahead and work on our RestrictedBoltzmannMachine class. For this class, we'll need to keep track of how many visible and hidden layers we have, the weights and learning rate we will use, and our training data:

```
public class RestrictedBoltzmannMachine
{
private RestrictedBoltzmannMachineLayer visibleLayers;
private RestrictedBoltzmannMachineLayer hiddenLayers;
private RestrictedBoltzmannMachineWeightSet weights;
private RestrictedBoltzmannMachineLearningRate learnrate;
private TrainingData trainingdata;
private int numVisibleLayers;
private int numHiddenLayers;
}
```

And, finally, with everything else in place, let's create our Autoencoder class:

```
public class Autoencoder
{
private int numlayers;
private bool pretraining = true;
```

```
private RestrictedBoltzmannMachineLayer[] layers;
private AutoencoderLearningRate learnrate;
private AutoencoderWeights recognitionweights;
private AutoencoderWeights generativeweights;
private TrainingData[] trainingdata;
private List<IErrorObserver> errorobservers;
}
```

Even though we know there will be a lot more required for some of these classes, this is the basic framework that we need to get started framing in the rest of the code. To do that, we should think about some things.

Since weights are a prominent aspect of our autoencoder, we are going to have to use and initialize weights quite often. But how should we initialize our weights, and with what values? We will provide two distinct choices. We will either initialize all weights to zero, or use a Gaussian. We will also have to initialize the biases as well. Let's go ahead and create an interface from which to do this so it will make it easier later to select the type of initialization we want (zero or Gaussian):

```
public interface IWeightInitializer
{
double InitializeWeight();
double InitializeBias();}
```

We mentioned earlier that we needed to have multiple types of RBM layer to use. Gaussian and binary were two that came to mind. We have already created the interface for that, so let's go ahead and put our base classes into the form, as we will need them shortly. To do this, we will need to expand our RBM layer class and add two abstract methods so that they can be cloned, and so that we can set the state of the layer:

```
public abstract void SetState(int PWhich, double PInput);
public abstract object Clone();
```

Our `RestrictedBoltzmannMachineLayer` class now looks like this:

```
public abstract class RestrictedBoltzmannMachineLayer
{
protected double[] state;
protected double[] bias;
protected double[] biasChange;
protected double[] activity;
protected int numNeurons = 0;
public abstract void SetState(int PWhich, double PInput);
public abstract object Clone();
}
```

With our very basic autoencoder in place, we should now turn our attention to how we will build our autoencoder. Let's try to keep things as modular as possible and, with that in mind, let's create an `AutoEncoderBuilder` class that we can have encapsulate things such as weight initialization, adding layers, and so forth. It will look something like the following:

```
public class AutoencoderBuilder
{
private List<RestrictedBoltzmannMachineLayer> layers = new
List<RestrictedBoltzmannMachineLayer>();
private AutoencoderLearningRate learnrate = new AutoencoderLearningRate();
private IWeightInitializer weightinitializer = new
GaussianWeightInitializer();
}
```

Now that we have this class blocked in, let's begin to add some meat to it in the form of functions. We know that when we build an autoencoder we are going to need to add layers. We can do that with this function. We will pass it the layer, and then update our internal learning-rate layer:

```
private void AddLayer(RestrictedBoltzmannMachineLayer PLayer)
{
learnrate.preLearningRateBiases.Add(0.001);
learnrate.preMomentumBiases.Add(0.5);
learnrate.fineLearningRateBiases.Add(0.001);
if (layers.Count >= 1)
{
learnrate.preLearningRateWeights.Add(0.001);
learnrate.preMomentumWeights.Add(0.5);
learnrate.fineLearningRateWeights.Add(0.001);
}
layers.Add(PLayer);
}
```

Once we have this base function, we can then add some higher-level functions, which will make it easier for us to add layers to our autoencoder:

```
public void AddBinaryLayer (int size)
{
AddLayer (new RestrictedBoltzmannMachineBinaryLayer(size));
}
public void AddGaussianLayer (int size)
{
AddLayer (new RestrictedBoltzmannMachineGaussianLayer(size));
}
```

Finally, let's add a `Build()` method to our autoencoder builder to make it easy to build:

```
public Autoencoder Build()
{
return new Autoencoder(layers, learnrate, weightinitializer);
}
```

Now let's turn our attention to our autoencoder itself. We are going to need a function to help us initialize our biases:

```
private void InitializeBiases(IWeightInitializer PWInitializer)
{
for (int i = 0; i < numlayers; i++)
{
for (int j = 0; j < layers[i].Count; j++)
{
layers[i].SetBias(j, PWInitializer.InitializeBias());
}
}
}
```

Next, we are going to need to initialize our training data. This will basically involve creating all the arrays that we need and setting their initial values to zero as follows:

```
private void InitializeTrainingData()
{
trainingdata = new TrainingData[numlayers - 1];
for (inti = 0; i < numlayers - 1; i++)
{
trainingdata[i].posVisible = new double[layers[i].Count];
Utility.SetArrayToZero(trainingdata[i].posVisible);
trainingdata[i].posHidden = new double[layers[i + 1].Count];
Utility.SetArrayToZero(trainingdata[i].posHidden);
trainingdata[i].negVisible = new double[layers[i].Count];
Utility.SetArrayToZero(trainingdata[i].negVisible);
trainingdata[i].negHidden = new double[layers[i + 1].Count];
Utility.SetArrayToZero(trainingdata[i].negHidden);
}
}
```

With that behind us, we're off to a good start. Let's start to use the software and see what we're missing. Let's create our `builder` object, add some binary and Gaussian layers, and see how it looks:

```
AutoencoderBuilder builder = new AutoencoderBuilder();
builder.AddBinaryLayer(4);
builder.AddBinaryLayer(3);
```

```
builder.AddGaussianLayer(3);
builder.AddGaussianLayer(1);
```

Not bad, right? So, what's next? Well, we've got our autoencoder created and have added layers. We now lack functions to allow us to fine tune and train learning rates and momentum. Let's see how they would look if we were to add them here as follows:

```
builder.SetFineTuningLearningRateBiases(0, 1.0);
builder.SetFineTuningLearningRateWeights(0, 1.0);
builder.SetPreTrainingLearningRateBiases(0, 1.0);
builder.SetPreTrainingLearningRateWeights(0, 1.0);
builder.SetPreTrainingMomentumBiases(0, 0.1);
builder.SetPreTrainingMomentumWeights(0, .05);
```

That looks about right. At this point, we should add these functions into our `autoencoderbuilder` object so we can use them. Let's see how that would look. Remember that with our builder object we automatically created our learning rate object, so now we just have to use it to populate things such as our weights and biases, along with the momentum weights and biases:

```
public void SetPreTrainingLearningRateWeights(int PWhich, double PLR)
{
learnrate.preLearningRateWeights[PWhich] = PLR;
}
public void SetPreTrainingLearningRateBiases(int PWhich, double PLR)
{
learnrate.preLearningRateBiases[PWhich] = PLR;
}
public void SetPreTrainingMomentumWeights(int PWhich, double PMom)
{
learnrate.preMomentumWeights[PWhich] = PMom;
}
public void SetPreTrainingMomentumBiases(int PWhich, double PMom)
{
learnrate.preMomentumBiases[PWhich] = PMom;
}
public void SetFineTuningLearningRateWeights(int PWhich, double PLR)
{
learnrate.fineLearningRateWeights[PWhich] = PLR;
}
public void SetFineTuningLearningRateBiases(int PWhich, double PLR)
{
learnrate.fineLearningRateBiases[PWhich] = PLR;
}
```

Well, let's now stop and take a look at what our sample program is turning out to look like:

```
AutoencoderBuilder builder = new AutoencoderBuilder();
builder.AddBinaryLayer(4);
builder.AddBinaryLayer(3);
builder.AddGaussianLayer(3);
builder.AddGaussianLayer(1);
builder.SetFineTuningLearningRateBiases(0, 1.0);
builder.SetFineTuningLearningRateWeights(0, 1.0);
builder.SetPreTrainingLearningRateBiases(0, 1.0);
builder.SetPreTrainingLearningRateWeights(0, 1.0);
builder.SetPreTrainingMomentumBiases(0, 0.1);
builder.SetPreTrainingMomentumWeights(0, .05);
```

Not bad. All we should need to do now is to call our `Build()` method on our `builder` and we should have the first version of our framework:

```
Autoencoder encoder = builder.Build();
```

With all this now complete, and looking back at the preceding code, I think at some point we are going to need to be able to gain access to our individual layers; what do you think? Just in case, we'd better provide a function to do that. Let's see how that would look:

```
RestrictedBoltzmannMachineLayer layer = encoder.GetLayer(0);
RestrictedBoltzmannMachineLayer layerHidden = encoder.GetLayer(1);
```

Since our internal layers are `RestrictedBoltzmannMachine` layers, that is the type that we should be returning, as you can see from the previous code. The `GetLayer()` function needs to reside inside our autoencoder object, though, not the builder. So, let's go ahead and add it now. We'll need to be good developers and make sure that we have a bounds check to ensure that we are passing a valid layer index before we try to use it. We'll store all those neat little utility functions in a class of their own, and we might as well call it `Utility`, since the name makes sense. I won't go into how we can code that function, as I am fairly confident that every reader already knows how to do bounds checks, so you can either make up your own or look at the accompanying source code to see how it's done in this instance:

```
public RestrictedBoltzmannMachineLayer GetLayer(int PWhichLayer)
{
Utility.WithinBounds("Layer index out of bounds!", PWhichLayer, numlayers);
return layers[PWhichLayer];
}
```

OK, so we can now create our autoencoders, set weights and biases, and gain access to individual layers. I think the next thing we need to start thinking about is training and testing. We'll need to take each separately, of course, so why don't we start with training?

We will need to be able to train our RBM, so why don't we create an object dedicated to doing this. We'll call it, no surprise here, `RestrictedBoltzmannMachineTrainer`. Again, we are going to need to deal with our `LearningRate`, object, and weight sets, so let's make sure we add them as variables right away:

```
public static class RestrictedBoltzmannMachineTrainer
{
private static RestrictedBoltzmannMachineLearningRate learnrate;
private static RestrictedBoltzmannMachineWeightSet weightset;
}
```

Now, what functions do you think we will need for our trainer? Obviously, a `Train()` method is required; otherwise, we named our object incorrectly. We'll also need to train our weights and layer biases:

```
private static void TrainWeight(int PWhichVis, int PWhichHid, double
PTrainAmount);
private static void TrainBias(RestrictedBoltzmannMachineLayer PLayer, int
PWhich, double PPosPhase, double PNegPhase);
```

Last, but not least, we should probably have a `helper` function that lets us know the training amount, which for us will involve taking the positive visible amount times the positive hidden amount and subtracting that from the negative visible amount times the negative hidden amount:

```
private static double CalculateTrainAmount(double PPosVis, double PPosHid,
double PNegVis, double PNegHid)
{
return ((PPosVis * PPosHid) - (PNegVis * PNegHid));
}
```

OK, let's see where our program stands:

```
AutoencoderBuilder builder = new AutoencoderBuilder();
builder.AddBinaryLayer(4);
builder.AddBinaryLayer(3);
builder.AddGaussianLayer(3);
builder.AddGaussianLayer(1);
builder.SetFineTuningLearningRateBiases(0, 1.0);
builder.SetFineTuningLearningRateWeights(0, 1.0);
builder.SetPreTrainingLearningRateBiases(0, 1.0);
builder.SetPreTrainingLearningRateWeights(0, 1.0);
builder.SetPreTrainingMomentumBiases(0, 0.1);
```

```
builder.SetPreTrainingMomentumWeights(0, .05);
Autoencoder encoder = builder.Build();
RestrictedBoltzmannMachineLayer layer = encoder.GetLayer(0);
RestrictedBoltzmannMachineLayer layerHidden = encoder.GetLayer(1);
```

Nice. Can you see how it's all starting to come together? Now it's time to consider how we are going to add data to our network. Before we do any kind of training on the network, we will need to load data. How will we do this? Let's consider the notion of pre-training. This is the act of loading data into the network manually before we train it. What would this function look like in the context of our program? How about something such as this?

```
encoder.PreTrain(0, new double[] {0.1, .05, .03, 0.8});
```

We would just need to tell our autoencoder which layer we want to populate with data, and then supply the data. That should work for us. If we did this, then the following is how our program would evolve:

```
AutoencoderBuilder builder = new AutoencoderBuilder();
builder.AddBinaryLayer(4);
builder.AddBinaryLayer(3);
builder.AddGaussianLayer(3);
builder.AddGaussianLayer(1);
builder.SetFineTuningLearningRateBiases(0, 1.0);
builder.SetFineTuningLearningRateWeights(0, 1.0);
builder.SetPreTrainingLearningRateBiases(0, 1.0);
builder.SetPreTrainingLearningRateWeights(0, 1.0);
builder.SetPreTrainingMomentumBiases(0, 0.1);
builder.SetPreTrainingMomentumWeights(0, .05);
Autoencoder encoder = builder.Build();
RestrictedBoltzmannMachineLayer layer = encoder.GetLayer(0);
RestrictedBoltzmannMachineLayer layerHidden = encoder.GetLayer(1);
encoder.PreTrain(0, new double[] {0.1, .05, .03, 0.8});
encoder.PreTrain(1, new double[] { 0.1, .05, .03, 0.9 });
encoder.PreTrain(2, new double[] { 0.1, .05, .03, 0.1 });
encoder.PreTrainingComplete();
```

What do you think so far? With this code, we would be able to populate three layers with data. I threw in an extra function, PreTrainingComplete, as a nice way to let our program know that we have finished pre-training. Now, let's figure out how those functions come together.

For pretraining, we will do this in batches. We can have from 1 to *n* number of batches. In many cases, the number of batches will be just 1. Once we determine the number of batches we want to use, we will iterate through each batch of data.

For each batch of data, we will process the data and determine whether our neurons were activated. We then set the layer state based upon that. We will move both forward and backward through the network, setting our states. Using the following diagram, we will move forward through layers like this $Y \rightarrow V \rightarrow W \rightarrow (Z)$:

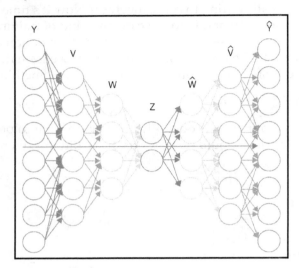

Once activations are set, we must perform the actual pre-training. We do this in the pre-synaptic layer, starting at layer 0. When we pre-train, we call our trainer object's `Train` method, which we created earlier and then pass the layer(s) and the training data, our recognition weights, and learning rate. To do this, we will need to create our actual function, which we will call `PerformPreTraining()`. The following is what this code would look like:

```
private void PerformPreTraining(int PPreSynapticLayer)
{
RestrictedBoltzmannMachineLearningRate sentlearnrate = new
RestrictedBoltzmannMachineLearningRate(learnrate.preLearningRateWeights[PPr
eSynapticLayer],learnrate.preLearningRateBiases[PPreSynapticLayer],learnrat
e.preMomentumWeights[PPreSynapticLayer],learnrate.preMomentumBiases[PPreSyn
apticLayer]);RestrictedBoltzmannMachineTrainer.Train(layers[PPreSynapticLay
er], layers[PPreSynapticLayer + 1],trainingdata[PPreSynapticLayer],
sentlearnrate, recognitionweights.GetWeightSet(PPreSynapticLayer)};
}
```

Once pre-training is complete, we now will need to calculate the error rate based upon the positive and negative visible data properties. That will complete our `pretraining` function, and our sample program will now look as follows:

```
AutoencoderBuilder builder = new AutoencoderBuilder();
builder.AddBinaryLayer(4);
builder.AddBinaryLayer(3);
builder.AddGaussianLayer(3);
builder.AddGaussianLayer(1);
builder.SetFineTuningLearningRateBiases(0, 1.0);
builder.SetFineTuningLearningRateWeights(0, 1.0);
builder.SetPreTrainingLearningRateBiases(0, 1.0);
builder.SetPreTrainingLearningRateWeights(0, 1.0);
builder.SetPreTrainingMomentumBiases(0, 0.1);
builder.SetPreTrainingMomentumWeights(0, .05);
Autoencoder encoder = builder.Build();
RestrictedBoltzmannMachineLayer layer = encoder.GetLayer(0);
RestrictedBoltzmannMachineLayer layerHidden = encoder.GetLayer(1);
encoder.PreTrain(0, new double[] {0.1, .05, .03, 0.8});
encoder.PreTrain(1, new double[] { 0.1, .05, .03, 0.9 });
encoder.PreTrain(2, new double[] { 0.1, .05, .03, 0.1 });
encoder.PreTrainingComplete();
```

With all this code behind us, all we need to do now is to save the autoencoder, and we should be all set. We will do this by creating a `Save()` function in the autoencoder, and call it as follows:

```
encoder.Save("testencoder.txt");
```

To implement this function, let's look at what we need to do. First, we need a filename to use for the autoencoder name. Once we open a **.NET TextWriter** object, we then save the learning rates, the recognition weights, and generative weights. Next, we iterate through all the layers, write out the layer type, and then save the data. If you decide to implement more types of RBM layers than we created, make sure that you in turn update the `Save()` and `Load()` methods so that your new layer data is saved and re-loaded correctly.

Let's look at our `Save` function:

```
public void Save(string PFilename)
{
TextWriter file = new StreamWriter(PFilename);
learnrate.Save(file);
recognitionweights.Save(file);
generativeweights.Save(file);
file.WriteLine(numlayers);
for (int i = 0; i < numlayers; i++)
{
```

```
if(layers[i].GetType() == typeof(RestrictedBoltzmannMachineGaussianLayer))
{
file.WriteLine("RestrictedBoltzmannMachineGaussianLayer");
}
else if (layers[i].GetType() ==
typeof(RestrictedBoltzmannMachineBinaryLayer))
{
file.WriteLine("RestrictedBoltzmannMachineBinaryLayer");
}
layers[i].Save(file);
}
file.WriteLine(pretraining);
file.Close();
}
```

With our autoencoder saved to disk, we now should really deal with the ability to reload that data into memory and create an autoencoder from it. So, we'll now need a `Load()` function. We'll need to basically follow the steps we did to write our autoencoder to disk but, this time, we'll read them in, instead of writing them out. Our weights, learning rate, and layers will have also a `Load()` function, just like each of the preceding items had a `Save()` function.

Our `Load()` function will be a bit different in its declaration. Since we are loading in a saved autoencoder, we have to assume that, at the time this call is made, an autoencoder object has not yet been created. Therefore, we will make this function `static()` on the autoencoder object itself, as it will return a newly created autoencoder for us. Here's how our function will look:

```
public static Autoencoder Load(string PFilename)
{
TextReader file = new StreamReader(PFilename);
Autoencoder retval = new Autoencoder();
retval.learnrate = new AutoencoderLearningRate();
retval.learnrate.Load(file);
retval.recognitionweights = new AutoencoderWeights();
retval.recognitionweights.Load(file);
retval.generativeweights = new AutoencoderWeights();
retval.generativeweights.Load(file);
retval.numlayers = int.Parse(file.ReadLine());
retval.layers = new RestrictedBoltzmannMachineLayer[retval.numlayers];
for (inti = 0; i < retval.numlayers; i++)
{
string type = file.ReadLine();
if (type == "RestrictedBoltzmannMachineGaussianLayer")
{
retval.layers[i] = new RestrictedBoltzmannMachineGaussianLayer();
```

```
}
else if (type == "RestrictedBoltzmannMachineBinaryLayer")
{
retval.layers[i] = new RestrictedBoltzmannMachineBinaryLayer();
}
retval.layers[i].Load(file);
}
retval.pretraining = bool.Parse(file.ReadLine());
retval.InitializeTrainingData();
retval.errorobservers = new List<IErrorObserver>();
file.Close();
return retval;
}
```

With that done, let's see how we would call our `Load()` function. It should be like the following:

```
Autoencoder newAutoencoder = Autoencoder.Load("testencoder.txt");
```

So, let's stop here and take a look at all we've accomplished. Let's see what our program can do, as follows:

```
AutoencoderBuilder builder = new AutoencoderBuilder();
builder.AddBinaryLayer(4);
builder.AddBinaryLayer(3);
builder.AddGaussianLayer(3);
builder.AddGaussianLayer(1);
builder.SetFineTuningLearningRateBiases(0, 1.0);
builder.SetFineTuningLearningRateWeights(0, 1.0);
builder.SetPreTrainingLearningRateBiases(0, 1.0);
builder.SetPreTrainingLearningRateWeights(0, 1.0);
builder.SetPreTrainingMomentumBiases(0, 0.1);
builder.SetPreTrainingMomentumWeights(0, .05);
Autoencoder encoder = builder.Build();
RestrictedBoltzmannMachineLayer layer = encoder.GetLayer(0);
RestrictedBoltzmannMachineLayer layerHidden = encoder.GetLayer(1);
encoder.PreTrain(0, new double[] {0.1, .05, .03, 0.8});
encoder.PreTrain(1, new double[] { 0.1, .05, .03, 0.9 });
encoder.PreTrain(2, new double[] { 0.1, .05, .03, 0.1 });
encoder.PreTrainingComplete();
encoder.Save("testencoder.txt");
Autoencoder newAutoencoder = Autoencoder.Load("testencoder.txt");
```

Summary

Well, folks, I think it's time to wrap this chapter up and move on. You should commend yourself, as you've written a complete autoencoder from start to (almost) finish. In the accompanying source code, I have added even more functions to make this more complete, and for you to have a better starting point from which to make this a powerful framework for you to use. As you are enhancing this, think about the things you need your autoencoder to do, block in those functions, and then complete them as we have done. Rather than learn to use an open-source framework, you've built your own—congratulations!

I have taken the liberty of developing a bit more of our autoencoder framework with the supplied source code. You can feel free to use it, discard it, or modify it to suit your needs. It's useful, but, as I mentioned, please feel free to embellish this and make it your own, even if it's just for educational purposes.

So, let's briefly recap what we have learned in this chapter: we learned about autoencoders and different variants, and we wrote our own autoencoder and created some powerful functionality. In the next chapter, we are going to move on to perhaps my most intense passion, and I hope it will soon be yours, **swarm intelligence**. There's going to be some theory, of course, but, once we're discussed that, I think you're going to be impressed with what particle swarm optimization algorithms can do!

References

- Vincent P, La Rochelle H, Bengio Y, and Manzagol P A (2008), *Extracting and Composing Robust Features with Denoising Autoencoders*, proceedings of the 25th international conference on machine learning (ICML, 2008), pages 1,096 - 1,103, ACM.
- Vincent, Pascal, et al, *Extracting and Composing Robust Features with De-noising Autoencoders.*, proceedings of the 25th international conference on machine learning. ACM, 2008.
- Kingma, Diederik P and Max Welling, *Auto-encoding variational bayes,* arXiv pre-print arXiv:1312.6114 (2013).
- Marc'Aurelio Ranzato, Christopher Poultney, Sumit Chopra, and Yann LeCun, *Efficient Learning of Sparse Representations with an Energy-Based Model*, proceedings of NIPS, 2007.
- Bourlard, Hervé, and Yves Kamp, *Auto Association by Multilayer Perceptrons and Singular Value Decomposition, Biological Cybernetics 59.4–5* (1988): 291-294.

Replacing Back Propagation with PSO

7

One of the latest examples of success with neural networks is the field of study known as **Swarm Intelligence**. Even though this field of study has been around for many years, advances in computer hardware combined with our understanding of studying animals has helped us to take this fascinating field out of the laboratory and into many different directions and real-world scenarios.

In this chapter, we are going to cover the following:

- Basic theory on Particle Swarm Optimization, or PSO for short
- The open-source machine-learning framework Encog
- Replacing the conventional back propagation with PSO

Technical requirements

You will require Microsoft Visual Studio and also might want refer `https://github.com/encog`.

Check out the following video to see Code in Action: `http://bit.ly/2QPd6Qo`.

Basic theory

OK, pop quiz time. What do a flock of birds, a school of fish, and a swarm of bees all have in common? Swarm intelligence—knowing how to cooperatively live and work near each other while optimally achieving the same objective. It's not about the intelligence of the individual, but rather the achievements of the group. No one individual has a clear path or directive, no one is at the top shouting orders, yet the optimal goal is always accomplished. Swarms of bees find new nests by doing waggle dances. Birds fly in great harmony, each taking turns being the leader. Fish swim collectively in beautiful architectures we call schools. But if we as humans always need someone at the top giving orders, and we still collectively don't always agree, how is it that millions of these little creatures have been doing it for years and we can't? Oops, going off on a tangent there, sorry!

Let's start off with a few quick definitions that will be used throughout to ensure we are all on the same page going forward.

Swarm intelligence

Swarm intelligence is the collective behavior of self-organizing systems, decentralized in nature. The swarm itself exhibits social cognitive behavior and achieves a goal that individual contributors would not achieve by themselves. The collective achieves the goals rather than the efforts of any individual contributor. This leads us to PSO itself.

Particle Swarm Optimization

Particle Swarm Optimization is a method (a population-based algorithm) that solves a problem by optimizing it iteratively while trying to improve a potential solution regarding its optimal quality. Every individual particle in the PSO algorithm learns from itself and another particle with a good fitness value. Each particle, which represents a solution, flies through the search space with a velocity that is dynamically adjusted according to its own and its companion's historical behaviors. The particles tend to fly toward better search areas over the course of the search process.

Types of Particle Swarm Optimizations

The following is a list of just some of the variants of Particle Swarm Optimization:

- Traditional Particle Swarm Optimization
- Canonical Particle Swarm Optimization
- Fully informed Particle Swarm Optimization

Let's now talk a little bit about the theory behind swarm intelligence, and then we'll move into two of the more specialized types of study in that field: Particle Swarm Optimization and ant swarm optimization, which are both direct drop-in replacements for back propagation!

However fascinating and intriguing you find this, please remember that nothing is perfect and there's no single shiny bullet that works for everything. This is a fascinating theory of study and entire books have been written on the subject. However, we always need to keep in mind the **No Free Lunch Theorem for Optimization**.

The No Free Lunch Theorem for Optimization states that no one can propose any one specific algorithm for solving all optimization problems. The success of an algorithm in solving one specific set of problems does not guarantee that it solves all optimization problems. More concretely, all optimization techniques perform equally well on average if you consider every optimization problem despite the performance on a subset of problems.

In a very well written paper titled *A time performance comparison of Particle Swarm Optimization in mobile devices*, written by Luis Antonio Beltrán Prieto, Zuzana Komínkova-Oplatková, Rubén Torres Frías, and Juan Luis Escoto Hernández, Particle Swarm Optimization is described like this:

"PSO is an optimization technique developed by Kennedy and Eberhart inspired by the collective behavior of animal groups, such as swarms of insects, to build a swarm of particles, i.e., a set of candidate solutions which flow through the parameter space generating trajectories driven by the best individuals. The initial population (swarm) consists of random solutions (particles) for the problem and is considered as a population of homogeneous agents which interact locally with other individuals without any central control. As a result, collective behavior is generated, thus evolution relies on cooperation and competition among individuals through the different epochs (generations). Each particle defines trajectories in the parameter space according to a motion function which is affected by velocity, inertia, cognitive coefficient and social coefficient. The objective is to find the global best solutions by stochastic weighting of the aforementioned elements. The process is iterative until a stopping criterion is met."

More intuitive analogies for Particle Swarm Optimization are birds and how they behave collaboratively, or a swarm of bees and how they determine which flowers to visit or which humans to attack! If you've ever watched a flock of birds flying or inadvertently knocked down a bee's nest then you know exactly what I am referring to.

Now, instead of dealing in just theory, let's take a hypothetical journey, a Treasure Hunt. I am intentionally going to make this as verbose as possible to ensure the analogy fits the problem space. It goes something like this.

You and several of your friends are in a mountainous region trying to find a hidden treasure worth a lot of money. We are not quite sure where the treasure is located, but we do know that it is in the deepest valley in the region. This equates to the minimum elevation in terms of height above sea level.

Let us also state that all our friends can communicate with one another using their cell phones (let's assume we have cell service here!). Let's also assume for now that our cell phones have GPS apps on them that tell us the elevation we are currently at. We will search each day for the treasure until we find it, and at the end of each day we will have either found the treasure and are rich, or we need to update our information and try again the next day. So, here's what each person has:

- A cell phone with a GPS app to determine elevation.
- Pen and paper to track our information at the end of each day. On this we will write the best position we have found (individually), which is our personal best, or **PBEST**. We will also write on this paper the best position that the entire team has found thus far, being our global best value or **GBEST**.

The following are the rules that we need to follow in our search:

- Each person will start in a random location and in a random direction. We determine our elevation right away and write it on our paper. It would be best for us if each person was spread out as much as possible so that we can be efficient and cover more ground, but this is not necessary.
- Our journey will take T number of days, to which at this point we are now aware of what that value is or will be.
- Every morning we will plan our day.
- Communications can only take place at the end of each day.
- Each morning, everyone compares the elevations they are at and updates **GBEST** on their paper.
- **GBEST** is the only piece of information each person can share (location and elevation).

- Each person will update **PBEST** on their paper if they find a better position.
- **PBEST** information is not shared; no one cares about anything but GBEST.
- Take notes of this one; to move each day, each person takes (for instance) x steps in the direction of the last day, y steps in the direction towards **PBEST**, and z steps in the direction of **GBEST**. Confused?
- Steps are random as we need some form of randomness in the search to make a stochastic search pattern for everyone as a collective group (that is, a flock or swarm of people).

With these few rules behind us, we can start our journey to the treasure. The team as a collective will keep locating different regions while watching the GBEST location found thus far. There is no guarantee of course that we will find the treasure, or that we will find it in the minimal number of days, but generally our search should be effective. Remember, no individual knows the exact location of the treasure, but cooperates with the swarm to develop collective intelligence to help find the treasure faster. For sure, it's better than a completely random search!

Let's try and plot out our steps in pseudo-pseudo-code:

1. Initialize a population of random solutions. For x number of decision variables, we have an x-space in which our solution exists as particles. Each particle has n variables and stores the best fitness for itself and the team.
2. For each iteration (either a number or a fitness value), calculate the fitness and store the best fitness variable (**PBEST**) and communicate this to the swarm.
3. Identify **GBEST** by comparing all the information we have received from the collective swarm.
4. Identify what will take us in the direction of **GBEST** considering our **PBEST** and **GBEST**.
5. Move in a specific time step in the direction of our velocity vector.
6. Over time, each team member (our particles in the swarm) will identify better **GBEST** variables and navigate towards them, thus also improving their **PBEST** at the same time.

With Particle Swarm Optimization we have three basic components that we should briefly discuss. They are, in no particular order:

- **Position**: Similar to the location in the preceding analogy, referring to the parameter values. This refers to where a particle (bird, bee, fish, and so on) is in an x-dimensional search space.
- **Velocity**: Similar to the movement direction in the preceding analogy, it is used for storing velocity, which will update each particle's position.
- **Fitness**: Similar to the elevation in the preceding analogy, this shows how fit the particle is.

Velocity is the main part of our Particle Swarm Optimization. It considers the current position of the particle, the best position found by the swarm (**GBEST**) (all particles), and the best position of the current particle (**PBEST**). Mathematically, it breaks down like this:

$$Velocity = r1 * currentVelocity + r2 * distancetoPBEST + r3 * distancetoGBEST.$$

$$Position = Position + Velocity$$

There are also three hyperparameters that we should mention as you will be hearing about them a lot.

Inertia Weight (W): The inertia weight controls the impact of the previous historical velocities on the current velocity. It regulates the trade-off between the global and local exploration abilities. If the inertia is high, particles are constrained in changing their direction and thus turn around much slower. This implies a larger exploration area and less possibility of convergence towards the optimum.

If inertia is small, then only a small amount of momentum is present from the previous time-step; this allows for much faster changes in direction. The problem here is that it could take quite a bit longer to converge.

By decreasing the inertia weight, it is easier to obtain a better global search ability and make the particles enter the optimal value area earlier. This means it will then be easier to have a better search ability and optimum value.

- **C1: Cognitive intelligence**
- *C2*: **Social intelligence**

It should be noted that C1 and C2 are positive constants that control how far an individual particle can move within a single iteration. Lower values will allow particles to stray further from the targeted regions before being reined in. Higher values will result in shorter, more abrupt movements toward, or past, the targeted region. By default, we will set both values to 2.0.

 You should experiment with the cognitive intelligence and social intelligence values, as sometimes different values lead to improved performance.

Original Particle Swarm Optimization strategy

As the particles (bees, birds, fish, termites) are moving along in the pre-designated search space to determine the best position, during each iteration of the cycle (where a *cycle* may be referred to as *max iterations*), each particle updates its velocity and position. Once the new velocity has been determined, it is used to compute the new particle position for the next time step.

Particle Swarm Optimization search strategy

For every particle over time, we will track the inertia (current velocity), the personal best (referred to as PBEST) and the global best (referred to as **GBEST**). As we mentioned, as we move through time to our global minimum, we will be tracking our personal best location, as well as the global best location of the swarm. This information will be communicated to the rest of the group so that the swarms' best location information can be communicated back to the group after each iteration is completed. We need to be either following the swarm or leading it in order to achieve our goals.

Particle Swarm Optimization search strategy pseudo-code

The following is pseudo-code for the logic we will be using to find our global minimum (the location of the treasure):

```
Initialize our hyperparameters
Initialize the population of particles
Do
For each particle
Calculate the objective
Update PBEST
Update GBEST
End for
```

```
Update Inertia weight
For each particle
Update Velocity (V)
Update Position (X)
End for
While the end condition is not satisfied
Return GBEST as the best global optimum estimation
```

Parameter effects on optimization

There are many varying theories for what each variable in Particle Swarm Optimization should look like. There are the theoretically acceptable values, and then there are the values determined over time with testing. The following are some of the recommendations I am making for your consideration.

The original (canonical) version of the Particle Swarm Optimization algorithm used values of 1, 2, and 2 respectively for Inertia, C1, and C2. These values do seem to work quite well. I have also found through testing, as have others, that values of 0.5, 1.5, and 1.5 respectively work even better, providing the best convergence rate depending upon the function and strategy used. Other values lead to slower or complete non-convergence. You, the reader, should perform your own testing based upon the strategy and function you prefer and determine which values you find suitable for your purpose.

Please note that, depending upon the strategy and function you select, your values should be different to provide proper convergence. For instance, using a minimization strategy and a Step function, I have seen optimal convergence happen using a global value of 0.729 for inertia. The cognitive intelligence (C1) is usually the same as the social intelligence (C2) with a pre-determined value of 2. I should point out however that, as you will see when we get to the chapter on building and using the visual workbench, the default value I use for C1 and C2 is 1.49445.

It is important to note that any of the values shown here are not pulled out of thin air. They come from a tremendous amount of optimization testing. In addition, they closely align with those tested by Clerc and Kennedy (2002) for implementation of constriction coefficients. Please feel free to use your own values and always keep in mind the No Free Lunch theorem.

The following is an example of how swarm optimization is affected by weight, social, and cognitive parameters:

 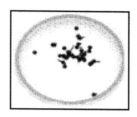 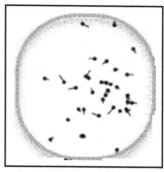

Iteration=31,w=0,c1=c2=2   Iteration=31,w=0.59,c1=c2=2   Iteration=31,w=1,c1=c2=2

Replacing back propagation with Particle Swarm Optimization

And now we come to the moment of truth. How does any of this apply to my code? In order to answer this question, we are going to use the open source Encog machine learning framework for our next demonstration. You can download our sample project following the instructions for the web location of the files for the book. Please make sure you have it loaded and open in Visual Studio before proceeding:

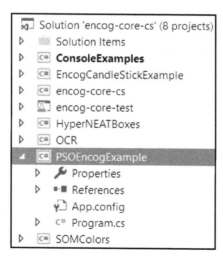

We are going to create a sample application that will demonstrate replacing back propagation with Particle Swarm Optimization. If all goes well, from the outside looking in you will not notice a difference.

You will be able to run this sample out of the box and follow along. We will be using the XOR problem solver, but instead of using back propagation it will be using the Particle Swarm Optimization we've been discussing. Let's dig a little deeper into the code. The following is the data that we will be using to implement this example:

```
/// Input for the XOR function.
public static double[][] XORInput = {new[] {0.0, 0.0},new[] {1.0,
0.0},new[] {0.0, 1.0},new[] {1.0, 1.0}};
/// Ideal output for the XOR function.
public static double[][] XORIdeal = {new[] {0.0},new[] {1.0},new[]
{1.0},new[] {0.0}};
```

Pretty straightforward.

Now let's look at the sample application itself. The following is how the XORPSO implementation is done:

```
///Create a basic training data set using the supplied data shown above
IMLDataSet trainingSet = new BasicMLDataSet(XORInput, XORIdeal);
///Create a simple feed forward network
BasicNetworknetwork = EncogUtility.SimpleFeedForward(2, 2, 0, 1, false);
///Create a scoring/fitness object
ICalculateScore score = new TrainingSetScore(trainingSet);
///Create a network weight initializer
IRandomizer randomizer = new NguyenWidrowRandomizer();
///Create the NN PSO trainer. This is our replacement function from back
prop
IMLTrain train = new NeuralPSO(network, randomizer, score, 20);
///Train the application until it reaches an error rate of 0.01
EncogUtility.TrainToError(train, 0.01);
network = (BasicNetwork)train.Method;
///Print out the results
EncogUtility.Evaluate(network, trainingSet);
```

When we run this sample application here is what it looks like. You will notice that it appears exactly like the normal XOR sample from the outside looking in:

```
■ C:\Development\AI\machinelearning\encog-...    —    □    ×
Iteration #43 Error:1.674299% Target Error: 1.000000%
Iteration #44 Error:1.340656% Target Error: 1.000000%
Iteration #45 Error:1.069344% Target Error: 1.000000%
Iteration #46 Error:1.069344% Target Error: 1.000000%
Iteration #47 Error:1.069344% Target Error: 1.000000%
Iteration #48 Error:1.069344% Target Error: 1.000000%
Iteration #49 Error:1.069344% Target Error: 1.000000%
Iteration #50 Error:1.069344% Target Error: 1.000000%
Iteration #51 Error:1.069344% Target Error: 1.000000%
Iteration #52 Error:1.069344% Target Error: 1.000000%
Iteration #53 Error:1.069344% Target Error: 1.000000%
Iteration #54 Error:1.069344% Target Error: 1.000000%
Iteration #55 Error:1.069344% Target Error: 1.000000%
Iteration #56 Error:1.069344% Target Error: 1.000000%
Iteration #57 Error:1.069344% Target Error: 1.000000%
Iteration #58 Error:1.069344% Target Error: 1.000000%
Iteration #59 Error:1.069344% Target Error: 1.000000%
Iteration #60 Error:1.069344% Target Error: 1.000000%
Iteration #61 Error:1.069344% Target Error: 1.000000%
Iteration #62 Error:1.069344% Target Error: 1.000000%
Iteration #63 Error:1.069344% Target Error: 1.000000%
Iteration #64 Error:0.870543% Target Error: 1.000000%
Neural Network Results:
Input=0.0000,0.0000, Actual=0.0600, Ideal=0.0000
Input=1.0000,0.0000, Actual=0.8981, Ideal=1.0000
Input=0.0000,1.0000, Actual=0.9310, Ideal=1.0000
Input=1.0000,1.0000, Actual=0.1268, Ideal=0.0000

Press any key to continue...                       v
```

You will notice that, when training is completed, we are very close to our ideal scores.

Now let's talk about the internals. Let's look at some of the internal variables used to make this work. The following is where you will see why we spent time early on with our basic theory. It should all be familiar to you now.

Declare the variable `m_populationSize`. A typical range is 20 - 40 for many problems. More difficult problems may need a much higher value. It must be low enough to keep the training process computationally efficient:

```
protected int m_populationSize = 30;
```

This determines the size of the search space. The positional components of particle will be bounded to [-maxPos, maxPos]. A well chosen range can improve the performance. -1 is a special value that represents boundless search space:

```
protected double m_maxPosition = -1;
```

This maximum change one particle can take during one iteration imposes a limit on the maximum absolute value of the velocity components of a particle, and affects the granularity of the search. If too high, particles can fly past the optimum solution. If too low, particles can get stuck in local minima. It is usually set to a fraction of the dynamic range of the search space (10% was shown to be good for high dimensional problems). -1 is a special value that represents boundless velocities:

```
protected double m_maxVelocity = 2;
```

For c1, cognitive learning rate >= 0 (the tendency to return to the personal best position):

```
protected double m_c1 = 2.0;
```

For c2, social learning rate >= 0 (tendency to move towards the swarm best position):

```
protected double m_c2 = 2.0;
```

Inertia weight, w, controls global (higher-value) versus local exploration of the search space. It is analogous to temperature in simulated annealing and must be chosen carefully or gradually decreased over time. The value is usually between 0 and 1:

```
protected double m_inertiaWeight = 0.4;
```

All these variables should be familiar to you. Next, the heart of what we are doing involves the `UpdateParticle` function, shown as follows. This function is responsible for updating the velocity, position, and personal best position of a particle:

```
public void UpdateParticle(int particleIndex, bool init)
{
int i = particleIndex;
double[] particlePosition = null;
if (init)
{
```

Create a new particle with random values (except the first particle, which has the same value as the network passed to the algorithm):

```
if (m_networks[i] == null)
{
m_networks[i] = (BasicNetwork)m_bestNetwork.Clone();
if (i > 0) m_randomizer.Randomize(m_networks[i]);
```

```
}
particlePosition = GetNetworkState(i);
m_bestVectors[i] = particlePosition;
```

Randomize the velocity:

```
m_va.Randomise(m_velocities[i], m_maxVelocity);
}
else
{
particlePosition = GetNetworkState(i);
UpdateVelocity(i, particlePosition);
```

Velocity clamping:

```
m_va.ClampComponents(m_velocities[i], m_maxVelocity);
```

New position $(Xt = Xt - 1 + Vt)$:

```
m_va.Add(particlePosition, m_velocities[i]);
```

Pin the particle against the boundary of the search space (only for components exceeding `maxPosition`):

```
m_va.ClampComponents(particlePosition, m_maxPosition);
SetNetworkState(i, particlePosition);
}
UpdatePersonalBestPosition(i, particlePosition);
}
```

Each particle will need to have its velocity updated, as you can see in the preceding code. This function will use the inertia weight, cognitive, and social terms to compute the velocity of the particle. This function encompasses the standard Particle Swarm Optimization formula as we described in the pseudo-code earlier in this chapter:

```
protected void UpdateVelocity(int particleIndex, double[] particlePosition)
{
int i = particleIndex;
double[] vtmp = new double[particlePosition.Length];
```

Standard PSO formula for inertia weight:

```
m_va.Mul(m_velocities[i], m_inertiaWeight);
```

Standard PSO formula for cognitive term:

```
m_va.Copy(vtmp, m_bestVectors[i])
m_va.Sub(vtmp, particlePosition);
m_va.MulRand(vtmp, m_c1);
m_va.Add(m_velocities[i], vtmp);
```

Standard PSO formula for social term:

```
if (i != m_bestVectorIndex)
{
m_va.Copy(vtmp, m_pseudoAsynchronousUpdate ?
m_bestVectors[m_bestVectorIndex] : m_bestVector);
m_va.Sub(vtmp, particlePosition);
m_va.MulRand(vtmp, m_c2);
m_va.Add(m_velocities[i], vtmp);
}
}
```

And this is how we substituted Particle Swarm Optimization for the standard backward propagation. Simple, right?

Summary

In this chapter we learned some basic theory behind Particle Swarm Optimization. We learned how this algorithm applies to, and has been influenced by flocks of birds, swarms of bees, schools of fish, and more. We also saw how we could replace the standard back propagation formula with Particle Swarm Optimization.

In the next chapter, we are going to learn how to delve into function optimization and show you how you can find optimal parameters, a process that will save you countless hours of testing!

Function Optimizations: How and Why

8

And now it's time to have some fun. We are going to develop a very powerful, three-dimensional application that you won't find anywhere else. This application will allow you to visualize how individual functions optimize over time, with a two and three-dimensional graphic of each. The source code for this application is located in the instructions given for access of the book's source code. This application will be very unique in that we will use a mixture of open source and third-party controls to create an unbelievably powerful application. Open source doesn't handle everything all the time, and for those of you serious about graphics I wanted to expose you to some controls aside from the open source standards such as ZedGraph, Microsoft Charting Controls, and others. As you will see in a moment, the difference is astounding and worth the ride. You can decide later if you want to change anything back to completely open source.

We are also going to show you how we can use Particle Swarm Optimization to enhance visualizations of function optimizations. By doing so you will see how each particle in the swarm converges to the optimal solution.

In this chapter, we are going to accomplish the following:

- Build a Visual Studio WinForms project
- Create a function optimization tester
- Implement graphic controls for our visualizations
- Talk about various third-party controls used in this project
- Learn about the various hyperparameters available
- Learn to tune and adjust hyperparameters
- Learn the effect of adjusting hyperparameters
- Learn about the purpose of functions
- Learn how to add new functions
- Demonstrate adding a new function and running a test

Technical requirements

You will be required to have a basic knowledge of .NET development using Microsoft Visual Studio and C#. You will need to download the code for this chapter from the book's website.

Check out the following video to see Code in Action: `http://bit.ly/2ppBmvI`.

Getting started

Before we get started, let me show you the product we are going to create. When we are done you will have an application that allows you to view graphically how a function minimizes or maximizes over iterations. This is contrary to the typical text-based representations of such systems, as follows:

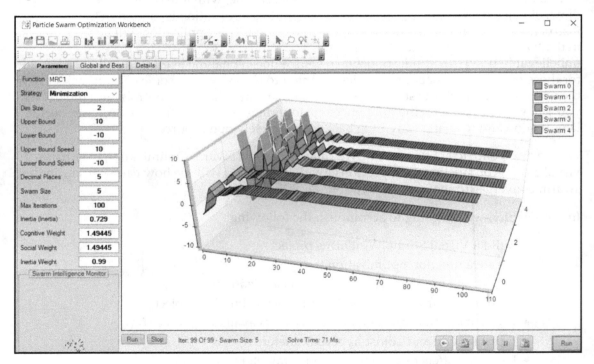

3D Plot

As you can see, this is a very visual application. Let's go ahead and break this down into sections that we will refer to as we progress.

The first section is the three-dimensional plot and is located on our main page. Three dimensions can provide much more insight into the path that each particle in the swarm takes, and the swarm itself is taking. It is also much easier to see when a particle or the swarm converges on the global minimum. For this plot we will use the incredible Nevron chart control. You can find more information about this Chart control at `https://www.nevron.com/products-open-vision-nov-chart-control-overview.aspx`. The main user interface is developed with DotNetBar. For those looking for a different user interface with all the bells and whistles such as crumbbars, tabs, grids, listviews, charts, sparklines, and more, this is a great and more affordable choice than say Infragistics or DevExpress. You can find more information about this suite of controls at `http://www.devcomponents.com/dotnetbar/`

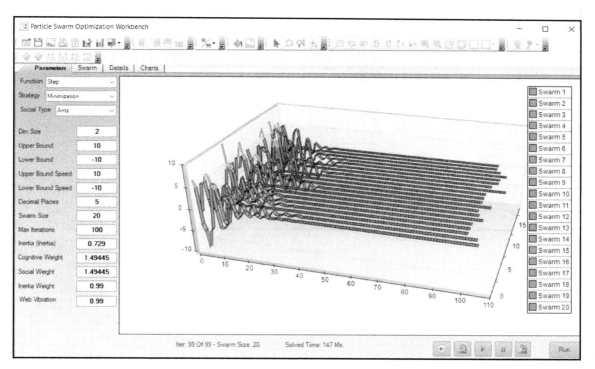

Main Page

The second section is the two-dimensional plot, and is located on our fourth page, the **Charts** tab. Some people would also call this type of plot a spaghetti plot. Its job is to plot the swarm on a two-dimensional plane. For this plot we will use the Microsoft Chart control. As you can see, this control becomes very busy when trying to plot on a two-dimensional surface. The more particles in the swarm that you have, the busier your chart will become:

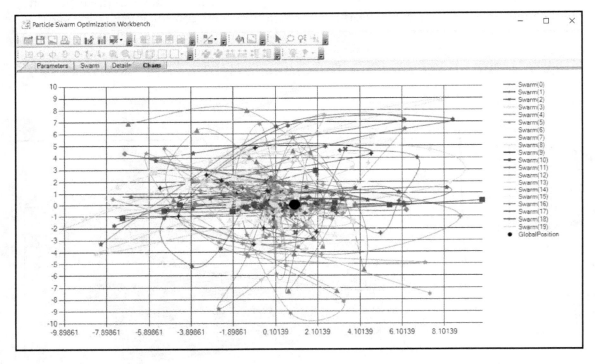

2D Visualization

The third section is the information tree, and is located on our third page, the **Details** tab. This tree houses detailed information from each iteration. The total number of iterations is a hyperparameter we will discuss shortly. Each iteration will track all swarm particle information such as position, speed, best position, and fitness, as follows:

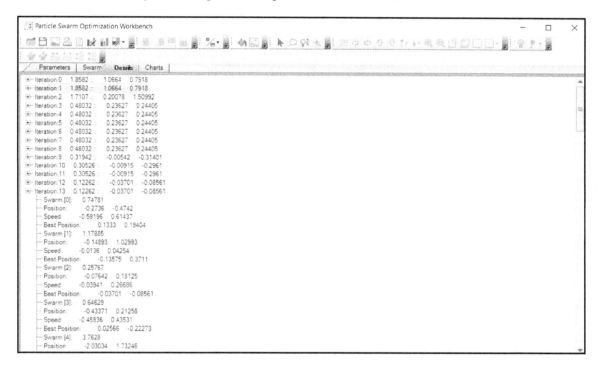

Information Tree

The fourth section is the function hyperparameters and is located on our main page. These parameters control the function and function optimizations and are essential for plotting both the two and three-dimensional plots. The individual parameters themselves will be discussed in a later section:

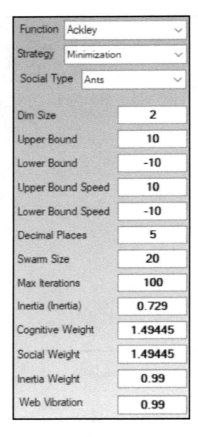

Parameters

The fifth section is the plot replay controls, also located on our main page at the bottom, underneath the hyperparameters. Aside from running the main function optimization iteration loop, they are responsible for replaying the function optimization plot for both the two and three-dimensional plots. You can play, pause, rewind, step forward, and step backward, as follows:

Run controls

With the details behind us, let's move on to discussing exactly how we are going to create our application. Let the fun begin!

Function minimization and maximization

Function minimization and maximization are the process of finding the smallest and largest value of a given function. Let's talk briefly about that value.

If the value is within a given range, then it is called the local extrema; if it is within the entire domain of a function then it is called the global extrema. Let's say we have a function f, and it's defined against a domain X. The maximum, or global, point at x* is f(x*) is greater than or equal to f(x) for all x in the domain X. Conversely, the function's global minimum point at x* is f(x*) is less than or equal to f(x) for all x in the domain X.

In a simpler fashion, the maximum point is also called the maximum value, and the minimum point is called the minimum value, of the function. The global maximum or minimum is either the highest or lowest function value in the entire domain space (search space), and the local maximum or minimum is the highest or lowest value in a defined neighborhood within that search space (it is not allowed to reside on the boundary at all), as follows:

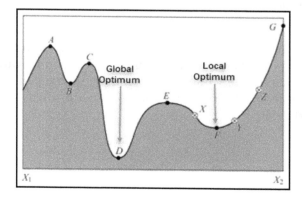

Global and Local Optimums

In this simple illustration, **D** is the global minimum and **G** is the global maximums. **A**, **C**, and **E** are local maximums (it is important to note that a function can have more than one global or local maximum or minimum). **B** and **F** are considered local minimum. **X**, **Y**, and **Z** exist around the minimum value **F**, since the value of **Y** is less than both **X** and **Z**:

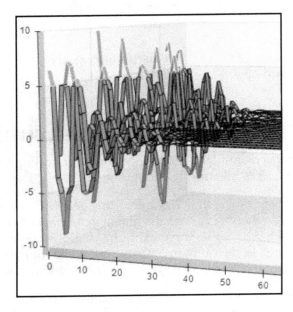

3D Tape Plot

Let's take a real example. Let's say we are using the function sin(x). The maximum value for this function is +1, and the minimum value would be -1. Therefore, we have the global minimum and maximum. Sin(x) can take on any value between negative and positive infinity, but over all of these values, the maximum can only be +1 and, the minimum can only be -1.

If we then restrict the search space (global domain) to between 0 and 90 (sometimes people call this the interval), sin(x) will now have a minimum of 0, and its value will be 0. However, the global or maximum value will now be 90 and the value is 1, because we restricted our search space to between 0 and 90. All values of sin(x) will lie between 0 and 1, within the interval of 0 to 90.

What is a particle?

One of the main components we are going to be dealing with is what is known as a
particle—hence, Particle Swarm Optimization. To briefly provide an analogy as to what a
particle is, let's look at it this way. Let's say that we see a flock of birds flying in the sky.
Each bird in this flock is a particle. We see a school of fish swimming in the water. Each fish
is a particle. We knocked down that bee hive and were attacked by hundreds of bees. Each
bee that attacked us was, you got it, a particle!

Each particle has fitness values which, once evaluated by the fitness function to be
optimized, will tell us how it ranks in the swarm. Additionally, we also have velocities that
direct the flying of each particle. The particles, like the birds, fly through our problem space
by following the *optimum* particle, which would be the leader of the flock of birds.

Now that we know exactly what a particle is, how do we describe it in computational
terms? We will define a structure like the following:

```
/// <summary> A particle. </summary>
public struct Particle
{
/// <summary> The position of the particle. </summary>
public double[] Position;
/// <summary> The speed of the particle. </summary>
public double[] Speed;
/// <summary> The fitness value of the particle. </summary>
public double FitnessValue;
/// <summary> The best position of the particle. </summary>
public double[] BestPosition;
/// <summary> The best fitness value of the particle. </summary>
public double BestFitnessValue;
}
```

With that behind us, let's go ahead and create our project. You should have Microsoft Visual Studio installed and open. If you have not installed Microsoft Visual Studio yet, you can install the free Community Version from the Microsoft web site. Once this is complete, open Microsoft Visual Studio and create a Windows Forms project as shown in the following screenshot. In our instance we are using .NET version 4.7.1. Feel free to use whatever version you have, but it needs to be at least version 4.5.2 or higher:

New Project Window

Next, let me mention that our user interface is created with a third-party product called **DotNetBar**. This is a fantastic, light weight user-interface library. It can be found here: http://www.devcomponents.com/dotnetbar/. We are now free to begin to focus on the formulation of our project. We will need to initialize some general areas of our program, such as the Swarm, the Chart, and the State.

Swarm initialization

To begin, we need to initialize our swarm and all the variables and properties that go along with it.

To begin the process, let's create a particle called `GlobalBest` (which I will refer to throughout the book as `gbest`) and initialize its best fitness value to either positive or negative infinity, depending upon whether the user has selected a strategy of `Minimization` or `Maximization`. We do so like this:

```
GlobalBest.BestFitnessValue = PSO_Type == PSOType.Minimization
? double.PositiveInfinity : double.NegativeInfinity;
```

Next, we will determine which swarm size the user desires, and then initialize all the particles in the swarm. Each particle will have several properties that will need to be initialized. They are:

Position:

```
Swarm[i].Position = Swarm_Random(lb_domXi, ub_domXi, dimSize);
```

Speed:

```
Swarm[i].Speed = Swarm_Random(lb_domXi, ub_domXi, dimSize);
```

Fitness value:

```
Swarm[i].FitnessValue = PSO_Round(Fitness(Swarm[i].Position));
```

Best fitness value:

```
Swarm[i].BestFitnessValue = Swarm[i].FitnessValue;
```

Best position:

```
Swarm[i].BestPosition = (double[])Swarm[i].Position.Clone();
```

With this done, we need to check and see if the individual particles' best fitness value (pbest) is better than the global particle (the team's) fitness value (gbest). If so we will update the global particle to that best position and fitness value and the other particles will follow it. We do so like this:

```
if (IsBetterPosition(Swarm[i].BestFitnessValue,
GlobalBest.BestFitnessValue, PSO_Type))
{
GlobalBest.BestPosition = (double[])Swarm[i].Position.Clone();
GlobalBest.BestFitnessValue = Swarm[i].BestFitnessValue;
}
```

Next, we will fill the swarm and global plot matrix like this:

```
FillPlotSwarmPosition(0, i, Swarm[i].Position);
FillPlotGlobalPosition(0, GlobalBest.BestPosition);
```

Once this is done, we will update our information tree with all the details associated with the swarm now. To do so we need to iterate through the entire swarm and record our information for display. Since we are using a Windows Tree Control, we will plot each swarm particle as a separate node, indicated by the identifier PSODisplayType.Swarm. The information underneath each node will be indicated by the identifier PSODisplayType.SwarmPosition. We accomplish this like this:

```
DisplayResult(PSODispType.GlobalBest, "Iter : 0 " +
GlobalBest.BestFitnessValue + " :: " + sResult(GlobalBest.BestPosition));
for (int i = 0; i < SwarmSize; i++)
{
DisplayResult(PSODispType.Swarm, "Swarm [" + i + "] : " +
Swarm[i].FitnessValue);
DisplayResult(PSODispType.SwarmPosition, "Position : " +
sResult(Swarm[i].Position));
DisplayResult(PSODispType.SwarmPosition, "Speed : " +
sResult(Swarm[i].Speed));
DisplayResult(PSODispType.SwarmPosition, "Best Pos : " +
sResult(Swarm[i].BestPosition));
}
```

Chart initialization

In our application, which we will call the workbench for short, we are dealing with two charts. The first chart is three-dimensional, the second is two-dimensional. Each one reflects the same data albeit from a different perspective. In our chart initialization function, we will initialize both charts at the same time.

- chartPSO is the name of our two-dimensional Microsoft Chart Control chart
- nChartControl2 is the name of our three-dimensional Nevron chart

Why not use the same control for both visualizations? That certainly could have been the case, but this way you, the reader, get exposure to two different types of control and can decide which you prefer.

The first thing that we will do is to create a random variable called _MarkerStyle. Each particle will have a different marker style in the two-dimensional plot, and we will use this random variable to control the correct creation of the style like this:

```
FastRandom _MarkerStyle = new FastRandom();
```

Next on our list of things to do is to clear the series data from both controls, just in case there is data left over. We do so with the following two lines of code. Remember, chartPSO is our two-dimensional chart and, nChartControl2 is our three-dimensional chart control:

```
chartPSO?.Series?.Clear();
nChartControl2?.Charts?[0]?.Series?.Clear();
```

To get the best visualization from our three-dimensional control, we need to ensure that it fits the entire chart area. We do that by setting the bounds mode like this:

```
nChartControl2.Charts[0].BoundsMode = BoundsMode.Stretch;
```

Now, we need to make sure that each particle in the swarm has an area of representation in both charts. We do that by iterating through the swarm size and setting each variable correctly. We start by adding the two-dimensional chart configuration first:

```
for (int i = 0; i < maxSwarm; i++)
{
chartPSO?.Series?.Add("Swarm(" + i + ")");
chartPSO.Series[i].ChartType = SeriesChartType.Spline;
chartPSO.Series[i].MarkerStyle = (MarkerStyle)_MarkerStyle.Next(1, 10);
chartPSO.Series[i].MarkerSize = 10;
```

And then the three-dimensional chart configuration, like this:

```
for (int i = 0; i < maxSwarm; i++)
{
NLineSeries m_Line1 =
(NLineSeries)nChartControl2.Charts[0].Series.Add(SeriesType.Line);
m_Line1.MultiLineMode = MultiLineMode.Series;
m_Line1.LineSegmentShape = LineSegmentShape.Tape;
m_Line1.DataLabelStyle.Visible = false;
m_Line1.DepthPercent = 50;
m_Line1.Name = "Swarm(" + i + ")";
```

Next, let's set the final variables of the two-dimensional chart as follows:

```
chartPSO?.Series?.Add("GlobalPosition");
chartPSO.Series[maxSwarm].ChartType = SeriesChartType.Point;
chartPSO.Series[maxSwarm].MarkerStyle = MarkerStyle.Diamond;
chartPSO.Series[maxSwarm].Color = Color.Black;
chartPSO.Series[maxSwarm].MarkerSize = 20;
```

And finally, to give our three-dimensional chart the most flexibility for use, we need to add the following toolbars:

```
nChartControl2.Controller?.Tools?.Add(new NTrackballTool());
nChartControl2.Controller?.Tools?.Add(new NZoomTool());
nChartControl2.Controller?.Tools?.Add(new NOffsetTool());
nChartControl2.Controller?.Tools?.Add(new NAxisScrollTool());
NPanelSelectorTool selector = new NPanelSelectorTool();
selector.Focus = true;
nChartControl2.Controller.Tools.Add(selector);
nChartControl2.Controller.Tools.Add(new NDataZoomTool());
```

State initialization

With the swarm and chart created and initialized, we now focus on initializing the state of the application itself. This means we are going to collect all the user-defined values and use them to initialize the hyperparameters themselves. We will delve into each in more detail in our chapter on hyperparameters, but for now you just need to be aware that they exist. Let's talk about each as it relates to state initialization.

First, we will determine the strategy we will use to initialize our function optimization. We will store this choice in a variable labeled `PSO_Type`. Our two choices of strategy are `Minimization` and `Maximization`. We determine the type like this:

```
switch (combType.SelectedIndex)
{
case 0:
PSO_Type = PSOType.Minimization;
break;
case 1:
PSO_Type = PSOType.Maximization;
break;
}
```

Next, we will initialize the number of dimensions, upper and lower bounds, and speed limits:

```
dimSize = Convert.ToInt32(txtdimSize.Text);
ub_domXi = Convert.ToDouble(txtUBXi.Text);
lb_domXi = Convert.ToDouble(txtLBXi.Text);
ub_SpeedXi = Convert.ToDouble(txtUbSpeedXi.Text);
lb_SpeedXi = Convert.ToDouble(txtLbSpeedXi.Text);
decP = Convert.ToInt32(txtdecP.Text);
```

We continue with initializing our inertia, cognitive, and social intelligence weights:

```
maxIter = Convert.ToInt32(txtmaxIter.Text);
Intertia = Convert.ToDouble(txtW.Text);
CognitiveWeight = Convert.ToDouble(txtC1.Text);
SocialWeight = Convert.ToDouble(txtC2.Text);
wMira = Convert.ToDouble(txtwMira.Text);
```

One of our most critical hyperparameters relates to our swarm and its population size – how many particles will be in the swarm. Remember, even though we have not placed boundary checks in the source code itself, this value should ideally be a value between 5 and 40. I often use a value of 5 to start my testing. We determine the swarm size by looking at the value that the user entered like this:

```
SwarmSize = Convert.ToInt32(txtSwarmSize.Text);
Swarm = new Particle[SwarmSize];
```

Finally, we initialize our global variables to track the maximum efficiency of the swarm:

```
PlotSwarm = new double[maxIter, SwarmSize, 2];
PlotGlobal = new double[maxIter, 2];
```

Controlling randomness

As the initialize process continues, position, speed, and fitness are initialized in the Swarm Initialization section. Here's a brief look at how we do randomization. We start with each of those hyperparameters, and then randomize the values between the upper and lower bounds we stated in our hyperparameters:

```
public double[] Swarm_Random(double a, double b, int n)
{
double[] x = new double[n];
for (int i = 0; i < n; i++)
{
x[i] = Swarm_Random(a, b);
}
return x;
}
public double Swarm_Round(double x) => decP != -1 ? Math.Round(x, decP) :
x;
public double Swarm_Random() => Swarm_Round(Randd.NextDouble());
public double Swarm_Random(double a, double b)
{
Return (a + (b - a) * Swarm_Random());
}
```

Updating the swarm position

The swarm position is the current position of the swarm relative to the global optimum – in this case, the hidden treasure. It is constrained within the upper and lower domain bounds as shown in the following. But remember, these two are hyperparameters entered in the same panel!:

```
private double UpdateSwarmPosition(double Pos, double Speed)
{
double OutPos = Pos + Speed;
return Math.Max(Math.Min(OutPos, upperBoundDomain), lowerBoundDomain);
}
```

Updating the swarm speed

The swarm speed is the speed at which the entire swarm heads towards the global optimum, that is, the hidden treasure. It is first calculated based upon the formula seen as follows, and then constrained within the upper and lower bound speed hyperparameter values. As you can see, we also apply various weights and randomization values to calculate and adjust the speed, like this:

```
// Update Swarm Speed
Swarm[i].Speed[j] = Inertia * Swarm[i].Speed[j] + CognitiveWeight *
Swarm_Random() * (Swarm[i].BestPosition[j] – Swarm[i].Position[j]) +
SocialWeight * Swarm_Random() * (GlobalBest.BestPosition[j] –
Swarm[i].Position[j]);
// Bound Speed
Swarm[i].Speed[j] = UpdateSwarmSpeed(Swarm[i].Speed[j]);
private double UpdateSwarmSpeed(double Speed)
{
return Math.Max(Math.Min(Speed, upperBoundSpeed), lowerBoundSpeed);
}
```

Main program initialization

When the main form initially loads, this is when our main initialization process begins. Let's walk through this method and talk about what exactly happens. In this method we are concerned with three-dimensional chart initialization.

First, we establish some general parameters for the chart:

```
// setup chart general parameters
NChart m_Chart = nChartControl2.Charts[0];
m_Chart.Enable3D = true;
m_Chart.Width = 60;
m_Chart.Height = 25;
m_Chart.Depth = 45;
m_Chart.Projection.Type = ProjectionType.Perspective;
m_Chart.Projection.Elevation = 28;
m_Chart.Projection.Rotation = -17;
m_Chart.LightModel.SetPredefinedLightModel(PredefinedLightModel.GlitterLeft
);
```

Next, we handle showing our interlaced strip on the back-left wall:

```
// add interlaced stripe to the Y axis
NScaleStripStyle stripStyle = new NScaleStripStyle(new
NColorFillStyle(Color.Beige), null, true, 0, 0, 1, 1);
```

```
stripStyle.SetShowAtWall(ChartWallType.Back, true);
stripStyle.SetShowAtWall(ChartWallType.Left, true);
stripStyle.Interlaced = true;
((NStandardScaleConfigurator)m_Chart.Axis(StandardAxis.PrimaryY).ScaleConfi
gurator).StripStyles.Add(stripStyle);
```

Finally, we handle showing our *x* axis gridlines like this:

```
// show the X axis gridlines
NOrdinalScaleConfigurator ordinalScale =
m_Chart.Axis(StandardAxis.PrimaryX).ScaleConfigurator as
NOrdinalScaleConfigurator;
ordinalScale.MajorGridStyle.SetShowAtWall(ChartWallType.Back, true);
ordinalScale.MajorGridStyle.SetShowAtWall(ChartWallType.Floor, true);
```

Running Particle Swarm Optimization

With our main functions in place and everything initialized from our hyperparameters, we can now focus on being able to run higher level functions. One of our PSO functions is the

PSORun method. This method is executed once the user clicks on the **Run** button .
Let's walk through this higher-level function now.

The first thing that we do is to initialize our state by calling our InitState function:

```
InitState();
```

After this we will clear out our information tree, create a new stopwatch responsible for timing our function, then run our Swarm_Run method. This will perform the actual function optimization behind the scenes, which usually will happen in just milliseconds depending upon the swarm size, iterations, and dimensions:

```
advTree1.Nodes.Clear();
SW = new Stopwatch();
SW.Start();
Swarm_Run();
SW.Stop();
```

Next, we create the variables responsible for tracking the global and individual positions of the entire swarm:

```
plotSwarmPositions = (double[,,])PlotSwarm.Clone();
plotGlobalPositions = (double[,])PlotGlobal.Clone();
maxIter = plotSwarmPositions.GetLength(0);
maxSwarm = plotSwarmPositions.GetLength(1);
```

And finally, we initialize our charts, and play back the swarm's plot at a much slower pace so the end user can see what has transpired. We do this via a call to the three methods as follows:

```
InitChart();
InitializeMeshSurfaceChart();
PlaybackPlot();
```

Our user interface

When we initially start our application, we have the proverbial blank slate. After initialization, we have completed the following items. Please note that the numbers relate to the screenshot showing the screen, shown as follows:

- Our parameters are initialized to the default values
- Our three-dimensional chart is initialized to the default values and has no series data:

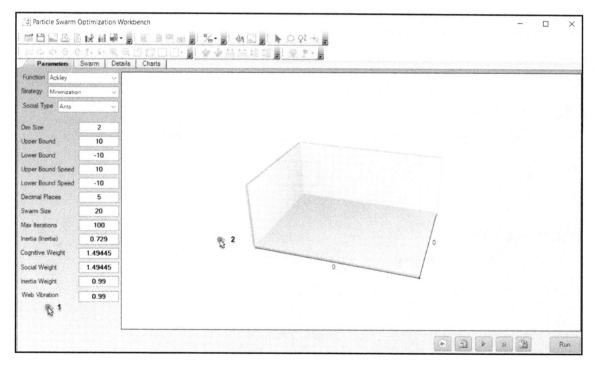

Blank 3D Chart

Run button

The run button executes the Particle Swarm Optimizer based upon the function and the strategy selected:

Rewind button

The Rewind button completely rewinds a PSO plot to the beginning:

Back button

The Back button takes one step backward in the particle swarm optimization test run:

Play button

The Play button replays a particle swarm optimization run from the beginning:

Pause button

The Pause button pauses a replay of a particle swarm optimization run:

Forward button

The Forward button takes one step forward in the particle swarm optimization test run:

Hyperparameters and tuning

Hyperparameters in general are parameters used for tuning various machine learning functions. This is no different in our application.

On the front screen of our application, the following is what our hyperparameter panel looks like. We will discuss each hyperparameter in detail:

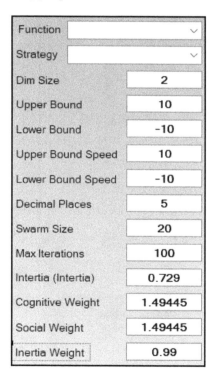

Parameters

Function

This is a list of all available functions for optimization. Simply select the function you would like to use, set the strategy and other parameters, and click the **Run** button. Please see the function optimization reference for more detailed information about each function. There are over 50 different functions currently available at the time of writing, and we will cover in a later chapter how you can add many of your own, as follows:

Functions

Strategy

There are two types of strategy one can apply to function optimization. You can either *maximize* or *minimize* your function optimization, as follows:

What do we mean by this? When we talk of maximizing or minimizing a function, what we mean is what the minimum or maximum value of that function can be. This is usually discussed in terms of either a *global range* or *local range*.

A global range would mean we want to determine the minimum or maximum value of the function over the whole range of input over which the function can be defined. This is commonly known as the domain of the function.

A local range, on the other hand, would mean we want to determine the minimum or maximum value of the function over the given local range, which will be a subset of the global range.

Dim size

Dimension size is used within the main loop (the final inner loop) to process the optimization for the function selected. 2 is the default value:

The relevant code is as follows:

```
// Main Loop
for (int iter = 1; iter < maxIter; iter++)
{
for (int i = 0; i < SwarmSize; i++)
{
for (int j = 0; j < dimSize; j++)
```

Upper bound

The upper bound is the upper limit of constraint which the swarm must adhere to. This is used to update the swarm position and to scale it within range. 10 is the default value:

Upper Bound	10

Please note that, depending upon the function you are optimizing, the upper and lower bounds could be quite different from the default. Consult the reference guide for your function and see what the upper and lower constraints are:

```
return Math.Max(Math.Min(OutPos, upperBoundDomain), lowerBoundDomain);
```

Upper Bound = 10:

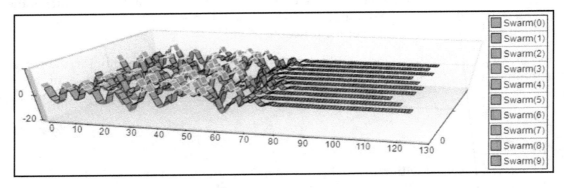

3D Plot

Upper Bound = 20:

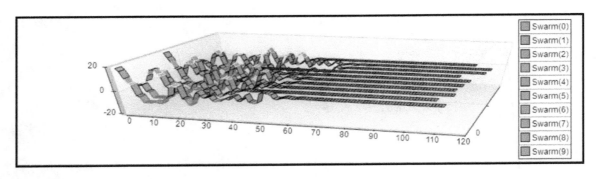

3D Plot

Lower bound

This is the lower limit of constraint which the swarm must adhere to. This is used to update the swarm position and to scale it within range. -10 is the default value:

The relevant code is as follows:

```
return Math.Max(Math.Min(OutPos, upperBoundDomain), lowerBoundDomain);
```

Upper bound speed

The upper bound speed is used to help determine the swarm speed. 10 is the default value:

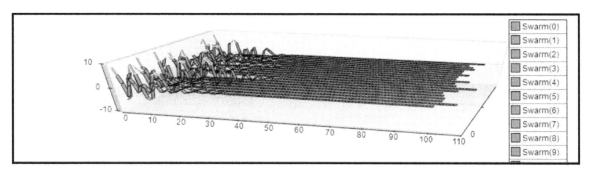

The code is as follows:

```
return Math.Max(Math.Min(Speed, upperBoundSpeed), lowerBoundSpeed);
```

Upper Bound Speed = 10:

3D Plot

Upper Bound Speed = 20:

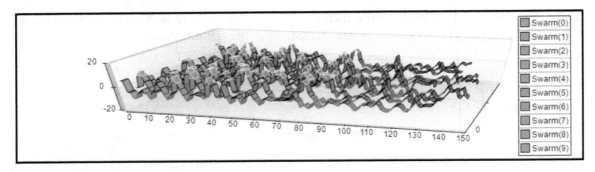

3D Plot

Lower bound speed

The lower bound speed is used to help determine the swarm speed. **-10** is the default value:

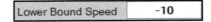

The code is as follows:

```
return Math.Max(Math.Min(Speed, upperBoundSpeed), lowerBoundSpeed);
```

Decimal places

This is the total number of decimal places rounding occurs to. 5 is the default value:

The code is as follows:

```
public double Swarm_Round(double x) => decimalPlaces != -1 ? Math.Round(x,
decimalPlaces)
```

Swarm size

The total size of the swarm. This equates to the total number of particles available for optimization. There is a considerable amount of theory as to the appropriate number to use here. Remember, as we stated before, no free lunch! Generally, a value of 20-40 seems to be the most widely acceptable. 20 is the default value:

Swarm Size	20

The code is as follows:

```
for (int i = 0; i < SwarmSize; i++)
```

Swarm Size = 10:

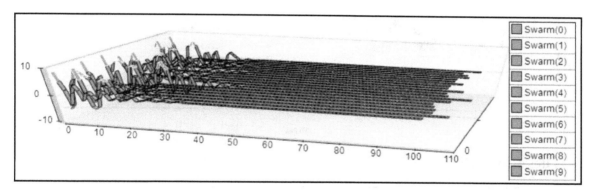

3D Plot

Swarm Size = 3:

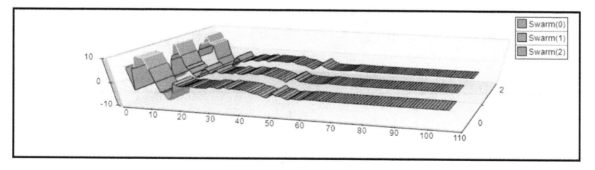

3D Plot

Max iterations

The total number of iterations used for testing. 100 is the default value:

The code is as follows:

```
for (int iter = 1; iter < maxIter; iter++)
```

Max Iterations = 100:

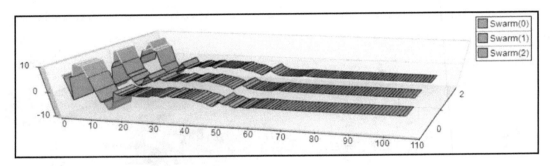

3D Plot

Max Iterations = 25:

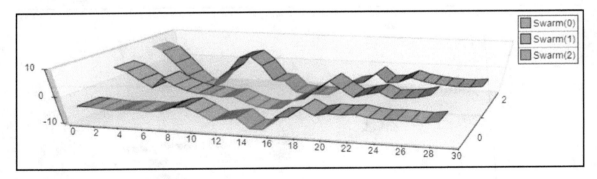

3D Plot

Inertia

Inertia weight was initially introduced to balance optimization between the global and local search abilities. In our case, inertia is multiplied by the inertia weight to adjust the swarm speed. Generally, the accepted values range from 0.4 to 1 for this variable. 0.729 is the default value:

Intertia (Intertia)	0.729

The code is as follows:

```
Swarm[i].Speed[j] = Inertia * Swarm[i].Speed[j]
```

Inertia = 0.729:

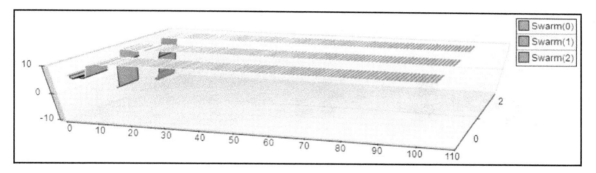

3D Plot

Inertia = 0.4:

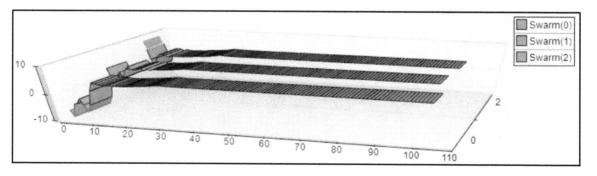

3D Plot

Social weight

Social weight is used to adjust the swarm speed. It is the factor that determines the extent to which the particle will follow the swarms' best solution. **1.49445** is the default value:

Social Weight	1.49445

The code is as follows:

```
// Update Swarm Speed
Swarm[i].Speed[j] = Intertia * Swarm[i].Speed[j]+ CognitiveWeight *
Swarm_Random() * (Swarm[i].BestPosition[j] - Swarm[i].Position[j])+
SocialWeight * Swarm_Random() * (GlobalBest.BestPosition[j] -
Swarm[i].Position[j]);
```

Social Weight = 1.49445:

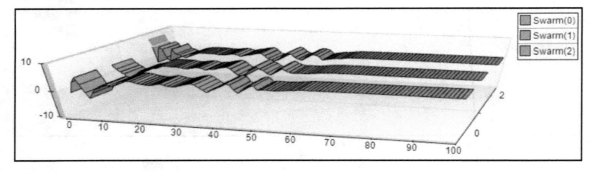

3D Plot

Social Weight = 1.19445:

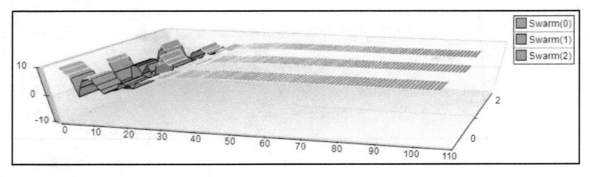

3D Plot

Cognitive weight

Cognitive weight is also used to adjust the swarm speed. It is the factor that determines the extent to which the particle will follow its own best solution. **1.49445** is the default value:

Cognitive Weight	1.49445

The code is as follows:

```
// Update Swarm Speed
Swarm[i].Speed[j] = Intertia * Swarm[i].Speed[j] + CognitiveWeight *
Swarm_Random() * (Swarm[i].BestPosition[j] – Swarm[i].Position[j])+
SocialWeight * Swarm_Random() * (GlobalBest.BestPosition[j] –
Swarm[i].Position[j]);
```

Cognitive Weight = 1.49445:

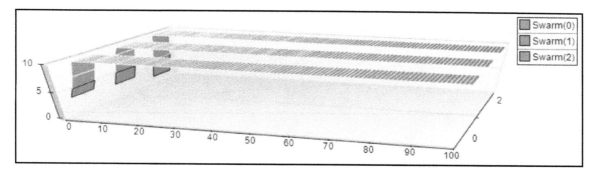

3D Plot

Cognitive Weight = 1.19445:

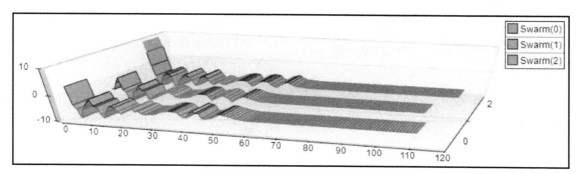

3D Plot

Inertia weight

The inertia weight is multiplied by the inertia during each iteration of function optimization. **0.99** is the default value:

Inertia Weight	**0.99**

The code is as follows:

```
Inertia *= InertiaWeight;
```

Inertia Weight = 0.99:

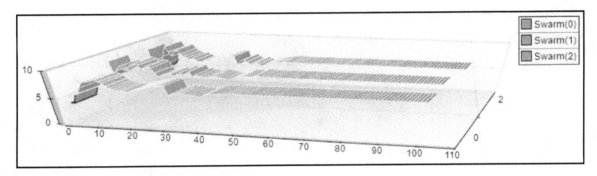

3D Plot

Inertia Weight = 0.75:

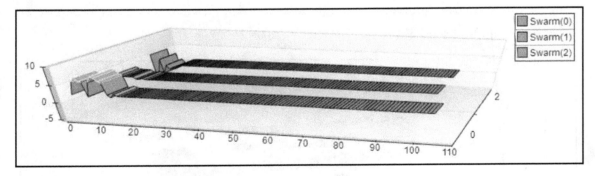

3D Plot

Understanding visualizations

In this section we will go over some of the many that you will see in our program. This includes both two and three dimensional plots.

Understanding two-dimensional visualizations

For our application, we have several two-dimensional visualizations that we need to explain. The first is the two-dimensional plot of the function optimization, be it maximized or minimized. This visualization is shown as follows. Remember, for this we are using Microsoft Chart control, which is available from: `https://www.microsoft.com/en-us/download/details.aspx?id=14422`:

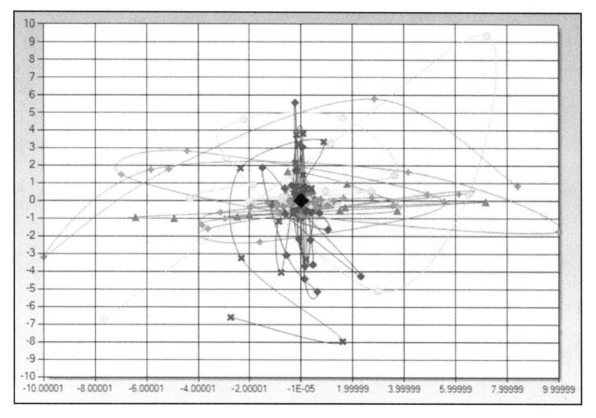

2D Visualization

For each particle that we are plotting (up to a maximum of 10), we will have a different marker style. A marker is the diamonds, circles, x's, and so on that you see plotted in the preceding diagram. We will also rotate colors based upon each particle being a different color. If you are not viewing this book in color, you hopefully will have shades of grey.

The lines you are seeing in the preceding diagram (or, to be more technically accurate, the splines you are seeing above them) are the plots of each particle in the swarm. The global optimum value (gbest) is the black diamond in the middle of the plot area. As you can see, we always remain within the bounds of our hyperparameters.

Understanding three-dimensional visualizations

In my opinion, the three-dimensional view is the easiest to interpret and the most intuitive, especially if it is a part of your model verification package that you will show to someone else. You can easily see in the following when each particle arrives (if it arrives) at a global optimum. The result is a flat line indicated by one or more line segments at the 0 axis:

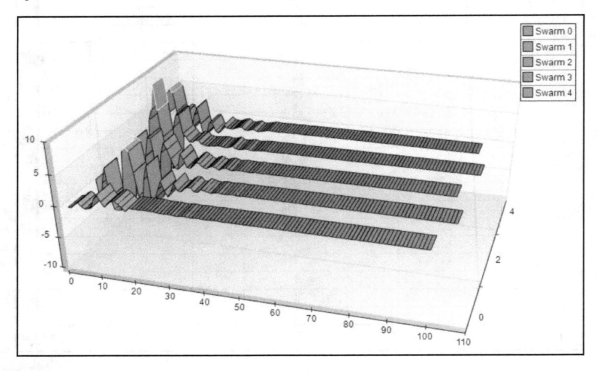

3D Visualization

There are several toolbars available for working with the three-dimensional view, of which you have rotational options, placement options, color options, and more:

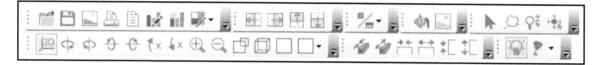

You can use the **Trackball** to rotate the chart to see the view from virtually any direction:

Just select the Trackball, and then select the chart, click on the left mouse button and drag the chart to your new view like this:

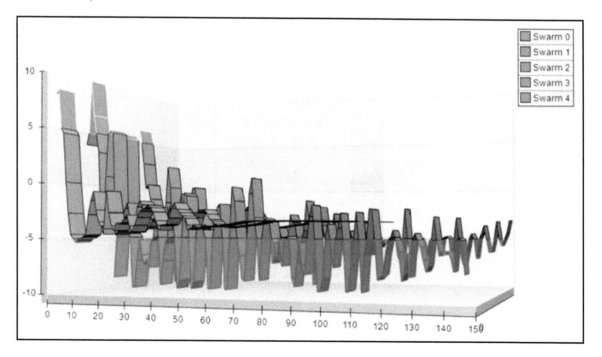

Rotating the View

You can change the lighting of the chart by changing the **Predefined Light Model**:

Pre-defined Light Models

You can then select from any of the predefined models, as follows:

Pre-defined Light Models

The depth and width controls allow you to change both dimensions on the chart to suit your needs:

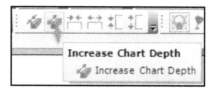

Simply click on the button you desire and continue to click to apply the transformation, as follows:

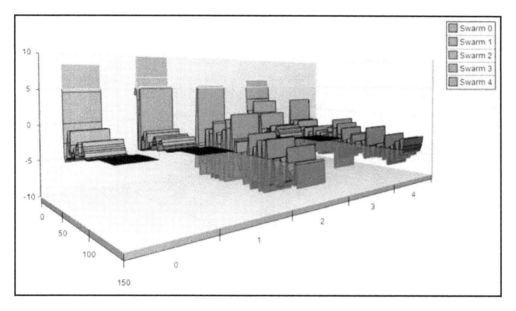

Transformations

Nudging allows you to make minor adjustments to the chart area and location. You can **Nudge** up, down, left, or right, as well as any combination of these, by simply clicking on the button(s) you desire, as follows:

In the main toolbar, you can open, save, and print charts, a valuable feature if you need to have images for a report based upon your testing. You can also use the Chart editor and Chart Wizard, as shown here:

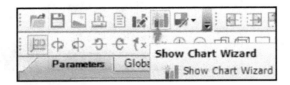

Simply select the button you desire, in this case **Show Chart Wizard**, and the wizard dialog will appear:

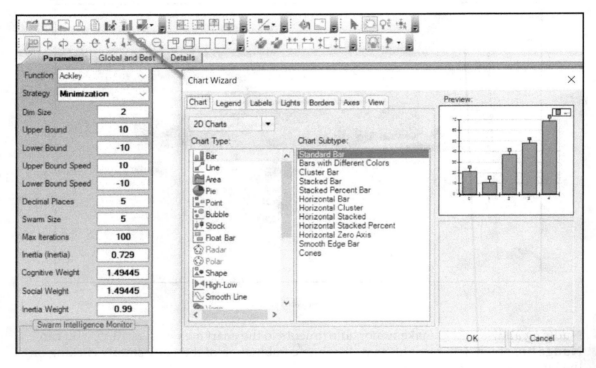

Chart Wizard

You can also use the 3D button to switch between two and three-dimensional views of the same chart.

The two dimensional view:

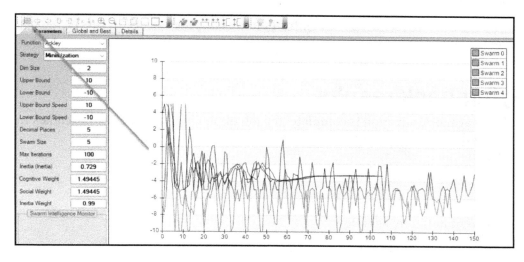

2D View

This can change to 3D with the click of a single button:

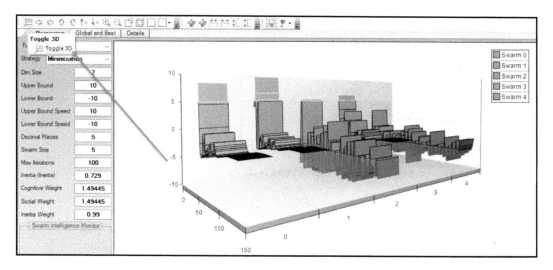

3D View

Plotting results

The following section details how our information is displayed once results have been obtained.

Playing back results

Once the swarm optimization is complete, the job of playing back the results comes to the forefront. Our main function in replaying plots is called `PlaybackPlot`. Let's discuss the function in detail:

```
private void PlaybackPlot()
{
```

Get our current iteration, as follows:

```
int iterN = GetCurrentIteration();
_Closing = false;
```

If we have played back all our points, then leave, as follows:

```
if (iterN >= maxIter)
return;
PlotStatusN = PlotStatus.Play;
```

Update the progress bar, as follows:

```
progressBarX1.Visible = true;
progressBarX1.Minimum = 0;
progressBarX1.Maximum = maxIter;
```

Go through all iterations, as follows:

```
for (int iter = iterN; iter < maxIter; iter++)
{
```

Update the progress bar value, as follows:

```
progressBarX1.Value = iter;
if (_Closing)
{
_Closing = false;
progressBarX1.Visible = false;
return;
}
```

Plot a single swarm iteration point, as follows:

```
PlotSwarmIterationPoint();
```

Briefly pause to allow the UI to remain responsive, as follows:

```
PauseForMilliSeconds(1);
ShowTitle();
}
PlotStatusN = PlotStatus.Pause;
progressBarX1.Visible = false;
}
```

You will notice in the preceding function a call to `PlotSwarmIterationPoint`. This function call (or method, if you prefer) is responsible for plotting a single movement of the particles. One step, if you will. Let's take you through that function and describe what is happening, as follows:

```
private void PlotSwarmIterationPoint()
{
```

If we have reached our final iteration, then leave, as follows:

```
int iterN = GetCurrentIteration();
if (iterN >= maxIter)
return;
NChart chart = nChartControl2.Charts[0];
chart.Axis(StandardAxis.PrimaryX).ScaleConfigurator = new
NLinearScaleConfigurator();
```

We need to plot a single point for each particle in the swarm, as follows:

```
for (int Swarm = 0; Swarm < maxSwarm; Swarm++)
{
```

Add a series for each point, as follows:

```
chartPSO.Series[Swarm].Points.AddXY(plotSwarmPositions[iterN, Swarm, 0],
plotSwarmPositions[iterN, Swarm, 1]);
```

Add a data point for the series we just created, as follows:

```
NLineSeries m_Line1 = (NLineSeries)nChartControl2.Charts[0].Series[Swarm];
m_Line1.AddDataPoint(new NDataPoint(plotSwarmPositions[iterN, Swarm, 0],
plotSwarmPositions[iterN, Swarm, 1]));
```

Dynamically handle the colors based upon the range values each particle is in, as follows:

```
ApplyLineColorRanges(new NRange1DD[] { new NRange1DD(-10, -5), new
NRange1DD(5, 10) },
new Color[] { Color.Red, Color.Yellow }, m_Line1);
}
```

Now, add a point for the optimal global position, as follows:

```
chartPSO.Series[maxSwarm].Points.Clear();
chartPSO.Series[maxSwarm].Points.AddXY(plotGlobalPositions[iterN, 0],
plotGlobalPositions[iterN, 1]);
```

Get the next iteration in line, paint the control, and show the text for what is going on:

```
iterN = Math.Min(iterN + 1, maxIter - 1);
nChartControl2.Refresh();
pictureBox1.Invalidate();
ShowTitle();
}
```

Updating the information tree

The information tree is on the **Details** tab page of our user interface. It houses the information treeview control. Depending upon the PSODispType, we will either create a new node or use the one previously created to write out our text:

```
private void DisplayResult(PSODispType DispType, string Text)
{
switch (DispType)
{
```

Create a brand-new node in the tree. This is the highest level for a particle in the tree and represents the global best values found, as follows:

```
case PSODispType.GlobalBest:
Node n1 = new Node();
n1.Text = Text;
lastNode = advTree1.Nodes.Add(n1);
break;
```

Add details to the previous node. This is an individual particle in the swarm, and its sub details will be plotted in our next function, as follows:

```
case PSODispType.Swarm:
Node n2 = new Node();
n2.Text = Text;
advTree1?.Nodes?[lastNode]?.Nodes?.Add(n2);
break;
```

Add details to the previous node. These are the exact details of the particle, and form the bottom-level node for this particle in the swarm, as follows:

```
case PSODispType.SwarmPosition:
Node n = new Node();
n.Text = Text;
advTree1?.Nodes?[lastNode]?.Nodes?.Add(n);
break;
}
}
```

And that's it. We now have a fully populated information tree!

Adding new optimization functions

One of the beautiful things about our visual test workbench is the ease of which we can add new optimization functions for testing.

The purpose of functions

Some problems are evaluated in terms of quality versus correct or incorrect. Such problems are known as optimization problems because the goal is the identification of the optimal value. Functions (sometimes called cost functions, objective functions, error functions, and so on.) achieve that goal by mapping n-dimensional real-valued items into one-dimensional real-valued items (some folks will prefer the termspaces over items' as it more closely aligns with the total search space we have talked about).

There are two types of function we will deal with. They are:

- **Minimization**: Looking for the solution with the smallest value
- **Maximization**: Looking for the solution with the largest value

It is not always the case that we can find the minimum or maximum, but sometimes must settle on a value that we deem sufficiently good enough for what we are trying to accomplish.

Adding new functions

Adding new functions is a very simple process comprised of only a few steps to follow. The steps are:

1. Create a new function based upon the signatures shown as follows
2. Add the new function name to the `GetFitnessValue` function
3. Add the new function name to the user interface

Let's now cover these steps on by one. First, we will deal with the function signature itself. The function signature is as follows:

```
Public double xxxxxx(double[] data)
{
}
```

Here, xxxxxx is the name of the function that will be displayed in the UI, as you can see in the following:

Optimization Function Window

After this, you must update the `GetFitnessValue` function so that it knows how to relate what is displayed on the user interface to an actual function. Here is a sample of what that function looks like. We will in fill this information later in the *Let's add a new function* section:

```
internal double GetFitnessValue(double x, double y)
{
```

```
double[] data = new double[2];
data[0] = x;
data[1] = y;
```

The `fitnessFunction` text is what appears in the user interface:

```
if (fitnessFunction == "Sphere")
return Swarm_Round(SphereFunction(data));
else if (fitnessFunction == "FitnessTest")
return Swarm_Round(FitnessTestFunction(data));
else if (fitnessFunction == "MSphere")
return Swarm_Round(MSphereFunction(data));
}
```

Let's add a new function

Now it's time for us to demonstrate how to add a new function. The function we are going to deal with is a modified version of the original `Levy` function and is the 13th version known to exist. This function is a minimization function.

The function itself, which you can find in the visual workbench source code, looks like this:

```
public double LevyFunction13(double[] data)
{
double x1 = data[0];
double x2 = data[1];
double term1 = Math.Pow(Math.Sin(3 * Math.PI * x1), 2);
double term2 = Math.Pow((x1 - 1), 2) * (1 + (Math.Pow(Math.Sin(3 * Math.PI
* x2),
2)));
double term3 = Math.Pow((x2 - 1), 2) * (1 + (Math.Pow(Math.Sin(2 * Math.PI
* x2), 2)));
return term1 + term2 + term3;
}
```

Definitely a lot of math there, right? Many times, functions such as this would be created in editors that make the math much easier to view. For instance, if I were to represent this code mathematically, it would look like this:

$$f(x,y) = \sin^2(3\pi x) + (x-1)^2 (1 + \sin^2(3\pi y)) + (y-1)^2 (1 + \sin^2(2\pi y))$$

If we were to take that and plot it with a tool such as MATLAB, here's what it would look like graphically:

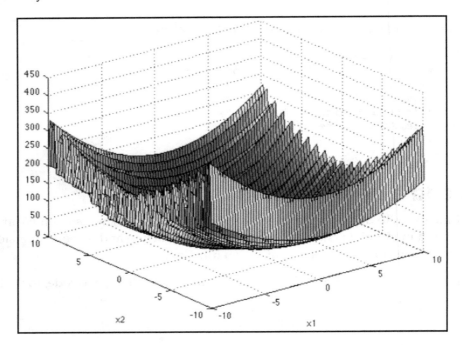

Our view under MATLAB

Why did I say and show all of that? Because, as you use this tool to validate your testing, you need to be able to relay, and sometimes justify, this information to others. No doubt just showing the C# code will not be enough, and the math and visualizations are many times what others expect to see. Don't let that put you off; you'll see how easy it is to create these functions, and our application makes it very easy to produce the kind of information you need.

Let's get back on track with adding that function.

Once we have added our new function, we now need to add it to the `GetFitnessValue` function so that what is selected in the user interface can relate to our specific function:

```
else if (fitnessFunction == "Shubert")
return Swarm_Round(ShubertFunction(data));
else if (fitnessFunction == "Levy13")
return Swarm_Round(LevyFunction13(data));
```

Once this is complete, we need to add it to our dropdown function list box on the user interface. Just select the combo box on the user interface, go to the **Items** property, and click on the button:

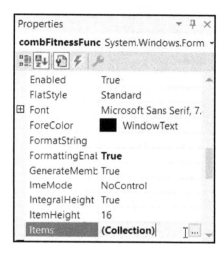

Next, simply add the text you want displayed, as follows:

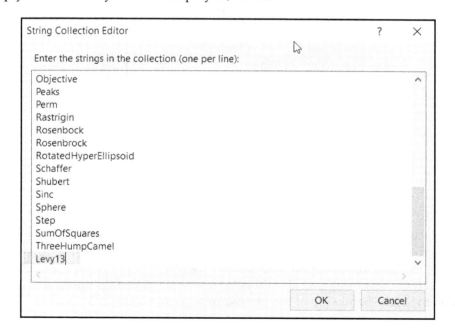

String Collection Editor

Once this is complete, build the project, run it, and you should see the function displayed in the dropdown:

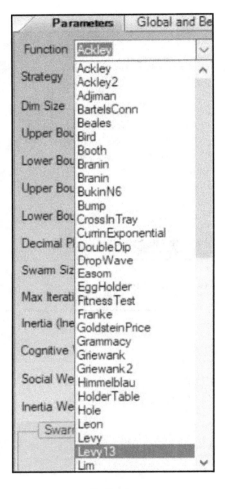

New Function

After you select the **Levy13** function, click on the **Run** button and voilà, you've successfully added a new function and tested its execution. You can view the two and three-dimensional plots as a validation of your success. Before you reach your maximum number of iterations (100 in this case), you should have reached a global optimum of 0 (the flat tape segments on the right-hand side of the three-dimensional plot):

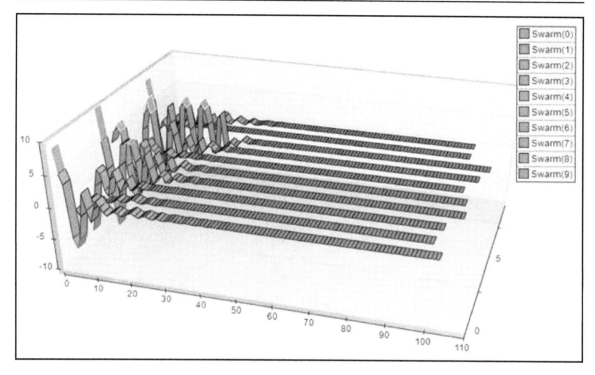

Swarm(0)
Swarm(1)
Swarm(2)
Swarm(3)
Swarm(4)
Swarm(5)
Swarm(6)
Swarm(7)
Swarm(8)
Swarm(9)

3D View

Summary

In this chapter, we discussed functions, what they are, and why we use them. We developed a very powerful and flexible application with which to test function optimization. We also showed you the complete process of adding a new function and how to run it once added. You are now free to add as many new functions as you like; just follow the process outlined herein and you should have no problems.

In the next chapter, we are going to learn how to replace back propagation with particle swarm-optimized algorithms, so hold on to your hats!

Finding Optimal Parameters 9

In this chapter, we will use the open source package SwarmOps, version 4.0, to help you better understand how you can use this tool to find optimal parameters for your functions. You can get the latest version of SwarmOps from the following location: `https://github.com/mattcolefla/SwarmOps`.

Once again, we must spend a little time on theory, where we will take you back to your academic days and lay a foundation so that we are all speaking the same language. It should be noted that SwarmOps is a highly research-oriented tool and should be used as such. We have worked hard to make this product open source, and the latest version has over 60 different optimization functions for you to use.

This chapter will cover the following topics:

- Fitness function
- Constraints
- Meta-optimization
- Optimization methods
- Parallelism

Ready? Here we go!

Technical requirements

You will be required to have a basic knowledge of .NET development using Microsoft Visual Studio and C#. You will need to download the code for this chapter from the book's website: SwarmOps (`https://github.com/mattcolefla/SwarmOps`).

Check out the following video to see Code in Action: `http://bit.ly/2QPddLO`.

Optimization

Solutions to some problems are not as cut and dry as *correct* or *incorrect*, but are rated in terms of quality. Such problems are known as **optimization problems** because the goal is to find the candidate solution with the best, that is, *optimal* quality.

What is a fitness function?

SwarmOps works for real-valued and single-objective optimization problems, that is, optimization problems that map candidate solutions from n-dimensional real-valued spaces to one-dimensional real-valued spaces. Mathematically speaking, we consider optimization problems to be functions f of the following form:

$$f : R^n \to R$$

In SwarmOps, it is assumed that f is a minimization problem, meaning that we are searching for the candidate solution $\vec{x} \in R^n$ with the smallest value $f(\vec{x})$. Mathematically, this may be written as the following:

Find $\vec{x}$, such that $\forall \vec{y} \in R^n : f(\vec{x}) \leq f(\vec{y})$.

Typically, however, it is not possible to locate the exact optimum; we must be satisfied with a candidate solution of sufficient quality that is perhaps not quite optimal. In this chapter, we refer to the optimization problem f as the `fitness` function, but it is can also be known as the cost function, objective function, error function, quality measure, and so on. We may also refer to candidate solutions as positions, agents, or particles, and to all possible candidate solutions as the search-space.

Maximization

SwarmOps can also be used with maximization problems. If $h : R^n \to R$ is a maximization problem, then the equivalent minimization problem is as follows: $f(\vec{x}) = -h(\vec{x})$.

Gradient-based optimization

The classic way of optimizing a fitness function f is to first deduce its gradient, that is, $\nabla f : R^n \rightarrow R^n$, which consists of the partial differentials of f, that is:

$$\nabla f = \left[\frac{\partial f}{\partial x1}, \ldots, \frac{\partial f}{\partial x_n} \right]$$

The gradient is then followed iteratively in the direction of the steepest descent; a quasi-Newton optimizer can also be used if necessary. This optimizer requires that not only for the fitness function f be differentiable, but time and patience as well. This is because the gradient can be very laborious to derive, and the execution can be very time-consuming.

Heuristic optimization

An alternative to gradient-based optimization methods is to let the optimization be guided solely by fitness values. This kind of optimization has no explicit knowledge of how the fitness landscape looks, but merely considers the fitness function to be a black box that takes candidate solutions as input and produces a fitness value as output. This is known in this chapter as Derivate-free optimization, direct search, heuristic optimization, meta-heuristics, black-box optimization, and so on. We will use these terms a lot!

Constraints

Constraints split the search-space into regions of feasible and infeasible candidate solutions. For instance, an engineering problem could have a mathematical model that should be optimized, but producing the solution in the real world puts some constraints on what is feasible. There are different ways of supporting and handling constraints in heuristic optimization.

Boundaries

A simple form of constraint is search-space boundaries. Instead of letting f map from the entire n-dimensional real-valued space, it is often practical to use only a part of this vast search-space. The lower and upper boundaries that constitute the search-space are denoted as $\vec{b}_{lo}$ and $\vec{b}_{up}$, so the fitness function is of the following form:

$$f : \left[\vec{b}_{lo}, \vec{b}_{up} \right] \rightarrow R$$

Such boundaries are typically enforced in optimization methods by moving candidate solutions back to the boundary value if they have exceeded the boundaries. This is the default type of constraint available in SwarmOps.

Penalty functions

More complicated constraints are supported transparently by any heuristic optimizer by penalizing infeasible candidate solutions, that is, by adding a penalty function to the fitness function. Examples can be found in the penalized benchmark problems section of the SwarmOps source code.

General constraints

SwarmOps supports general constraints by taking feasibility (constraint satisfaction) into account when comparing candidate solutions. Normally, we determine whether candidate solution $\vec{x}$ is better than $\vec{y}$ by comparing their fitness with $f(\vec{x}) < f(\vec{y})$, but it is also possible to take feasibility into account. Feasibility is a Boolean; either a candidate solution is feasible or it is infeasible. The comparison operator is as shown in the following diagram:

($\vec{x}$ is better than $\vec{y}$)

$\Updownarrow$

($\vec{y}$ is infeasible and $\vec{x}$ is feasible) or

($\vec{y}$ is infeasible and $\vec{x}$ is infeasible and $f(\vec{x}) < f(\vec{y})$)   or

($\vec{y}$ is feasible and $\vec{x}$ is feasible and $f(\vec{x}) < f(\vec{y})$)

Note in the preceding diagram that the actual implementation of this comparison is simplified somewhat. Also note that when $\vec{y}$ is feasible and $\vec{x}$ is infeasible, their fitness need not be computed. This is because $\vec{x}$ is worse than $\vec{y}$ due to their mutual feasibility. This is used in the implementation to avoid fitness computations when possible.

Constrained optimization phases

Using the earlier comparison operator means that optimization has two phases. First, the optimizer will likely only find infeasible candidate solutions, so it optimizes the fitness of infeasible solutions. Then, at some point, the optimizer hopefully discovers a feasible candidate solution; regardless of its fitness, it will then become the best-found solution of the optimizer and will form the basis of the further search. This is essentially the optimization of a feasible solution's fitness.

Constrained optimization difficulties

While SwarmOps gives you the ability to implement any constraint imaginable, constraints themselves will make it increasingly difficult for the optimizer to find feasibly optimal solutions because constraints narrow the feasible regions of the search-space. You should therefore also narrow the initialization and search-space boundaries to be as close to the feasible region as possible.

Implementation

There are two methods in the `problem` class where you can implement constraints; they are as follows:

- `EnforceConstraints()` allows you to make repairs to a candidate solution before its feasibility and fitness are evaluated. For example, when search-space boundaries are used as constraints then the repairing would consist of moving candidate solutions back between boundaries if they were overstepped. This is done by default.

- `Feasible()` evaluates and returns the feasibility of a candidate solution without altering it.

Meta-optimization

Optimization methods usually have several user-defined parameters that govern the behavior and efficacy of the optimization method. These are called the optimizer's behavioral or control parameters. Finding a good choice of these behavioral parameters has previously been done manually by hand-tuning, and sometimes even by using coarse mathematical analysis. It has also become a common belief among researchers that behavioral parameters can be adapted during optimization to improve overall optimization performance; however, this has been demonstrated to be mostly unlikely. Tuning behavioral parameters can be considered an optimization problem and hence can be solved by an overlaid optimization method. This is known here as meta-optimization, but is also known in the chapter as meta-evolution, super-optimization, parameter calibration, and so on. The success of SwarmOps when doing meta-optimization relies mainly on the following three factors:

1. SwarmOps features an optimization method that is particularly suitable as the overlaid meta-optimizer because it quickly discovers well-performing behavioral parameters (this is the LUS method described in this chapter).
2. SwarmOps employs a simple technique for reducing computational time called pre-emptive fitness evaluation.
3. SwarmOps uses the same function-interface for both optimization problems and optimization methods. Several scientific publications use SwarmOps for meta-optimization and have more elaborate descriptions than those given here, as well as having literature surveys and experimental results. The concept of meta-optimization can be illustrated schematically as follows:

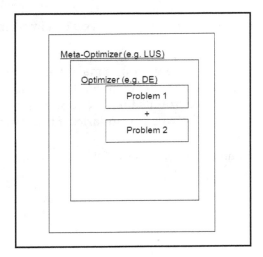

In the preceding diagram, the optimizer whose behavioral parameters are to be tuned is taken to the DE method, which we will look at later on in this chapter. The SwarmOps framework allows for parameters to be tuned regarding multiple optimization problems, which is sometimes necessary to make the performance of the behavioral parameters respond better to more general problems.

In the preceding example, the DE parameters are tuned for two specific problems.

Fitness normalization

Fitness functions must be non-negative to work properly with meta-optimization in SwarmOps. This is because pre-emptive fitness evaluation works by summing fitness values for several optimization runs and aborting the summation when the fitness sum becomes worse than that needed for the new candidate solution to be considered an improvement. This means that fitness values must be non-negative, so the fitness sum is only able to grow worse and the evaluation can thus be aborted safely. SwarmOps for C# does this normalization automatically, provided you accurately implement the **MinFitness** field of the `problem` class. For example, you may have a fitness function f which maps to, for example, $[-4, \infty]$. In this case, you would have to set **MinFitness** to -4. It is best to make **MinFitness** accurate so that $f\vec{x} - MinFitness = 0$ for the optimum $\vec{x}$, that is, **MinFitness** should be the fitness of the optimum. You should be able to estimate a lower fitness boundary for most real-world problems, and if you are unsure what the theoretical boundary value is, you may choose some boundary fitness value of ample—but not extreme—magnitude.

Fitness weights for multiple problems

If you are using multiple problems in meta-optimization, you may need to experiment with weights on each problem to make their influence on the meta-optimization process more equal.

Advice

The LUS method is generally recommended as the overlaid meta-optimizer. The tutorial source code contains suggestions for experimental settings that have been found to work well. It is best if you perform meta-optimization regarding the problems you are ultimately going to use the optimization method for. However, if your fitness function is very expensive to evaluate, then you may try and resort to using benchmark problems as a temporary replacement when meta-optimizing the behavioral parameters of your optimizer—provided you use multiple benchmark problems and the optimization settings are the same as those used in a real-world application. In other words, you should use benchmark problems of similar dimensionality and with a similar number of optimization iterations to what you would use for the actual problem you will ultimately optimize.

Constraints and meta-optimization

Two issues regarding constraints in meta-optimization should be mentioned; they are as follows:

- Constraints can be made on an optimizer's control parameters in the same manner as for an optimization problem by implementing the EnforceConstraints() and Feasible() methods in the optimizer's class. This means the meta-optimizer will search for control parameters that are feasibly optimal, allowing you to search for control parameters that meet certain criteria; for example, they have certain relationships with each other, such as one parameter being smaller than the other, and so on. See the source code of the MOL optimizer for an example of this.
- Constraint satisfaction is ignored when determining how well an optimizer performs in making up the meta-fitness measure. This is an open research topic, but experiments suggest that an optimizer's control parameters should be meta-optimized for unconstrained problems. This will also yield good performance on constrained problems.

Meta-meta-optimization

When using meta-optimization to find the best performing parameters of an optimizer, one may naturally wonder what the best performing parameters for the meta-optimizer itself are. It makes good sense to find the best meta-optimizer if one is going to use it often. The best parameters for the meta-optimizer can be found by employing yet another layer of optimization, which may be termed meta-meta-optimization.

Optimization methods

This section will give you a brief description of the optimization methods that are supplied with SwarmOps and some recommendations for their use.

Choosing an optimizer

When faced with a new optimization problem, the first optimizer you may want to try is the PS method, which is often sufficient and has the advantage of converging (or stagnating) very quickly. In addition, PS does not have any behavioral parameters that need tuning, so it either works or it doesn't. If the PS method fails at optimizing your problem, you may want to try the LUS method. You may need to run both PS and LUS several times as they may converge to sub-optimal solutions. If PS and LUS both fail, you may try the DE, MOL, or PSO methods and experiment with their behavioral parameters.

As a rule of thumb, the PS and LUS methods stagnate rather quickly, say, after $40.n$ iterations, where n is the dimensionality of the search-space. On the other hand, the DE, MOL, and PSO methods require substantially more iterations, say, $500.n$ or $2000.n$, and sometimes even more than that.

If these optimizers fail, you either need to tune their behavioral parameters using meta-optimization or use another optimizer altogether.

Gradient descent (GD)

A classic way of minimizing a fitness function ($f : R^n \rightarrow R$) is to repeatedly follow the gradient in the direction of steepest descent. The gradient function $\nabla f : R^n \rightarrow R^n$ is defined as the vector of the partial differentials of f, which is denoted as follows:

$$\nabla f = \left[\frac{\partial f}{\partial x1}, \ldots, \frac{\partial f}{\partial x_n} \right]$$

How it works

The position $\vec{x}$ is first chosen randomly from the search-space and then updated iteratively according to the following formula, regardless of fitness improvement:

$$\vec{x} \leftarrow \vec{x} - d. \frac{\nabla f(\vec{x})}{||\nabla f(\vec{x})||}$$

As shown in the preceding formula, $d > 0$ is the step-size. When f is a minimization problem, the descent direction is followed, that is, we subtract the gradient from the current position instead of adding it—as we would have done for ascending a maximization problem.

Drawbacks

The GD method has some drawbacks, namely that it requires the gradient ∇f to be defined. The gradient may also be expensive to compute, and GD may approach the optimum too slowly.

Pattern Search (PS)

The optimization method known as **Pattern Search** (**PS**) was originally by Fermi and Metropolis, as described in [6], and is a similar method used by Hooke and Jeeves [7]. The implementation presented here is the variant from [4].

How it works

PS uses one agent or position in the search-space that is being moved around. Let the position be denoted as $\vec{x} \in R^n$, which is initially picked at random from the entire search-space. The initial sampling range is the entire search-space: $\vec{d} = \vec{b}_{up} - \vec{b}_{lo}$. The potential new position is denoted as $\vec{y}$ and is sampled as follows.

First, pick an index ($R \in 1, \dots, n$) at random and let $Y_R = X_R + d_R$ and $Y_i = X_i$ for all $i \neq R$. If $\vec{y}$ improves on the fitness of $\vec{x}$ then move to $\vec{y}$. Otherwise, halve and reverse the sampling range for the Rth dimension with $d_R \leftarrow -d_R/2$. Repeat this several times.

Local Unimodal Sampling (LUS)

The LUS optimization method performs local sampling by moving a single agent around the search-space to decrease the sampling range during optimization. The LUS method was presented in [4] [8].

How it works

The agent's current position is denoted as $\vec{x} \in R^n$ and is initially picked at random from the entire search-space. The potential new position is denoted as $\vec{y}$ and is sampled from the neighborhood of $\vec{x}$ by letting $\vec{y} = \vec{x} + \vec{a}$, where $\vec{a} \sim U(-\vec{d}, \vec{d})$ is a random vector picked uniformly from the range $(-\vec{d}, \vec{d})$, which is initially $\vec{d} = \vec{b}_{up} - \vec{b}_{lo}$. In other words, the full range of the entire search-space is defined by its upper boundaries, $\vec{b}_{up}$, and its lower boundaries, $\vec{b}_{lo}$. LUS moves from position $\vec{x}$ to position $\vec{y}$ in the event of any improvement in the fitness. Upon each failure for $\vec{y}$ to improve on the fitness of $\vec{x}$, the sampling range is decreased by multiplication with a factor of q, as follows:

$$\vec{d} \leftarrow q.\vec{d}$$

Here, the decrease factor q is then defined as follows:

$$q = \sqrt[m]{1/2} = \left(\frac{1}{2}\right)^{\gamma n}$$

The preceding formula denotes n as the dimensionality of the search-space and γ as a user-defined parameter used to adjust the rate of sampling-range decrease. A value of $\gamma = 3$ has been found to work well for many optimization problems.

Differential Evolution (DE)

The multi-agent optimization method known as **Differential Evolution** (DE) was originally devised by Storn and Price [9]. Many DE variants exist and a simple one is implemented in the DE class. Several different DE variants are available through the DE Suite and JDE classes.

How it works

DE uses a population of agents. Let $\vec{x}$ denote the position of an agent being updated and which has been picked at random from the entire population. Let $\vec{y} = [y_1, \ldots, y_n]$ be its new potential position computed as follows (this is the so-called **DE/rand/1/bin variant**):

$$y_i = \begin{cases} ai + F(b_i - c_i), i = R \vee r_i < CR \\ x_i, else \end{cases}$$

Here, the vectors $\vec{a}$, $\vec{b}$, and $\vec{c}$ are the positions of distinct and randomly-picked agents from the population. The index $R \in \{1, \ldots, n\}$ is randomly-picked and $r_i \sim U(0, 1)$ is also picked randomly for each dimension, i. A move is made to the new position $\vec{y}$ if it improves on the fitness of $\vec{x}$. The user-defined parameters consist of the differential weight F, the crossover probability CR, and the population-size NP.

Particle Swarm Optimization (PSO)

The optimization method known as **Particle Swarm Optimization (PSO)** was originally devised by Kennedy, Eberhart, and Shi [10] [11]. It works by having a swarm of candidate solutions called particles, with each particle having a velocity that is updated recurrently and added to the particle's current position to move it to a new one.

How it works

Let $\vec{x}$ denote the current position of a particle from the swarm. The particle's velocity $\vec{v}$ is then updated as follows:

$$\vec{v} \leftarrow \omega\vec{v} + \phi_p \gamma_p (\vec{p} - \vec{x}) + \phi_g \gamma_g (\vec{g} - \vec{x})$$

Here, the user-defined parameter ω is called the inertia weight and the user-defined parameters ϕ_p and ϕ_g are weights on the attraction toward the particle's own best-known position, $\vec{p}$, and the swarm's best-known position, $\vec{g}$. These are also weighted by the random numbers $\gamma_1, \gamma_2 \sim U(0,1)$. In addition to this, the user also determines the swarm-size, S. In the SwarmOps implementation, the velocity is bounded to the full range of the search-space, so an agent cannot move further than one search space boundary to the other in a single move.

Once the agent's velocity has been computed it is added to the agent's position, as follows:

$$\vec{x} \leftarrow \vec{x} + \vec{v}$$

Many Optimizing Liaisons (MOL)

A simplification of PSO is called **Many Optimizing Liaisons** (MOL) and was originally suggested by Kennedy [12], who called it the *Social Only* PSO. The name MOL is used in [5], where more thorough studies were made. MOL differs from PSO in that it eliminates the particle's best-known position, $\vec{p}$. This has been found to improve performance on some problems and makes it easier to tune behavioral parameters.

Mesh (MESH)

Fitness can be computed at regular intervals of the search-space using the MESH method. For increasing search-space dimensionality, this incurs an exponentially increasing number of mesh-points to retain a similar interval size. This phenomenon is what is known as the Curse of Dimensionality. The MESH method is used as any other optimization method in SwarmOps is and will indeed return the mesh-point found to have the best fitness as its solution. The quality of this solution will depend on how coarse or fine the mesh is. The MESH method is mostly used to make plots of the fitness landscape for simpler optimization problems, or for studying how different choices of behavioral parameters influence an optimization method's performance, that is, how the meta-fitness landscape looks.

The MESH method is not intended to be used as an optimizer.

Parallelism

Computers with multiple processing units are becoming increasingly popular and there are different ways of using this parallelism.

Parallelizing the optimization problem

Some optimization problems can be parallelized internally. The advantage of this is that all optimization methods in SwarmOps can be used without modification. The disadvantage is that each optimization problem must be parallelized, and this process does not take advantage of the natural parallel structure of population-based optimizers.

Parallel optimization methods

SwarmOps provides parallelized versions of the DE, PSO, and MOL methods, all of which merely assume that the implementation of the fitness function is thread-safe. These parallelized optimizers are best suited for fitness functions that are time-consuming to compute, otherwise the parallelization overhead cancels out the gain.

Necessary parameter tuning

Parallel optimizer variants are implemented somewhat differently from their sequential versions. The typical way of parallelizing a multi-agent optimizer is to maintain and update the population of agents on one execution thread and then distribute only the computation of the fitness to multiple execution threads. This makes it easier to synchronize access to the data. However, this also means the entire population must be processed before improvements can become effective and be used in the computation of new candidate solutions. This changes the dynamic behavior of the optimizer and means it requires different behavioral parameters to work well, which may not necessarily work as well as the optimizer's sequential version.

And finally, the code

Assuming you have already downloaded the code we described at the beginning of the chapter, let's now take a look at what's happening. To start, let's open the `TestParallelMetaBenchmarks` project and open the `main.cs` file. This is the file we will be working with for the following code.

First, we need to create some very important variables which will become settings for the optimization layer. We have commented each so that you know what they are for, shown as follows:

```
// Set this close to 50 and a multiple of the number of processors, e.g. 8.
static readonly int NumRuns = 64;
// The total dimensions.
static readonly int Dim = 5;
// The dimension factor.
static readonly int DimFactor = 2000;
// The total number of times we will loop to determine optimal parameters.
static readonly int NumIterations = DimFactor * Dim;
```

Next, we are going to create our optimizer. There are several optimizers included with SwarmOps, but for our purposes we will use the MOL optimizer. **MOL** stands for **Many Optimizing Liaisons**, which is devised as a simplification to the original Particle Swarm Optimization method from Eberhart et al [1][2]. The Many Optimizing Liaisons method does not have any attraction to the particles' own best-known position, and the algorithm also randomly selects which particle to update instead of iterating over the entire swarm. It is similar to the Social Only Particle Swarm Optimization suggested by Kennedy [3] and was studied more thoroughly by Pedersen et al [4], who found that it can outperform the standard Particle Swarm Optimization approach and has more easily-tunable control parameters. Whew, that was a mouthful, wasn't it?

```
// The optimizer whose control parameters are to be tuned.
static Optimizer Optimizer = new MOL();
```

Next is the problem(s) that we want to optimize. You can choose to have one or multiple problems solved at the same time, but it is often easier to solve one optimization tuning problem at a time.

The optimizer is having its control parameters tuned to work well on the included problem(s), shown as follows. The numbers are the weights that signify the mutual importance of the problems in tuning. The higher the weight, the more important it is, as shown in the following code:

```
static WeightedProblem[] WeightedProblems = new WeightedProblem[]
{
new WeightedProblem(1.0, new Sphere(Dim, NumIterations)),
};
Next we have our settings for the meta-optimization layer.
static readonly int MetaNumRuns = 5;
static readonly int MetaDim = Optimizer.Dimensionality;
static readonly int MetaDimFactor = 20;
static readonly int MetaNumIterations = MetaDimFactor * MetaDim;
```

The meta-fitness aspect consists of computing optimization performance for the problems we listed over several optimization runs and summing the results. For ease of use, we wrap the optimizer in a `MetaFitness` object which takes care of this for us, as follows:

```
static SwarmOps.Optimizers.Parallel.MetaFitness MetaFitness = new
SwarmOps.Optimizers.Parallel.MetaFitness(Optimizer, WeightedProblems,
NumRuns, MetaNumIterations);
```

Now we need to create out meta-optimizer object, as shown in the following snippet. For this, we will use the **Local Unimodal Sampling (LUS)** optimizer originally created by Pedersen 1. This object does local sampling with an exponential deduction of the sampling range. It works well for many optimization problems, especially when only short runs are used or allowed. It is particularly well-suited as the overlaying meta-optimizer when tuning parameters for another optimizer:

```
static Optimizer MetaOptimizer = new LUS(LogSolutions);
```

Finally, we will wrap the meta-optimizer in a `Statistics` object to log our results. We then repeat a number of meta-optimization runs using the `MetaRepeat` object, shown as follows:

```
static readonly bool StatisticsOnlyFeasible = true;
static Statistics Statistics = new Statistics(MetaOptimizer,
StatisticsOnlyFeasible);
static Repeat MetaRepeat = new RepeatMin(Statistics, MetaNumRuns);
```

Performing meta-optimization

If you look at the project, the main method in our optimizer appears to be a large method that performs the meta-optimization run, but instead it only takes the following line of code:

```
double fitness = MetaRepeat.Fitness(MetaParameters);
```

That's it! Everything else involves logging and printing results and information to the user.

Computing fitness

The next block of code that we should look at is how we calculate our solution. Our main loop calls our fitness function as follows:

```
Statistics.Compute();
```

Now let's dive into the `Fitness` function. For ease, we have placed the entire function in the following snippet. We will dissect each line relative to its importance in the function. Our ultimate objective here is to compute the meta-fitness measure by passing the parameters to our optimizer. We perform optimization runs on the array of problem(s) until the fitness exceeds the `fitnessLimit` parameter:

```
public override double Fitness(double[] parameters, double fitnessLimit)
{
double fitnessSum = 0;
// Iterate over the problems.
for (int i = 0; i < ProblemIndex.Count && fitnessSum<fitnessLimit; i++)
{
// Assign the problem to the optimizer.
Optimizer.Problem = ProblemIndex.GetProblem(i);
// Get the weight associated with this problem.
double weight = ProblemIndex.GetWeight(i);
// Use another fitness summation because we need to keep
// track of the performance on each problem.
double fitnessSumInner = 0;
// Perform a number of optimization runs.
for (int j = 0; j < NumRuns && fitnessSum < fitnessLimit; j++)
{
// Perform one optimization run on the problem.
Result result = Optimizer.Optimize(parameters, fitnessLimit -fitnessSum);
// Get the best fitness result from optimization and adjust it
// by subtracting its minimum possible value.
double fitness = result.Fitness;
double fitnessAdjusted = fitness - Optimizer.MinFitness;
// Ensure adjusted fitness is non-negative, otherwise Preemptive
// Fitness Evaluation does not work.
Debug.Assert(fitnessAdjusted >= 0);
// Apply weight to the adjusted fitness.
fitnessAdjusted *= weight;
// Accumulate both fitness sums.
fitnessSumInner += fitnessAdjusted;
fitnessSum += fitnessAdjusted;
}
// Set the fitness result achieved on the problem.
// This was why we needed an extra summation variable.
ProblemIndex.SetFitness(i, fitnessSumInner);
}
// Sort the optimization problems so that the worst
// performing will be attempted optimized first, when
// this method is called again.
ProblemIndex.Sort();
return fitnessSum;
}
```

Now let's look at our code in action, as shown in the following screenshot:

```
C:\Development\AI\Swarm\SwarmOps\SwarmOps\TestParallelMetaBenchmarks\bin\D...    —    □    ×

Best found parameters for MOL optimizer:
        S = 58.0149
        omega = 0.1357
        phi = 1.9972
Parameters written in array notation:
        { 58.0149, 0.1357, 1.9972 }
Best parameters have meta-fitness: 7.69e-60
Worst meta-fitness: 2.59
Mean meta-fitness: 0.98
StdDev for meta-fitness: 1.21

Best 20 found parameters:
        Parameters: 58.0149 0.1357 1.9972      Fitness: 7.69e-60    Feasible: 1
        Parameters: 49.8081 0.1565 2.0998      Fitness: 8.23e-60    Feasible: 1
        Parameters: 52.6214 0.1842 1.8799      Fitness: 8.41e-60    Feasible: 1
        Parameters: 48.9351 0.2837 1.7609      Fitness: 8.73e-60    Feasible: 1
        Parameters: 43.695 0.2269 2.0808       Fitness: 9.04e-60    Feasible: 1
        Parameters: 80.3562 0.0652 1.8813      Fitness: 3.17e-56    Feasible: 1
        Parameters: 92.1368 0.128 1.6697       Fitness: 4.91e-54    Feasible: 1
        Parameters: 69.6763 0.2668 1.3818      Fitness: 1.5e-52     Feasible: 1
        Parameters: 92.3687 0.1479 1.5309      Fitness: 4.78e-52    Feasible: 1
        Parameters: 64.2127 0.0428 2.836       Fitness: 3.76e-42    Feasible: 1
        Parameters: 109.2663 0.0014 1.8643     Fitness: 3.69e-37    Feasible: 1
        Parameters: 132.8459 -0.0557 2.2995    Fitness: 2.26e-35    Feasible: 1
        Parameters: 90.9603 0.3014 2.1532      Fitness: 4.45e-33    Feasible: 1
        Parameters: 122.3657 0.0578 3.1469     Fitness: 7.27e-23    Feasible: 1
        Parameters: 101.1935 -0.1856 3.2472    Fitness: 1.97e-14    Feasible: 1
        Parameters: 171.2163 -0.2945 2.3516    Fitness: 8.31e-14    Feasible: 1
        Parameters: 222.4041 -0.2481 2.4496    Fitness: 4.46e-12    Feasible: 1
        Parameters: 210.2644 0.1508 4.0521     Fitness: 1.89e-5     Feasible: 1
        Parameters: 244.3359 -0.0257 4.772     Fitness: 0.02     Feasible: 1
        Parameters: 236.3843 -0.5211 -3.7727   Fitness: 2.32     Feasible: 1

Time usage: 0:00:00:08.6458844
Press any key to exit ...
```

As you can see, the goal of the program is to output the most optimal parameters so that you can tune your network using the same function optimization.

But what can you do if you have a function that is not one of those included in SwarmOps? Luckily, you can define a custom problem of your own and use it. Let's take a look at how that's used. First, let's look at the `TestCustomProblem` project, as shown in the following screenshot:

TestCustomProblem Project

Testing custom problems

Before we get into creating and testing our own custom problem, let's talk about a more general problem. We have already outlined what we define as a problem earlier in this chapter, but now is a good time to show you the code for our base object `Problem` before we design our own. So, let's move on.

Base problem

The following is the base class `Problem` that is used in every optimization:

```
public abstract class Problem
{
public Problem() : this(0, true)
{
}
public Problem(int maxIterations) : this(maxIterations, true)
{
}
public Problem(int maxIterations, bool requireFeasible)
{
MaxIterations = maxIterations;
RequireFeasible = requireFeasible;
}
```

The maximum number of optimization iterations to perform is as follows:

```
public int MaxIterations
```

The following command checks that the solution is feasible (that it satisfies constraints):

```
public bool RequireFeasible
```

Then, the name of the optimization problem is returned with the following command:

```
public abstract string Name
```

This includes an array with the names of the parameters, as follows:

```
public virtual string[] ParameterName => null;
```

To lower the search-space boundary, use the following command:

```
public abstract double[] LowerBound
```

To increase the upper search-space boundary, use the following command:

```
public abstract double[] UpperBound
```

The lower initialization boundary, if different from the search-space boundary, is denoted as follows:

```
public virtual double[] LowerInit => LowerBound;
```

The upper initialization boundary, if different from the search-space boundary, is denoted as follows:

```
public virtual double[] UpperInit => UpperBound;
```

The following command details the maximum (that is, the worst) fitness possible, as follows:

```
public virtual double MaxFitness => double.MaxValue;
```

The following command details the minimum (that is, the best) fitness possible. This is especially important if using meta-optimization where fitness is assumed to be non-negative; this should be roughly equivalent among all the problems we meta-optimize:

```
public abstract double MinFitness
```

The threshold for an acceptable fitness value is denoted as follows:

```
public virtual double AcceptableFitness => MinFitness;
```

To return the dimensionality of the problem, that is, the number of parameters in a candidate solution, use the following command:

```
public abstract int Dimensionality
```

The following line checks if the gradient has been implemented:

```
public virtual bool HasGradient => false;
```

The following command computes and returns fitness for the given parameters:

```
public virtual double Fitness(double[] parameters)
{
return Fitness(parameters, true);
}
```

The fitness evaluation is aborted preemptively if the fitness becomes higher (that is, worse) than `fitnessLimit()`, or if it is not possible for the fitness to improve, as follows:

```
public virtual double Fitness(double[] parameters, double fitnessLimit){
return Fitness(parameters);
}
```

We compute and return fitness for the given parameters. The fitness evaluation is aborted preemptively if feasibility of the new candidate solution is the same as or better than that of the old candidate solution—or if the fitness becomes higher (that is, worse) than `fitnessLimit()` and it is not possible for the fitness to improve, as follows:

```
public virtual double Fitness(double[] parameters, double fitnessLimit,
bool oldFeasible, bool newFeasible)
{
return Tools.BetterFeasible(oldFeasible, newFeasible)? Fitness(parameters,
fitnessLimit) : Fitness(parameters);
}
```

Compute and return fitness for the given parameters as follows:

```
public virtual double Fitness(double[] parameters, bool feasible)
{
return Fitness(parameters, MaxFitness, feasible, feasible);
}
```

Compute the gradient of the fitness-function with the following command relating to the computation time-complexity factor. For example, if fitness takes time O(n) to compute and gradient takes time O(n*n) to compute, then `return n. </returns>`:

```
public virtual int Gradient(double[] x, ref double[] v)
{
throw new NotImplementedException();
}
```

Enforce constraints and evaluate feasibility with the following command. If you do not wish to enforce constraints, you should make the call `Feasible()`:

```
public virtual bool EnforceConstraints(ref double[] parameters)
{
```

By default, we bound the candidate solution to the search-space boundaries, as follows:

```
Tools.Bound(ref parameters, LowerBound, UpperBound);
```

Since we know that the candidate solution is now within bounds and this is all that is required for feasibility, we could just return `true` here. As shown in the following snippet, `Feasible` is called for educational purposes, as most optimizers call `EnforceConstraints()`.

```
return Feasible(parameters);
}
```

Evaluate feasibility (constraint satisfaction) with the following code:

```
public virtual bool Feasible(double[] parameters)
{
return Tools.BetweenBounds(parameters, LowerBound, UpperBound);
}
```

The following is called at the beginning of an optimization run:

```
public virtual void BeginOptimizationRun()
```

The following is called at the end of an optimization run:

```
public virtual void EndOptimizationRun()
```

To return whether optimization is allowed to continue, use the following code:

```
public virtual bool Continue(int iterations, double fitness, bool feasible)
{
return (iterations < MaxIterations &&!(fitness <= AcceptableFitness &&
(!RequireFeasible || feasible)));
}
}
```

Creating a custom problem

Now that we have that out of the way, let's create a custom problem based upon our base problem class. The code will look like the following example.

The following is the two-dimensional Rosenbrock problem with some example constraints; its optimal feasible solution seems to be as follows:

```
<summary>
a ~ 1.5937
b ~ 2.5416
 </summary>
Class CustomProblem :Problem
{
public double GetA(double[] parameters)
{
return parameters[0];
}
public double GetB(double[] parameters)
{
return parameters[1];
}
```

Here, the base-class overrides the name of the optimizer, as follows:

```
public override string Name => "CustomProblem";
```

The dimensionality of the problem is as follows:

```
public override int Dimensionality => 2;
double[] _lowerBound = { -100, -100 };
```

The following is the lower search-space boundary:

```
public override double[] LowerBound => _lowerBound;
double[] _upperBound = { 100, 100 };
```

The following is the upper search-space boundary:

```
public override double[] UpperBound => _upperBound;
```

The lower initialization boundary is as follows:

```
public override double[] LowerInit => LowerBound;
```

The upper initialization boundary is as follows:

```
public override double[] UpperInit => UpperBound;
```

The minimum possible fitness for this problem is worked out using the following line:

```
public override double MinFitness => 0;
```

The acceptable fitness threshold is as follows:

```
public override double AcceptableFitness => 0.4;
string[] _parameterName = { "a", "b" };
```

The names of the parameters for the problem are as follows:

```
public override string[] ParameterName => _parameterName;
```

To compute and return fitness for the given parameters, use the following code:

```
public override double Fitness(double[] x)
{
Debug.Assert(x != null && x.Length == Dimensionality);
double a = GetA(x);
double b = GetB(x);
double t1 = 1 - a;
double t2 = b - a * a;
return t1 * t1 + 100 * t2 * t2;
}
```

To enforce and evaluate constraints, use the following code:

```
public override bool EnforceConstraints(ref double[] x)
{
// Enforce boundaries.
SwarmOps.Tools.Bound(ref x, LowerBound, UpperBound);
return Feasible(x);
}
// Evaluate constraints.
public override bool Feasible(double[] x)
{
Debug.Assert(x != null && x.Length == Dimensionality);
double a = GetA(x);
double b = GetB(x);
// Radius.
double r = Math.Sqrt(a * a + b * b);
return ((r < 0.7) || ((r > 3) && (r < 5))) && (a < b * b);
}
}
}
```

Our Custom Problem

Now, create an object of the custom problem, as follows:

```
static Problem Problem = new CustomProblem();
```

The optimization settings should be as follows:

```
static readonly int NumRuns = 50;
static readonly int DimFactor = 4000;
static readonly int Dim = Problem.Dimensionality;
static readonly int NumIterations = DimFactor * Dim;
```

Create the optimizer object as follows:

```
static Optimizer Optimizer = new DE(Problem);
```

The control parameters for the optimizer should be as follows:

```
static readonly double[] Parameters = Optimizer.DefaultParameters;
```

Wrap the optimizer in a logger of result-statistics, as follows:

```
static readonly bool StatisticsOnlyFeasible = true;
static Statistics Statistics = new Statistics(Optimizer,
StatisticsOnlyFeasible);
```

Wrap it again in the following repeater:

```
static Repeat Repeat = new RepeatSum(Statistics, NumRuns);
static void Main(string[] args)
{
```

Next, initialize the parallel random number generator, as follows:

```
Globals.Random = new RandomOps.MersenneTwister();
```

Then, set the maximum number of optimization iterations to perform with the following:

```
Problem.MaxIterations = NumIterations;
```

Create a fitness trace for tracing the progress of optimization with the following code:

```
int NumMeanIntervals = 3000;
FitnessTrace fitnessTrace = new FitnessTraceMean(NumIterations,
NumMeanIntervals);
FeasibleTrace feasibleTrace = new FeasibleTrace(NumIterations,
NumMeanIntervals, fitnessTrace);
```

Then, assign the fitness trace to the optimizer as follows:

```
Optimizer.FitnessTrace = feasibleTrace;
```

Perform the optimizations as follows:

```
double fitness = Repeat.Fitness(Parameters);
if (Statistics.FeasibleFraction > 0)
{
```

Compute the result-statistics with the following line:

```
Statistics.Compute();
```

Output the best result, as well as result-statistics, with the following code:

```
Console.WriteLine("Best feasible solution found:", Color.Yellow);
Tools.PrintParameters(Problem, Statistics.BestParameters);
Console.WriteLine();
Console.WriteLine("Result Statistics:", Color.Yellow);
Console.WriteLine("\tFeasible: \t{0} of solutions found.",
Tools.FormatPercent(Statistics.FeasibleFraction), Color.Yellow);
Console.WriteLine("\tBest Fitness: \t{0}",
Tools.FormatNumber(Statistics.FitnessMin), Color.Yellow);
Console.WriteLine("\tWorst: \t\t{0}",
Tools.FormatNumber(Statistics.FitnessMax), Color.Yellow);
Console.WriteLine("\tMean: \t\t{0}",
```

```
Tools.FormatNumber(Statistics.FitnessMean), Color.Yellow);
Console.WriteLine("\tStd.Dev.: \t{0}",
Tools.FormatNumber(Statistics.FitnessStdDev), Color.Yellow);
Console.WriteLine();
Console.WriteLine("Iterations used per run:", Color.Yellow);
Console.WriteLine("\tMean: {0}",
Tools.FormatNumber(Statistics.IterationsMean), Color.Yellow);
}
else
{
Console.WriteLine("No feasible solutions found.", Color.Red);
}
}
```

When we run our program, it should look like the following screenshot:

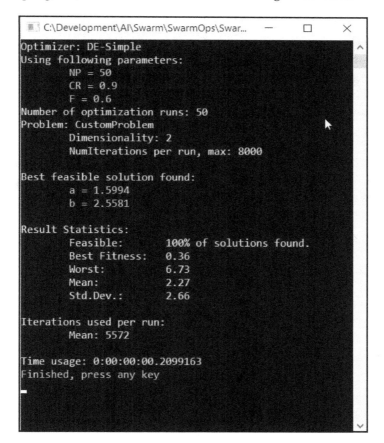

The output result of our problem

Summary

In this chapter, we learned how to use SwarmOps to help us optimize parameters for our function optimization. We learned how to use the built-in functions of SwarmOps, as well as how to define our own. In the next chapter, we will move on to image detection and will use the great open source package, TensorFlowSharp.

References

- J. Kennedy and R. Eberhart. Particle swarm optimization in Proceedings of IEEE International Conference on Neural Networks, volume IV, pages 1942-1948, Pert, Australia, 1995
- Y. Shi and R.C. Eberhart. A modified particle swarm optimizer. In Proceedings of the IEEE International Conference on Evolutionary Computation, pages 69-73, Anchorage, AK, USA, 1998.
- J. Kennedy. The particle swarm: social adaptation of knowledge. In Proceedings of the IEEE International Conference on Evolutionary Computation, Indianapolis, USA, 1997.
- M.E.H Pederson and A.J. Chipperfield. Simplified particle swarm optimization. Applied Soft Computing, 10, P. 618-628, 2010.
- Simplifying Particle Swarm Optimization. Pedersen, M.E.H. and Chipperfield, A.J. s.l. : Applied Soft Computing, 2010, Vol. 10, pp. 618-628.
- Variable metric method for minimization. Davidon, W.C. 1, s.l. : SIAM Journal on Optimization, 1991, Vol. 1, pp. 1-17.
- "Direct Search" solution for numerical and statistical problems. Hooke, R. and Jeeves, T.A. 2, s.l. : Journal of the Association for Computing Machinery (ACM), 1961, Vol. 8, pp. 212-229.
- Pedersen, M.E.H. and Chipperfield, A.J.Local Unimodal Sampling. s.l. : Hvass Laboratories, 2008. HL0801.
- Differential evolution - a simple and efficient heuristic for global optimization over continuous space. Storn, R. and Price, K. s.l. : Journal of Global Optimization, 1997, Vol. 11, pp. 341-359.

- Particle Swarm Optimization. Kennedy, J. and Eberhart, R. Perth, Australia : IEEE Internation Conference on Neural Networks, 1995.
- A Modified Particle Swarm Optimizer. Shi, Y. and Eberhart, R. Anchorage, AK, USA : IEEE International Conference on Evolutionary Computation, 1998.
- The particle swarm: social adaptation of knowledge. Kennedy, J. Indianapolis, USA : Proceedings of the IEEE International Conference on Evolutionary Computation, 1997.

10
Object Detection with TensorFlowSharp

In this chapter, we are going to introduce you to an open source package called TensorFlowSharp. More specifically, we will be using the TensorFlow[1] Object Detection API, which is an open source framework built on top of TensorFlow, which makes it easy to construct, train, and deploy various forms of object detection models.

For those not familiar with TensorFlow, the following is an excerpt from the TensorFlow website[2]:

> *"TensorFlow is an open source software library for high performance numerical computation. Its flexible architecture allows easy deployment of computation across a variety of platforms (such as CPUs, GPUs, and TPUs), and from desktops to clusters of servers to mobile and edge devices. Originally developed by researchers and engineers from the Google Brain team within Google's AI organization, it comes with strong support for machine learning and deep learning and the flexible numerical computation core is used across many other scientific domains."*

TensorFlowSharp provides .NET bindings to the TensorFlow library, which are published here in case you ever need them: `https://github.com/tensorflow/tensorflow`.

The topics included in this chapter are as follows:

- Working with Tensors
- TensorFlowSharp
- Developing your own TensorFlow application
- Detecting images
- Minimum score for object highlighting

Technical requirements

You will be required to have a basic knowledge of .NET development using Microsoft Visual Studio and C#. You will need to download the code for this chapter from this book's website: TensorFlowSharp (`https://github.com/migueldeicaza/TensorFlowSharp`).

Check out the following video to see Code in Action: `http://bit.ly/2pqEiZ9`.

Working with Tensors

Let's set the stage by talking about exactly what a Tensor is. To do so, we should also talk a little bit about vectors and matrices as well. You can skip this section if you are already familiar, but it is short and if you already know about matrices and vectors, who knows, you might remember something you've forgotten! So go ahead and read it anyway!

Now, before we talk, let me show you a graphic that may make things a tad easier to visualize:

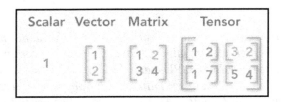

A vector is an array of numbers, as you can see here:

$$x = \begin{bmatrix} x_1 \\ x_2 \\ \dots \\ x_n \end{bmatrix}$$

A matrix is a grid of *n x m* numbers, a two-dimensional array. We can do all kinds of neat operations on a matrix, such as addition and subtraction, so long as the sizes are compatible:

$$A = \begin{bmatrix} A_{1,1} & A_{1,2} & \dots & A_{1,n} \\ A_{2,1} & A_{2,2} & \dots & A_{2,n} \\ \dots & \dots & \dots & \dots \\ A_{m,1} & A_{m,2} & \dots & A_{m,n} \end{bmatrix}$$

We can multiply matrices if we so desire, like this:

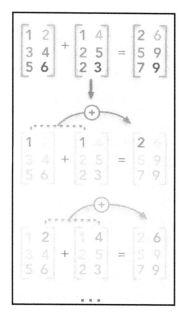

And matrices can be added together, like this:

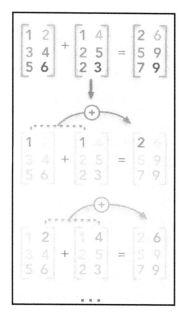

In both cases, we are working within a two-dimensional space. So, what can we do if our requirement is to work out of an *n* dimensional space to where *n* > 2? This where Tensors come in.

A Tensor is basically a matrix but is not two-dimensional (although it could be). It could be a three-dimensional matrix (a vector is a tensor is a matrix) or some incredibly crazy dimension that we do not yet know how to visualize. And to show you how powerful Tensors really are, a tensor can be covariant in one dimension and contravariant in another. The dimension of a tensor is usually called its **rank**.

More formally, a tensor is really what is called a **mathematical entity**, which lives inside a structure and interacts with other entities inside that structure. If one of the entities gets transformed, the tensor must obey what is referred to as a **related transformation rule**. This is really what differentiates a matrix from a tensor. The tensor must allow the entities to shift around when transformations occur.

Now that we've got that all squared away and under our belts, let's look at how we can work with Tensors by walking through a bit of example code:

```
void BasicVariables ()
{
Console.WriteLine ("Using placerholders");
using (var g = new TFGraph ())
{
var s = new TFSession (g);
```

Notice the variable type must match the cast in the `TFTensor`:

```
var var_a = g.Placeholder (TFDataType.Int16);
var var_b = g.Placeholder (TFDataType.Int16);
```

We are going to do addition and multiplication:

```
var add = g.Add (var_a, var_b);
var mul = g.Mul (var_a, var_b);
varrunner = s.GetRunner ();
```

Let's add two Tensors together (this is the variable type cast mentioned previously):

```
runner.AddInput (var_a, new TFTensor ((short)3));
runner.AddInput (var_b, new TFTensor ((short)2));
Console.WriteLine ("a+b={0}", runner.Run (add).GetValue ());
```

Now let's multiply two Tensors together:

```
runner = s.GetRunner ();
runner.AddInput (var_a, new TFTensor ((short)3));
runner.AddInput (var_b, new TFTensor ((short)2));
Console.WriteLine ("a*b={0}", runner.Run (mul).GetValue ());
}
}
```

TensorFlowSharp

Now that we've talked about and shown you Tensors, let's look at how we would typically use the TensorFlowSharp API itself.

Your application will typically create a graph (TFGraph), set up the operations there, then create a session from it (TFSession). This session will then use the session runner to set up inputs and outputs and execute the pipeline. Let's look at a quick example of how that might flow:

```
using(var graph = new TFGraph ())
{
graph.Import (File.ReadAllBytes ("MySavedModel"));
var session = new TFSession (graph);
var runner = session.GetRunner ();
runner.AddInput (graph ["input"] [0], tensor);
runner.Fetch (graph ["output"] [0]);
var output = runner.Run ();
```

Fetch the results from the output:

```
TFTensor result = output [0];
}
```

In scenarios where you do not need to set up the graph independently, the session will create one automatically for you. The following example shows how to use TensorFlow to compute the sum of two numbers. We will have the session automatically create the graph for us:

```
using (var session = new TFSession())
{
var graph = session.Graph;
var a = graph.Const(2);
var b = graph.Const(3);
Console.WriteLine("a=2 b=3");
```

Add two constants:

```
var addingResults = session.GetRunner().Run(graph.Add(a, b));
var addingResultValue = addingResults.GetValue();
Console.WriteLine("a+b={0}", addingResultValue);
```

Multiply two constants:

```
var multiplyResults = session.GetRunner().Run(graph.Mul(a, b));
var multiplyResultValue = multiplyResults.GetValue();
Console.WriteLine("a*b={0}", multiplyResultValue);
}
```

Developing your own TensorFlow application

Now that we've shown you some preliminary code samples, let's move on to our example project—how to use TensorFlowSharp from a console application to detect objects within an image. This code is easy enough for you to be able to add into your solution if you so desire. Just tweak the input and output names, perhaps allow for user adjusted hyperparameters, and you're off!

To run this solution, you should have the source code for this chapter downloaded from the website and open in Microsoft Visual Studio. Please follow the instructions for downloading code for this book:

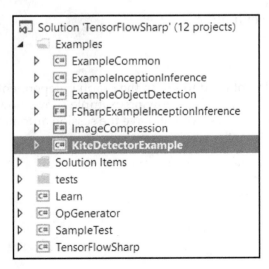

Before we dive into the code, let's talk about one very important variable:

```
private static double MIN_SCORE_FOR_OBJECT_HIGHLIGHTING = 0.5;
```

This variable is our threshold for identifying and highlighting objects in our base image. At 0.5, there is a reasonable synchronicity between detection reliability and accuracy. As we lower this number, we will find that more objects are identified, however, the identification accuracy begins to suffer. The lower we go, the greater the chance we have of identifying objects incorrectly. We will identify them, but they may not be what we intended, as you will see in a bit.

Now, let's have a quick look at the main function of this sample and walk through what it's doing:

```
static void Main(string[] args)
{
```

Load the default model and data:

```
_catalogPath = DownloadDefaultTexts(_currentDir);
_modelPath = DownloadDefaultModel(_currentDir);
_catalog = CatalogUtil.ReadCatalogItems(_catalogPath);
var fileTuples = new List<(string input, string output)>() { (_input,
_output) };
string modelFile = _modelPath;
```

Let's create our TensorFlowSharp graph object here:

```
using (var graph = new TFGraph())
{
```

Read all of the data into our graph object:

```
graph.Import(new TFBuffer(File.ReadAllBytes(modelFile)));
```

Create a new TensorFlowSharp session to work with:

```
using (var session = new TFSession(graph))
{
Console.WriteLine("Detecting objects", Color.Yellow);
foreach (var tuple in fileTuples)
{
```

Create our tensor from our image file:

```
var tensor = ImageUtil.CreateTensorFromImageFile(tuple.input,
TFDataType.UInt8);
var runner = session.GetRunner();
```

```
runner.AddInput(graph["image_tensor"][0],
tensor).Fetch(graph["detection_boxes"][0],graph["detection_scores"][0],grap
h["detection_classes"][0],graph["num_detections"][0]);var output =
runner.Run();
var boxes = (float[,,])output[0].GetValue();
var scores = (float[,])output[1].GetValue();
var classes = (float[,])output[2].GetValue();
Console.WriteLine("Highlighting object...", Color.Green);
```

After all variables are processed, let's identify and draw the boxes of the objects we have detected on our sample image:

```
DrawBoxesOnImage(boxes, scores, classes, tuple.input, tuple.output,
MIN_SCORE_FOR_OBJECT_HIGHLIGHTING);
Console.WriteLine($"Done. See {_output_relative}. Press any key",
Color.Yellow);
Console.ReadKey();
}
}
}
```

Well, that is all well and good for a simple operation, but what if what we really need to do is a more complicated operation, let's say multiplying a matrix? We can do that as follows:

```
void BasicMultidimensionalArray ()
{
```

Create our `TFGraph` object:

```
using (var g = new TFGraph ())
{
```

Create our `TFSession` object:

```
var s = new TFSession (g);
```

Create a placeholder for our variable for multiplication:

```
var var_a = g.Placeholder (TFDataType.Int32);
var mul = g.Mul (var_a, g.Const (2));
```

Do the multiplication:

```
var a = new int[,,] { { { 0, 1 } , { 2, 3 } } , { { 4, 5 }, { 6, 7 } } };
var result = s.GetRunner ().AddInput (var_a, a).Fetch (mul).Run () [0];
```

Test the results:

```
var actual = (int[,,])result.GetValue ();
var expected = new int[,,] { { {0, 2} , {4, 6} } , { {8, 10}, {12, 14} } };
Console.WriteLine ("Actual: " + RowOrderJoin (actual));
Console.WriteLine ("Expected: " + RowOrderJoin (expected));
Assert(expected.Cast<int> ().SequenceEqual (actual.Cast<int> ()));
};
}
private static string RowOrderJoin(int[,,] array) => string.Join (", ",
array.Cast<int> ());
```

Detecting images

Now it's time to move on to a real project. In this example, we are going to take our base image (seen as follows) and use it to have the computer detect objects in the image. As you can see, there are several instances of people and kites in the photograph. This is the same base image used in all TensorFlowSharp examples. You are going to see the detection and highlighting progresses changes as we change our minimum allowed threshold.

Here is our base sample image, a photograph:

Minimum score for object highlighting

We talked before about the minimum score for highlighting. Let's see exactly what that means by taking a look at what happens when we use different minimum scores for object highlighting. Let's start out with a value of 0.5 and see what objects are detected within our photograph:

As you can see, we have two kites selected with a fairly good accuracy score attached to each. The boxes are drawn in green to indicate high confidence targets. Not bad. But there are still a lot of objects out there that I think we should be picking up. There are a few more kites and several people that should be easy to detect. Why haven't we done so?

What if we lowered our minimum threshold to 0.3 instead of 0.5? Let's see the result:

Well, as you can see, we do pick up other kites, albeit with a lower confidence score due to their distance in the photograph, but we have also, more importantly, now started to recognize people. Any box drawn in red is a low confidence target, green is high, and yellow is medium.

Now, what if we went one step further and lowered our minimum threshold all the way down to 0.1? If our pattern follows, we should be able to identify more images, albeit with lower confidence scores, of course.

If you look at the following version of the photograph, you can see that we do, in fact, have many more objects selected. Unfortunately, the accuracy has diminished considerably, as we suspected. Kites were confused with people, and in one case a tree was confused with a person as well. But the positive note is that our recognition changes as we adjust our threshold. Could this be done adaptively in a more advanced application? Absolutely, and it's those kinds of thoughts I want to nurture so that you can embellish the code and make truly earth-shaking applications:

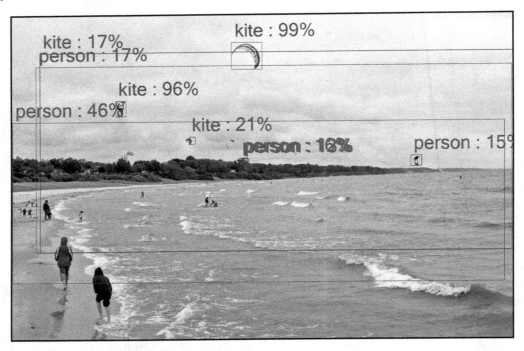

OK, there's one final example that I think you will like. In this example, I have dropped the minimum threshold down to 0.01. If our hunch is right, the screen should light up with low confidence targets now. Let's see whether we're right:

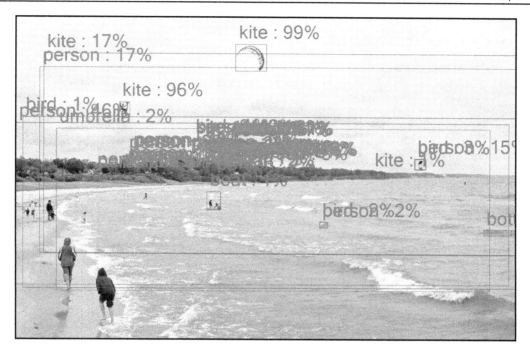

It looks like our hunch was right. I know the screen labeling is cluttered, but the point is that we have increased our object detection, albeit for a lower confidence threshold.

You should now take some time and consider all of the exciting applications for such technology. From face and object detection to autonomous vehicles, Tensors are used everywhere today and it's something you should get familiar with.

Summary

TensorFlowSharp is an exciting open source project that makes working with Tensors and TensorFlow incredibly easy. In this chapter, we showed you what Tensors are and how you can work with them. We also built an incredibly powerful sample application that allows you to detect and label images within a picture.

In our next chapter, we will learn about long short-term memory networks and how you can use them to enhance your applications and processes.

References

- [1]"Speed/accuracy trade-offs for modern convolutional object detectors."Huang J, Rathod V, Sun C, Zhu M, Korattikara A, Fathi A, Fischer I, Wojna Z, Song Y, Guadarrama S, Murphy K, CVPR 2017
- [2] www.tensorflow.org
- [3] JEAN, Hadrien. *Deep Learning Book Series 2.1 Scalars Vectors Matrices and Tensors* Web blog post. hadrienj.github.io. 26 Mar. 2018.

11
Time Series Prediction and LSTM Using CNTK

This chapter is dedicated to helping you understand more of the Microsoft Cognitive Toolkit, or CNTK. The inspiration for the examples contained within this chapter comes from the Python version of **CNTK 106: Part A – Time Series prediction with LSTM (Basics)**. As C# developers, the Python code is not what we will be using (although there are several ways in which we could) so we made our own C# example to mirror that tutorial. To make our example easy and intuitive, we will use the Sine function to predict future time-series data. Specifically, and more concretely, we will be using a **long short-term memory recurrent neural network**, sometimes called an **LSTM-RNN** or just **LSTM**. There are many variants of the LSTM; we will be working with the original.

In this chapter, we will cover the following topics:

- LSTM
- Tensors
- Static and dynamic axis
- Loading datasets
- Plotting data
- Creating models
- Creating mini-batches
- And more…

Technical requirements

You will be required to have basic knowledge of .NET development using Microsoft Visual Studio and C#. You will need to download the code for this chapter from the book's website.

Check out the following video to see Code in Action: `http://bit.ly/2xtDTto`.

Long short-term memory

Long short-term memory (**LSTM**) networks are a specialized form of recurrent neural network. They have the ability to retain long-term memory of things they have encountered in the past. In an LSTM, each neuron is replaced by what is known as a **memory unit**. This memory unit is activated and deactivated at the appropriate time, and is actually what is known as a **recurrent self-connection**.

If we step back for a second and look at the back-propagation phase of a regular recurrent network, the gradient signal can end up being multiplied many times by the weight matrix of the synapses between the neurons within the hidden layer. What does this mean exactly? Well, it means that the magnitude of those weights can then have a stronger impact on the learning process. This can be both good and bad.

If the weights are small they can lead to what is known as **vanishing gradients**, a scenario where the signal gets so small that learning slows to an unbearable pace or even, worse, comes to a complete stop. On the other hand, if the weights are large, this can lead to a situation where the signal is so large that learning diverges rather than converges. Both scenarios are undesirable but are handled by an item within the LSTM model known as a **memory cell**. Let's talk a little about this memory cell now.

A memory cell has four different parts. They are:

- Input gate, with a constant weight of 1.0
- Self-recurrent connection neuron
- Forget gate, allowing cells to remember or forget its previous state
- Output gate, allowing the memory cell state to have an effect (or no effect) on other neurons

Let's take a look at this and try and make it all come together:

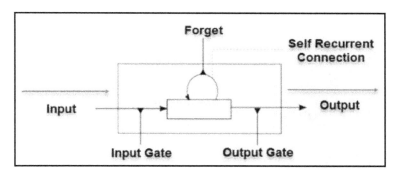

Memory Cell

LSTM variants

There are many variants of the LSTM network. Some of these variants include:

- Gated recurrent neural network
- LSTM4
- LSTM4a
- LSTM5
- LSTM5a
- LSMT6

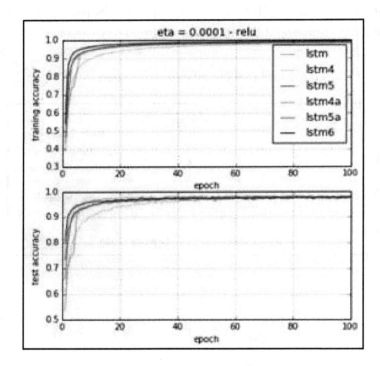

Training and Test accuracy, σ = relu, η = 1e −4

One of those variants, a slightly more dramatic version of the LSTM, is called the gated recurrent unit, or GRU/GRNN. It combines the forget and input gates of the LSTM into a single gate called an **update gate**. This makes it simpler than the standard LSTM and has been increasingly growing in popularity.

Here is what a LSTM looks like:

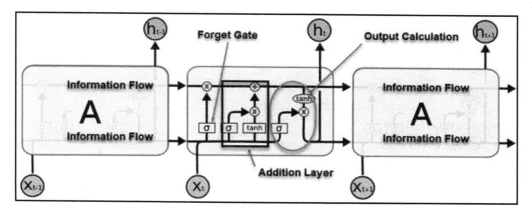

LSTM

As you can see, there are various memory *gates* in the LSTM that the RNN does not have. This allows it to effortlessly retain both long-and short-term memory. So, if we want to understand text and need to look ahead or behind in time, LSTM is made for just such a scenario. Let's talk about the different gates for a moment. As we mentioned, there are 3 of them. Let's use the following phrase to explain how each of these works.

Bob lives in New York City. John talks to people on the phone all day, and commutes on the train.

Forget Gate: As soon as we get to the period after the word City, the forget gate realizes that there may be a change of context in the works. As a result, the subject Bob is forgotten and the place where the subject was is now empty. As soon as the sentence turns to John, the subject is now John. This process is caused by the forget gate.

Input Gate: So the important facts are that Bob lives in New York City, and that John commutes on the train and talks to people all day. However, the fact that he talks to people over the phone is not as important and can be ignored. The process of adding new information is done via the input gate.

Output Gate: If we were to have a sentence *Bob was a great man. We salute ____*. In this sentence we have an empty space with many possibilities. What we do know is that we are going to salute whatever is in this empty space, and this is a verb describing a noun. Therefore, we would be safe in assuming that the empty space will be filled with a noun. So, a good candidate could be *Bob*. The job of selecting what information is useful from the current cell state and showing it as an output is the job of the output gate.

Applications of LSTM

The following are just a few of the applications of LSTM stacked networks:

- Speech recognition
- Handwriting recognition
- Time series prediction and anomaly detection
- Business process management
- Robotic control
- And many more...

Time series prediction itself can have a dramatic effect on the business's bottom line. We may need to predict in which day of the month, which quarter, or which year certain large expenses will occur. We may also have concerns over the Consumer Price Index over the course of time relative to our business. Increased prediction accuracy can lead to definite improvements to our bottom line.

CNTK terminology

It is important that we understand some of the terminology used within the Microsoft CNTK toolkit. Let's look at some of that terminology now:

- **Tensors**: All CNTK inputs, outputs and parameters are organized as tensors. It should also be noted that *minibatches* are tensors as well.
- **Rank**: Each tensor has a rank. Scalars are tensors with a rank of 0, vectors are tensors and have a rank of 1, and matrices are tensors with a rank of 2.
- **Static axis**: The dimensions listed in 2 are referred to as **axes**. Every tensor has *static* and *dynamic* axes. A Static axis has the same length throughout its entire life.
- **Dynamic axis**: Dynamic axes, however, can vary their length from instance to instance. Their length is typically not known before each minibatch is presented. Additionally, they may be ordered.
- **Minibatch**: A minibatch is also a tensor. It has a dynamic axis, which is called the **batch axis**. The length of this axis can change from minibatch to minibatch.

At the time of writing of CNTK supports one additional single additional dynamic axis, also known as the **sequence axis**. This axis allows the user to work with sequences in a more abstract, higher-level manner. The beauty of sequence is that whenever an operation is performed on a sequence, the CNTK toolkit does a type-checking operation to determine safety:

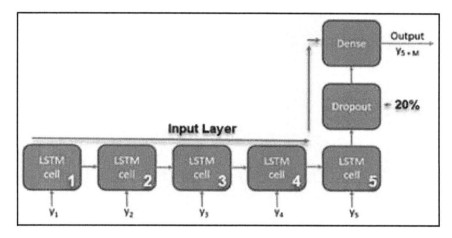

Sequence Axis

Our example

So now that we have covered some basics for both CNTK and LSTM, it's time to dive into our example application. You can find this project with the code that accompanies this book. Make sure you have it open in Microsoft Visual Studio before proceeding. You can follow the instructions in the upcoming *The Code* section if you need further instructions.

The example we are creating uses Microsoft CNTK as a back-end and will use a simple sine wave as our function. The sine wave was plotted earlier and is used due to it's being widely familiar to most individuals.

Here are screenshots of what our example application looks like:

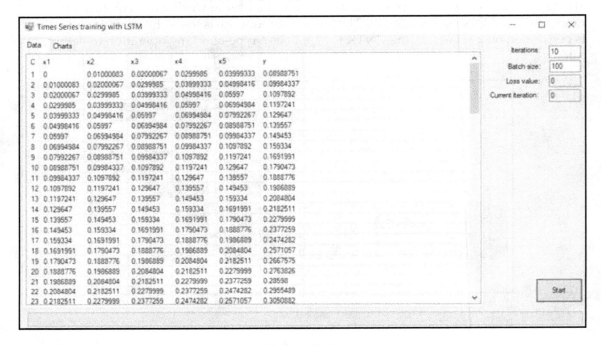

Main page – training data

The preceding screenshot shows our main screen, displaying our sine wave data points, our training data. The goal is to get our training data (blue) to match the red as closely as possible in shape, as follows:

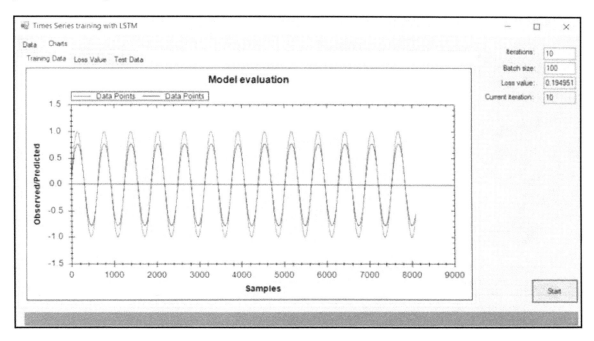

Main Page - Charts

The following screen allows us to plot our loss function:

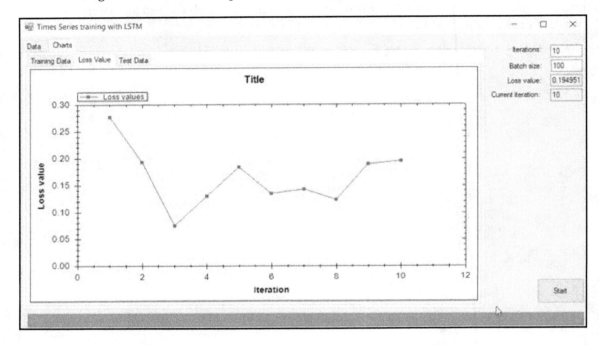

Plotting the loss value (Loss Value tab)

The following screen allows us to plot our observed versus predicted values. The goal is to have the predicted values (blue) match as closely as possible the actual values (shown in red):

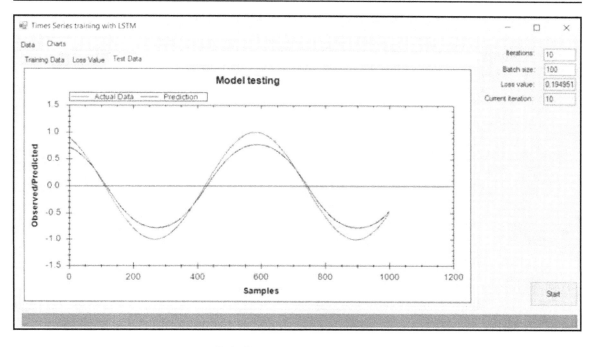

Plotting Observed versus Predicted (Test Data tab)

Coding our application

Let's now look at our code. For this you will need to reference the LSTMTimeSeriesDemo project that accompanies this book. Open the project in Microsoft Visual Studio. All the required CNTK libraries are already referenced in this project for you and included in the Debug/bin directory. The main library we will be using is Cntk.Core.Managed. We are using version 2.5.1 for this example, in case you were wondering!

Loading data and graphs

To load our data and graphs, we have two main functions that we will use; LoadTrainingData() and PopulateGraphs(). Pretty straightforward, right?:

```
private void Example_Load(object sender, EventArgs e)
{
  LoadTrainingData(DataSet?["features"].train, DataSet?["label"].train);
  PopulateGraphs(DataSet?["label"].train, DataSet?["label"].test);
}
```

Loading training data

For this example, we are simply making up our test and training data on-the-fly. The `LoadTrainingData()` function does just that:

```
private void LoadTrainingData(float[][] X, float[][] Y)
{
//clear the list first
listView1.Clear();
listView1.GridLines = true;
listView1.HideSelection = false;
if (X == null || Y == null )
return;

//add features
listView1.Columns.Add(new ColumnHeader() {Width=20});
for (int i=0; i < inDim ;i++)
{
var col1 = new ColumnHeader
{
Text = $"x{i + 1}",
Width = 70
};
listView1.Columns.Add(col1);
}

//Add label
var col = new ColumnHeader
{
Text = $"y",
Width = 70
};
listView1.Columns.Add(col);
for (int i = 0; i < 100; i++)
{
var itm = listView1.Items.Add($"{(i+1).ToString()}");
for (int j = 0; j < X[i].Length; j++)
itm.SubItems.Add(X[i][j].ToString(CultureInfo.InvariantCulture));
itm.SubItems.Add(Y[i][0].ToString(CultureInfo.InvariantCulture));
}
}
```

Populating the graphs

This function populates the graphs with training and test data:

```
private void PopulateGraphs(float[][] train, float[][] test)
 {
 if (train == null)
 throw new ArgumentException("TrainNetwork parameter cannot be null");
 if (test == null)
 throw new ArgumentException("test parameter cannot be null");
 for (int i=0; i<train.Length; i++)
 trainingDataLine?.AddPoint(new PointPair(i + 1, train[i][0]));
 for (int i = 0; i < test.Length; i++)
 testDataLine?.AddPoint(new PointPair(i + 1, test[i][0]));
 zedGraphControl1?.RestoreScale(zedGraphControl1.GraphPane);
 zedGraphControl3?.RestoreScale(zedGraphControl3.GraphPane);
 }
```

Splitting data

With this function we mirror frameworks such as Python, which make it very easy to split training and testing data from the main dataset. We have created our own function to do the same thing:

```
static (float[][] train, float[][] valid, float[][] test)
SplitDataForTrainingAndTesting(float[][] data, float valSize = 0.1f, float
testSize = 0.1f)
{
 if (data == null)
 throw new ArgumentException("data parameter cannot be null");
//Calculate the data needed
var posTest = (int)(data.Length * (1 - testSize));
 var posVal = (int)(posTest * (1 - valSize));
 return (
 data.Skip(0).Take(posVal).ToArray(),
 data.Skip(posVal).Take(posTest - posVal).ToArray(),
 data.Skip(posTest).ToArray());
 }
```

Running the application

Once we click the **Run** button, we will execute the function outlined as follows. We first determine the number of iterations the user wants to use, as well as the batch size. After setting up our progress bar and some internal variables, we call our `TrainNetwork()` function:

```
private void btnStart_Click(object sender, EventArgs e)
{
int iteration = int.Parse(textBox1.Text);
 batchSize = int.Parse(textBox2.Text);
progressBar1.Maximum = iteration;
progressBar1.Value = 1;
inDim = 5;
 ouDim = 1;
 int hiDim = 1;
 int cellDim = inDim;
Task.Run(() => TrainNetwork(DataSet, hiDim, cellDim, iteration, batchSize,
ReportProgress));
}
```

Training the network

In every neural network we must train the network in order for it to recognize whatever we are providing it. Our `TrainNetwork()` function does just that:

```
private void TrainNetwork(Dictionary<string, (float[][] train, float[][]
valid, float[][] test)> dataSet, int hiDim, int cellDim, int iteration, int
batchSize, Action<Trainer, Function, int, DeviceDescriptor> progressReport)
{
Split the dataset on TrainNetwork into validate and test parts
var featureSet = dataSet["features"];
var labelSet = dataSet["label"];
```

Create the model, as follows:

```
var feature = Variable.InputVariable(new int[] { inDim }, DataType.Float,
featuresName, null, false /*isSparse*/);
 var label = Variable.InputVariable(new int[] { ouDim }, DataType.Float,
labelsName, new List<CNTK.Axis>() { CNTK.Axis.DefaultBatchAxis() }, false);
 var lstmModel = LSTMHelper.CreateModel(feature, ouDim, hiDim, cellDim,
DeviceDescriptor.CPUDevice, "timeSeriesOutput");
 Function trainingLoss = CNTKLib.SquaredError(lstmModel, label,
"squarederrorLoss");
 Function prediction = CNTKLib.SquaredError(lstmModel, label,
"squarederrorEval");
```

Prepare for training:

```
TrainingParameterScheduleDouble learningRatePerSample = new
TrainingParameterScheduleDouble(0.0005, 1);
TrainingParameterScheduleDouble momentumTimeConstant =
CNTKLib.MomentumAsTimeConstantSchedule(256);
IList<Learner> parameterLearners = new List<Learner>()
{
Learner.MomentumSGDLearner(lstmModel?.Parameters(), learningRatePerSample,
momentumTimeConstant, /*unitGainMomentum = */true)
};
```

Create the trainer, as follows:

```
        var trainer = Trainer.CreateTrainer(lstmModel, trainingLoss,
    prediction, parameterLearners);
```

Train the model, as follows:

```
for (int i = 1; i <= iteration; i++)
{
```

Get the next minibatch amount of data, as follows:

```
foreach (var batchData infrom miniBatchData in
GetNextDataBatch(featureSet.train, labelSet.train, batchSize)
let xValues = Value.CreateBatch(new NDShape(1, inDim), miniBatchData.X,
DeviceDescriptor.CPUDevice)
let yValues = Value.CreateBatch(new NDShape(1, ouDim), miniBatchData.Y,
DeviceDescriptor.CPUDevice)
select new Dictionary<Variable, Value>
{
{ feature, xValues },
{ label, yValues }})
{
```

Train, as follows:

```
trainer?.TrainMinibatch(batchData, DeviceDescriptor.CPUDevice);
}
if (InvokeRequired)
{
Invoke(new Action(() => progressReport?.Invoke(trainer, lstmModel.Clone(),
i, DeviceDescriptor.CPUDevice)));
}
else
{
progressReport?.Invoke(trainer, lstmModel.Clone(), i,
DeviceDescriptor.CPUDevice);
```

```
        }
    }
}
```

Creating a model

To create a model, we are going to build a one-directional recurrent neural network that contains **long short-term memory (LSTM)** cells as shown in the following:

```
public static Function CreateModel(Variable input, int outDim, int LSTMDim,
int cellDim, DeviceDescriptor device, string outputName)
{
Func<Variable, Function> pastValueRecurrenceHook = (x) =>
CNTKLib.PastValue(x);
```

Create a LSTM cell for each input variable, as follows:

```
Function LSTMFunction = LSTMPComponentWithSelfStabilization<float>(input,
new[] { LSTMDim }, new[] { cellDim }, pastValueRecurrenceHook,
pastValueRecurrenceHook, device)?.Item1;
```

After the LSTM sequence is created, return the last cell in order to continue generating the network, as follows:

```
pre>        Function lastCell = CNTKLib.SequenceLast(LSTMFunction);
```

Implement dropout for 20%, as follows:

```
        var dropOut = CNTKLib.Dropout(lastCell, 0.2, 1);
```

Create the last dense layer before the output, as follows:

```
    return FullyConnectedLinearLayer(dropOut, outDim, device, outputName);
}
```

Getting the next data batch

We get our next batch of data in an enumerable fashion. We first verify parameters, and then call the `CreateBatch()` function, which is listed after this function:

```
private static IEnumerable<(float[] X, float[] Y)>
GetNextDataBatch(float[][] X, float[][] Y, int mMSize)
{
if (X == null)
 throw new ArgumentException("X parameter cannot be null");
 if (Y == null)
 throw new ArgumentException("Y parameter cannot be null");
for (int i = 0; i <= X.Length - 1; i += mMSize)
 {
 var size = X.Length - i;
 if (size > 0 && size > mMSize)
 size = mMSize;
var x = CreateBatch(X, i, size);
 var y = CreateBatch(Y, i, size);
yield return (x, y);
 }
}
```

Creating a batch of data

Given a dataset, this function will create *batches* of data for use in traversing the total data set in more manageable segments. You can see how it is called from the `GetNextDataBatch()` function shown previously:

```
internal static float[] CreateBatch(float[][] data, int start, int count)
{
 var lst = new List<float>();
 for (int i = start; i < start + count; i++)
 {
 if (i >= data.Length)
 break;
lst.AddRange(data[i]);
 }
return lst.ToArray();
 }
```

How well do LSTMs perform?

We tested LSTMs against predictions and historical values for sunspot data prediction, a very famous test in deep learning. As you can see, the red plot, which is our predictions, melded into the trend exactly, which is a tremendously encouraging sign:

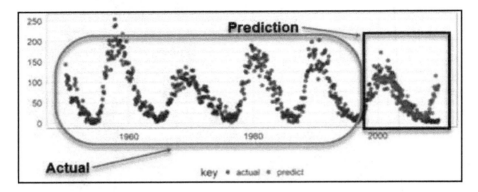

Prediction versus Performance

Summary

In this chapter, we learned about long short-term memory recurrent neural networks. We programmed an example application showing how to use them, and we learned some basic terminology along the way. We covered topics such as LSTMs, tensors, static and dynamic axes, loading datasets, plotting data, creating models, and creating minibatches. In our next chapter, we will visit a very close cousin of LSTM networks: gated recurrent units.

References

- Hochreiter, S., & Schmidhuber, J. (1997). Long short-term memory. Neural computation, 9(8), 1735-1780.
- Gers, F. A., Schmidhuber, J., & Cummins, F. (2000). Learning to forget: Continual prediction with LSTM. Neural computation, 12(10), 2451-2471.
- Graves, Alex. Supervised sequence labeling with recurrent neural networks. Vol. 385. Springer, 2012.

- Y. Bengio, P. Simard, and P. Frasconi. Learning long-term dependencies with gradient descent is difficult. IEE TRANSACTIONS ON NEURAL NETWORKS, 5, 1994.

- F. Chollet. Keras github.

- J. Chung, C. Gulcehre, K. Cho, and Y. Bengio. Empirical evaluation of gated recurrent neural networks on sequence modeling, 2014.

- S. Hochreiter and J. Schmidhuber. Long short-term memory. Neural Computation, 9:1735–1780, 1997.

- Q. V. Le, N. Jaitly, and H. G. E. A simple way to initialize recurrent networks of rectified linear units. 2015.

- Y. Lu and F. Salem. Simplified gating in long short-term memory (lstm) recurrent neural networks. arXiv:1701.03441, 2017.

- F. M. Salem. A basic recurrent neural network model. arXiv preprint arXiv:1612.09022, 2016.

- F. M. Salem. Reduced parameterization of gated recurrent neural networks. MSU Memorandum, 7.11.2016.

12
GRUs Compared to LSTMs, RNNs, and Feedforward networks

In this chapter, we're going to talk about **gated recurrent units (GRU)**. We will also compare them to LSTMs, which we learned about in the previous chapter. As you know, LSTMs have been around since 1987 and are among the most widely used models in Deep Learning for NLP today. GRUs, however, were first presented in 2014, are a simpler variant of LSTMs that share many of the same properties, train easier and faster, and typically have less computational complexity.

In this chapter, we will learn about the following:

- GRUs
- How GRUs differ from LSTMs
- How to implement a GRU
- GRU, LTSM, RNN, and Feedforward comparisons
- Network differences

Technical requirements

You will be required to have a basic knowledge of .NET development using Microsoft Visual Studio and C#. You will need to download the code for this chapter from the book website.

Check out the following video to see Code in Action: http://bit.ly/2OHd7o5.

QuickNN

To follow along with the code, you should have the QuickNN solution open inside Microsoft Visual Studio. We will be using this code to explain in detail some of the finer points as well as comparisons between coding the different networks. Here is the solution you should have loaded:

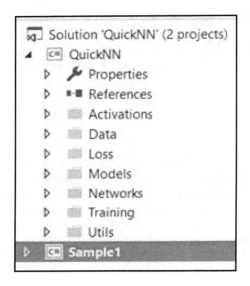

Solution

Understanding GRUs

GRUs are a cousin to the long short-term memory recurrent neural networks. Both LSTM and GRU networks have additional parameters that control when and how their internal memory is updated. Both can capture long- and short-term dependencies in sequences. The GRU networks, however, involve less parameters than their LSTM cousins, and as a result, are faster to train. The GRU learns how to use its reset and forget gates in order to make longer term predictions while enforcing memory protection. Let's look at a simple diagram of a GRU:

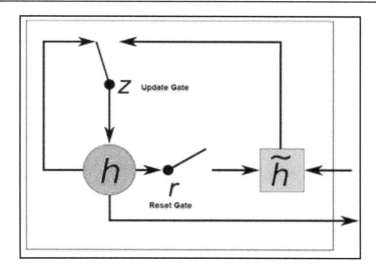

GRU

Differences between LSTM and GRU

There are a few subtle differences between a LSTM and a GRU, although to be perfectly honest, there are more similarities than differences! For starters, a GRU has one less gate than an LSTM. As you can see in the following diagram, an LSTM has an input gate, a forget gate, and an output gate. A GRU, on the other hand, has only two gates, a reset gate and an update gate. The reset gate determines how to combine new inputs with the previous memory, and the update gate defines how much of the previous memory remains:

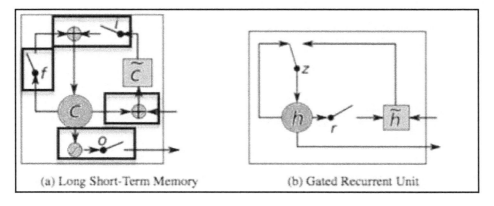

LSTM vs GRU

Another interesting fact is that if we set the reset gate to all 1s and the update gate to all 0s, do you know what we have? If you guessed a plain old recurrent neural network, you'd be right!

Here are the key differences between a LSTM and a GRU:

- A GRU has two gates, a LSTM has three.
- GRUs do not have an internal memory cell that is different from the exposed hidden state. This is because the output gate that the LSTM has does.
- The input and forget gates are coupled by an update gate that weighs the old and new content.
- The reset gate is applied directly to the previous hidden state.
- We do not apply a second non-linearity when computing the GRU output.
- There is no output gate, the weighted sum is what becomes the output.

Using a GRU versus a LSTM

Since GRUs are relatively new, the question usually arises as to which network type to use and when. To be honest, there really is no clear winner here, as GRUs have yet to mature, and LSTM variants seem to pop up every month. GRUs do have fewer parameters, and theoretically may train a bit faster than a LSTM. It may also theoretically need less data than a LSTM. On the other hand, if you have a lot of data, the extra power of the LSTM may work better for you.

Coding different networks

In this section, we are going to look at the sample code we described earlier in this chapter. We specifically are going to look at how we build different networks. The `NetworkBuilder` is our main object for building the four different types of networks we need for this exercise. You can feel free to modify it and add additional networks if you so desire. Currently, it supports the following networks:

- LSTM
- RNN
- GRU
- Feedforward

The one thing that you will notice in our sample network is that the only difference between networks is how the network itself is created via the `NetworkBuilder`. All the remaining code stays the same. You will also note if you look through the example source code that the number of iterations or epochs is much lower in the GRU sample. This is because GRUs are typically easier to train and therefore require fewer iterations. While our normal RNN training is complete somewhere around 50,000 iterations (we let it go to 100,000 just in case), our GRU training loop completes usually in under 10,000 iterations, which is a very large computational saving.

Coding an LSTM

To construct a LSTM, we simply call the `MakeLstm()` function of our `NetworkBuilder`. This function will ingest several input parameters and return to us a network object:

```
INetwork nn = NetworkBuilder.MakeLstm(inputDimension,
hiddenDimension,hiddenLayers,outputDimension,data.GetModelOutputUnitToUse()
,
initParamsStdDev, rng);
```

As you can see, internally this calls our `MakeLSTM()` function inside the `NetworkBuilder` object. Here is a look at that code:

```
public static NeuralNetwork MakeLstm(int inputDimension, int
hiddenDimension, int hiddenLayers, int outputDimension, INonlinearity
decoderUnit, double initParamsStdDev, Random rng)
{
List<ILayer> layers = new List<ILayer>();
for (int h = 0; h<hiddenLayers; h++)
{
```

Add all of the hidden layers:

```
layers.Add(h == 0? new LstmLayer(inputDimension, hiddenDimension,
initParamsStdDev, rng): new LstmLayer(hiddenDimension, hiddenDimension,
initParamsStdDev, rng));
}
```

Add the feed forward layer:

```
layers.Add(new FeedForwardLayer(hiddenDimension, outputDimension,
decoderUnit, initParamsStdDev, rng));
```

Create the network:

```
return new NeuralNetwork(layers);
}
```

Coding a GRU

To construct a gated recurrent unit, we simply call the `MakeGru()` function of our `NetworkBuilder` as shown here:

```
INetwork nn = NetworkBuilder.MakeGru(inputDimension,
hiddenDimension,
hiddenLayers,
outputDimension,
data.GetModelOutputUnitToUse(),
initParamsStdDev, rng);
```

The `MakeGru()` function calls the same named function internally to construct our GRU network. Here is a look at how it does it:

```
public static NeuralNetwork MakeGru(int inputDimension, int
hiddenDimension, int hiddenLayers, int outputDimension, INonlinearity
decoderUnit, double initParamsStdDev, Random rng)
{
List<ILayer> layers = new List<ILayer>();
for (int h = 0; h<hiddenLayers; h++)
  {
  layers.Add(h == 0
  ? newGruLayer(inputDimension, hiddenDimension, initParamsStdDev, rng)
  : newGruLayer(hiddenDimension, hiddenDimension, initParamsStdDev, rng));
  }
layers.Add(new FeedForwardLayer(hiddenDimension, outputDimension,
decoderUnit, initParamsStdDev, rng));
return new NeuralNetwork(layers);
}
```

Comparing LSTM, GRU, Feedforward, and RNN operations

In order to help you see the difference in both the creation and results of all the network objects we have been dealing with, I created the sample code that follows. This sample will allow you to see the difference in training times for all four of the network types we have here. As stated previously, the GRU is the easiest to train and therefore will complete faster (in less iterations) than the other networks. When executing the code, you will see that the GRU achieves the optimal error rate typically in under 10,000 iterations, while a conventional RNN and/or LSTM can take 50,000 or more iterations to converge properly.

Here is what our sample code looks like:

```
static void Main(string[] args)
{
Console.WriteLine("Running GRU sample", Color.Yellow);
Console.ReadKey();
ExampleGRU.Run();
Console.ReadKey();
Console.WriteLine("Running LSTM sample", Color.Yellow);
Console.ReadKey();
ExampleLSTM.Run();
Console.ReadKey();
Console.WriteLine("Running RNN sample", Color.Yellow);
Console.ReadKey();
ExampleRNN.Run();
Console.ReadKey();
Console.WriteLine("Running Feed Forward sample", Color.Yellow);
Console.ReadKey();
ExampleFeedForward.Run();
Console.ReadKey();
}
```

And here is the output from the sample running:

```
C:\Users\mattc\OneDrive\Documents\Visual Studio 2017\Projects\QuickNN\Sample1\bin\Debug\S...
epoch[9977/10000]       train loss = 0.12506    valid loss = 0.12500    test loss  = 0.12500
epoch[9978/10000]       train loss = 0.12506    valid loss = 0.12500    test loss  = 0.12500
epoch[9979/10000]       train loss = 0.12506    valid loss = 0.12500    test loss  = 0.12500
epoch[9980/10000]       train loss = 0.12506    valid loss = 0.12500    test loss  = 0.12500
epoch[9981/10000]       train loss = 0.12506    valid loss = 0.12500    test loss  = 0.12500
epoch[9982/10000]       train loss = 0.12506    valid loss = 0.12500    test loss  = 0.12500
epoch[9983/10000]       train loss = 0.12506    valid loss = 0.12500    test loss  = 0.12500
epoch[9984/10000]       train loss = 0.12506    valid loss = 0.12500    test loss  = 0.12500
epoch[9985/10000]       train loss = 0.12506    valid loss = 0.12500    test loss  = 0.12500
epoch[9986/10000]       train loss = 0.12506    valid loss = 0.12500    test loss  = 0.12500
epoch[9987/10000]       train loss = 0.12506    valid loss = 0.12500    test loss  = 0.12500
epoch[9988/10000]       train loss = 0.12506    valid loss = 0.12500    test loss  = 0.12500
epoch[9989/10000]       train loss = 0.12506    valid loss = 0.12500    test loss  = 0.12500
epoch[9990/10000]       train loss = 0.12506    valid loss = 0.12500    test loss  = 0.12500
epoch[9991/10000]       train loss = 0.12506    valid loss = 0.12500    test loss  = 0.12500
epoch[9992/10000]       train loss = 0.12506    valid loss = 0.12500    test loss  = 0.12500
epoch[9993/10000]       train loss = 0.12506    valid loss = 0.12500    test loss  = 0.12500
epoch[9994/10000]       train loss = 0.12506    valid loss = 0.12500    test loss  = 0.12500
epoch[9995/10000]       train loss = 0.12506    valid loss = 0.12500    test loss  = 0.12500
epoch[9996/10000]       train loss = 0.12506    valid loss = 0.12500    test loss  = 0.12500
epoch[9997/10000]       train loss = 0.12506    valid loss = 0.12500    test loss  = 0.12500
epoch[9998/10000]       train loss = 0.12506    valid loss = 0.12500    test loss  = 0.12500
epoch[9999/10000]       train loss = 0.12506    valid loss = 0.12500    test loss  = 0.12500
epoch[10000/10000]      train loss = 0.12506    valid loss = 0.12500    test loss  = 0.12500
Training Completed.
Test: 1,1
Test: 1,1. Output:0.499749999992807
Test: 0,1. Output:0.499749999992807
Complete
```

Output 1

Output 2

Now, let's look at how we create the GRU network and run the program. In the following code segment, we will use our XOR Dataset generator to generate random data for us. For our network, we will have 2 inputs, 1 hidden layer with 3 neurons, and 1 output. Our learning rate is set to 0.001 and our standard deviation is set to 0.08.

We call our `NetworkBuilder` object, which is responsible for creating all our network variants. We pass all our described parameters to the `NetworkBuilder`. Once our network object is created we pass this variable to our trainer and train the network. Once the network training is completed we then test our network to ensure our results are satisfactory. When we create our Graph object for testing, we are sure to pass false to the constructor to let it know that we do not need back propagation:

```
public class ExampleGRU
  {
public static void Run()
  {
```

```
Random rng = new Random();
DataSet data = new XorDataSetGenerator();
int inputDimension = 2;
int hiddenDimension = 3;
int outputDimension = 1;
int hiddenLayers = 1;
double learningRate = 0.001;
double initParamsStdDev = 0.08;

INetwork nn = NetworkBuilder.MakeGru(inputDimension,
hiddenDimension, hiddenLayers, outputDimension, newSigmoidUnit(),
initParamsStdDev, rng);

int reportEveryNthEpoch = 10;
int trainingEpochs = 10000; // GRU's typically need less training
Trainer.train<NeuralNetwork>(trainingEpochs, learningRate, nn, data,
reportEveryNthEpoch, rng);
Console.WriteLine("Training Completed.", Color.Green);
Console.WriteLine("Test: 1,1", Color.Yellow);
Matrix input = new Matrix(new double[] { 1, 1 });
Matrix output = nn.Activate(input, new Graph(false));
Console.WriteLine("Test: 1,1. Output:" + output.W[0], Color.Yellow);
Matrix input1 = new Matrix(new double[] { 0, 1 });
Matrix output1 = nn.Activate(input1, new Graph(false));
Console.WriteLine("Test: 0,1. Output:" + output1.W[0], Color.Yellow);
Console.WriteLine("Complete", Color.Yellow);
 }
 }
```

Network differences

As mentioned earlier, the only difference between our networks are the layers that are created and added to the network object. In an LSTM we will add LSTM layers, and in a GRU, unsurprisingly, we will add GRU layers, and so forth. All four types of creation functions are displayed as follows for you to compare:

```
public static NeuralNetwork MakeLstm(int inputDimension, int
hiddenDimension, int hiddenLayers, int outputDimension, INonlinearity
decoderUnit, double initParamsStdDev, Random rng)
{
    List<ILayer> layers = new List<ILayer>();
    for (int h = 0; h<hiddenLayers; h++)
    {
        layers.Add(h == 0
        ? new LstmLayer(inputDimension, hiddenDimension, initParamsStdDev,
rng)
```

```
                : new LstmLayer(hiddenDimension, hiddenDimension,
initParamsStdDev, rng));
    }
    layers.Add(new FeedForwardLayer(hiddenDimension, outputDimension,
decoderUnit,           initParamsStdDev, rng));
    return new NeuralNetwork(layers);
}


public static NeuralNetwork MakeFeedForward(int inputDimension, int
hiddenDimension, inthiddenLayers, int outputDimension, INonlinearity
hiddenUnit, INonlinearity decoderUnit, double initParamsStdDev, Random rng)
{
    List<ILayer> layers = new List<ILayer>();
    for (int h = 0; h<hiddenLayers; h++)
    {
        layers.Add(h == 0? new FeedForwardLayer(inputDimension,
hiddenDimension,           hiddenUnit, initParamsStdDev, rng): new
FeedForwardLayer(hiddenDimension,           hiddenDimension, hiddenUnit,
initParamsStdDev, rng));
    }
    layers.Add(new FeedForwardLayer(hiddenDimension, outputDimension,
decoderUnit, initParamsStdDev, rng));
    return new NeuralNetwork(layers);
  }


public static NeuralNetwork MakeGru(int inputDimension, int
hiddenDimension, int hiddenLayers, int outputDimension, INonlinearity
decoderUnit, double initParamsStdDev, Random rng)
{
    List<ILayer> layers = new List<ILayer>();
    for (int h = 0; h<hiddenLayers; h++)
    {
        layers.Add(h == 0? new GruLayer(inputDimension, hiddenDimension,
initParamsStdDev, rng): new GruLayer(hiddenDimension, hiddenDimension,
initParamsStdDev, rng));
    }
    layers.Add(new FeedForwardLayer(hiddenDimension, outputDimension,
decoderUnit, initParamsStdDev, rng));
    return new NeuralNetwork(layers);
}


public static NeuralNetwork MakeRnn(int inputDimension, int
hiddenDimension, int hiddenLayers, int outputDimension, INonlinearity
hiddenUnit, INonlinearity decoderUnit, double initParamsStdDev, Random rng)
{
```

```
    List<ILayer> layers = new List<ILayer>();
    for (int h = 0; h<hiddenLayers; h++)
    {
        layers.Add(h == 0? new RnnLayer(inputDimension, hiddenDimension,
hiddenUnit, initParamsStdDev, rng)
        : new RnnLayer(hiddenDimension, hiddenDimension, hiddenUnit,
initParamsStdDev, rng));
    }
    layers.Add(new FeedForwardLayer(hiddenDimension, outputDimension,
decoderUnit, initParamsStdDev, rng));
    return new NeuralNetwork(layers);
}
```

Summary

In this chapter, we learned about GRUs. We showed how they compared to, and differed from, LSTM Networks. We also showed you an example program that tested all the network types we discussed and produced their outputs. We also compared how these networks are created.

I hope you enjoyed your journey with me throughout this book. As we as authors try and better understand what readers would like to see and hear, I welcome your constructive comments and feedback, which will only help to make the book and source code better. Till the next book, happy coding!

Activation Function Timings

The following images show different activation functions and their respective plots. Use this as a visual reference when dealing with individual function plots:

Method	Jit	Platform	Mean [us]
LogisticFunctionSteepDouble	LegacyJit	X64	17,938.40
LogisticFunctionSteepDouble	RyuJit	X64	17,986.50
LogisticFunctionSteepFloat	LegacyJit	X64	20,345.40
LogisticFunctionSteepFloat	RyuJit	X64	19,126.60
LogisticApproximantSteepDouble	LegacyJit	X64	10,405.70
LogisticApproximantSteepDouble	RyuJit	X64	10,381.50
LogisticApproximantSteepFloat	LegacyJit	X64	11,115.70
LogisticApproximantSteepFloat	RyuJit	X64	7,907.00
SoftSignDouble	LegacyJit	X64	10,353.10
SoftSignDouble	RyuJit	X64	10,323.40
SoftSignFloat	LegacyJit	X64	8,017.20
SoftSignFloat	RyuJit	X64	4,013.80
PolynomialApproximantDouble	LegacyJit	X64	14,044.90
PolynomialApproximantDouble	RyuJit	X64	16,130.00
PolynomialApproximantFloat	LegacyJit	X64	13,581.90
PolynomialApproximantFloat	RyuJit	X64	11,433.00
QuadraticSigmoidDouble	LegacyJit	X64	8,172.50
QuadraticSigmoidDouble	RyuJit	X64	7,697.00
QuadraticSigmoidFloat	LegacyJit	X64	13,394.50
QuadraticSigmoidFloat	RyuJit	X64	13,661.80
ReLUDouble	LegacyJit	X64	4,103.00
ReLUDouble	RyuJit	X64	9,556.20
ReLUFloat	LegacyJit	X64	4,051.10
ReLUFloat	RyuJit	X64	4,015.80

Method	Jit	Platform	Mean [us]
LeakyReLUDouble	LegacyJit	X64	4,092.50
LeakyReLUDouble	RyuJit	X64	8,770.30
LeakyReLUFloat	LegacyJit	X64	4,080.30
LeakyReLUFloat	RyuJit	X64	4,023.10
LeakyReLUShiftedDouble	LegacyJit	X64	4,365.00
LeakyReLUShiftedDouble	RyuJit	X64	6,448.50
LeakyReLUShiftedFloat	LegacyJit	X64	4,006.80
LeakyReLUShiftedFloat	RyuJit	X64	4,015.40
SReLUDouble	LegacyJit	X64	4,659.40
SReLUDouble	RyuJit	X64	4,558.00
SReLUFloat	LegacyJit	X64	6,579.80
SReLUFloat	RyuJit	X64	6,897.80
SReLUShiftedDouble	LegacyJit	X64	5,346.70
SReLUShiftedDouble	RyuJit	X64	4,769.10
SReLUShiftedFloat	LegacyJit	X64	6,211.00
SReLUShiftedFloat	RyuJit	X64	8,832.10
ArcTanDouble	LegacyJit	X64	22,159.30
ArcTanDouble	RyuJit	X64	20,893.20
ArcTanFloat	LegacyJit	X64	22,102.70
ArcTanFloat	RyuJit	X64	4,019.60
TanHDouble	LegacyJit	X64	27,611.30
TanHDouble	RyuJit	X64	27,182.50
TanHFloat	LegacyJit	X64	27,380.30
TanHFloat	RyuJit	X64	4,014.50

Activation Method	Jit	Mean [us]
ActivationFunction_SReLU	LegacyJit	1,361.70
ActivationFunction_SReLU	RyuJit	1,171.20
ActivationFunction_SReLUShifted	LegacyJit	1,415.60
ActivationFunction_SReLUShifted	RyuJit	1,205.50
ActivationFunction_Linear	LegacyJit	1,337.90
ActivationFunction_Linear	RyuJit	1,055.10
ActivationFunction_Sine	LegacyJit	4,751.90
ActivationFunction_Sine	RyuJit	4,987.20
ActivationFunction_Absolute	LegacyJit	1,332.00
ActivationFunction_Absolute	RyuJit	1,066.00
ActivationFunction_AbsoluteRoot	LegacyJit	1,332.90
ActivationFunction_AbsoluteRoot	RyuJit	1,194.50
ActivationFunction_StepFunction	LegacyJit	1,257.70
ActivationFunction_StepFunction	RyuJit	1,084.70
ActivationFunction_ArcSinH	LegacyJit	4,638.80
ActivationFunction_ArcSinH	RyuJit	4,290.90
ActivationFunction_ArcTan	LegacyJit	2,507.50
ActivationFunction_ArcTan	RyuJit	2,346.40
ActivationFunction_LogisticApproximantSteep	LegacyJit	1,335.90
ActivationFunction_LogisticApproximantSteep	RyuJit	1,153.50
ActivationFunction_LogisticFunction	LegacyJit	2,442.10
ActivationFunction_LogisticFunction	RyuJit	2,239.20
ActivationFunction_MaxMinusOne	LegacyJit	1,255.20
ActivationFunction_MaxMinusOne	RyuJit	1,057.40
ActivationFunction_PolynomialApproximantSteep	LegacyJit	1,777.20
ActivationFunction_PolynomialApproximantSteep	RyuJit	1,758.90
ActivationFunction_ScaledELU	LegacyJit	1,337.40
ActivationFunction_ScaledELU	RyuJit	1,088.90
ActivationFunction_SoftSignSteep	LegacyJit	1,330.20
ActivationFunction_SoftSignSteep	RyuJit	1,120.50
ActivationFunction_TanH	LegacyJit	3,763.20
ActivationFunction_TanH	RyuJit	3,569.10

Activation Method	Jit	Mean [us]
ActivationFunction_BipolarGaussian	LegacyJit	10,072.10
ActivationFunction_BipolarGaussian	RyuJit	10,009.50
ActivationFunction_Gaussian	LegacyJit	9,972.40
ActivationFunction_Gaussian	RyuJit	9,954.30
ActivationFunction_RbfGaussian	LegacyJit	4,998.40
ActivationFunction_RbfGaussian	RyuJit	4,979.00
ActivationFunction_BipolarSigmoid	LegacyJit	2,372.70
ActivationFunction_BipolarSigmoid	RyuJit	3,527.80
ActivationFunction_InverseAbsoluteSigmoid	LegacyJit	1,345.20
ActivationFunction_InverseAbsoluteSigmoid	RyuJit	1,122.80
ActivationFunction_PlainSigmoid	LegacyJit	2,444.30
ActivationFunction_PlainSigmoid	RyuJit	2,230.20
ActivationFunction_ReducedSigmoid	LegacyJit	2,501.10
ActivationFunction_ReducedSigmoid	RyuJit	2,250.90
ActivationFunction_SteepenedSigmoid	LegacyJit	2,308.30
ActivationFunction_SteepenedSigmoid	RyuJit	2,121.90
ActivationFunction_SteepenedSigmoidApproximation	LegacyJit	1,315.00
ActivationFunction_SteepenedSigmoidApproximation	RyuJit	1,202.10
ActivationFunction_QuadraticSigmoid	LegacyJit	1,521.80
ActivationFunction_QuadraticSigmoid	RyuJit	1,363.60
ActivationFunction_LeakyReLU	LegacyJit	1,363.30
ActivationFunction_LeakyReLU	RyuJit	1,169.60
ActivationFunction_LeakyReLUShifted	LegacyJit	1,356.40
ActivationFunction_LeakyReLUShifted	RyuJit	1,203.80

Function Optimization Reference

The Currin Exponential function

The following is a pictorial representation of Currin Exponential function:

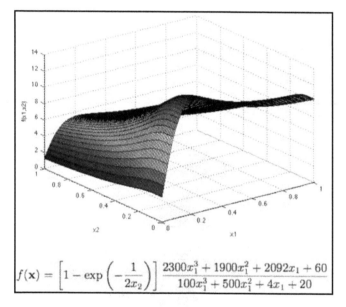

$$f(\mathbf{x}) = \left[1 - \exp\left(-\frac{1}{2x_2}\right)\right] \frac{2300x_1^3 + 1900x_1^2 + 2092x_1 + 60}{100x_1^3 + 500x_1^2 + 4x_1 + 20}$$

Currin Exponential function

Description

Dimensions: 2
This function is a simple two-dimensional example that occurs several times in the literature on computer experiments.

Input domain

The function is evaluated on the xi ∈ [0, 1] square, for all i = 1, 2.

Modifications and alternative forms

For the purpose of multi-fidelity simulation, Xiong et al. (2013) use the following function for the lower fidelity code:

$$f_L = \frac{1}{4}[f(x_1 + 0.05, x_2 + 0.05) + f(x_1 + 0.05, max(0, x_2 - 0.05))] + \frac{1}{4}[f(x_1 - 0.05, x_2 + 0.05) + f(x_1 - 0.05, max(0, x_2 - 0.05))]$$

The Webster function

The following is the Webster function:

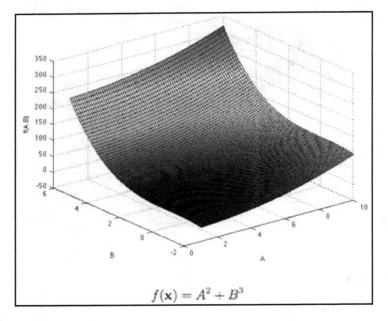

$$f(\mathbf{x}) = A^2 + B^3$$

Webster function

Description

Dimensions: 2

This function is used by Webster et al. (1996), with the assumption that the relationship between A, B, and Y is a black box.

Input distributions

The distributions of the input random variables are A ~ Uniform[1, 10], and B ~ N(μ=2, σ=1).

The Oakley & O'Hagan function

The pictorial representation of the Oakley & O'Hagan function is:

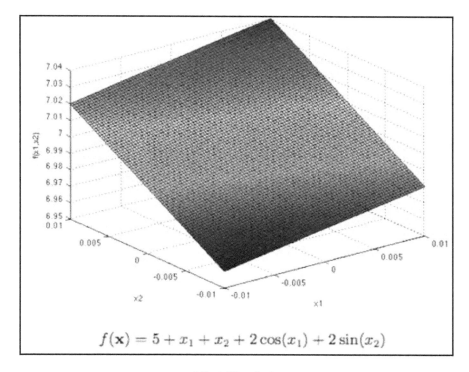

$$f(\mathbf{x}) = 5 + x_1 + x_2 + 2\cos(x_1) + 2\sin(x_2)$$

Oakley & O'Hagan function

Description

Dimensions: 2

This function is used by Oakley & O'Hagan (2002) as a simple illustrative example to show the discontinuity in the calculation of the posterior mean of the distribution function of the output.

Input domain

The domain of the random input variables is the xi ∈ [-0.01, 0.01] square, for all i = 1, 2.

The Grammacy function

The following is the Grammacy function:

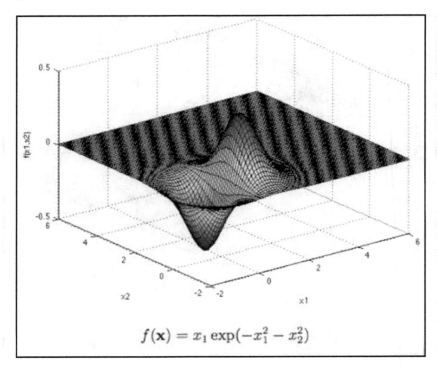

$$f(\mathbf{x}) = x_1 \exp(-x_1^2 - x_2^2)$$

Grammacy function

Description

Dimensions: 2

This function is a simple two-dimensional example used to illustrate methods of modeling computer-experiment output.

Input fomain

This function is evaluated on the xi ∈ [-2, 6] square, for all i = 1, 2.

Franke's function

The Franke's function is shown as follow:

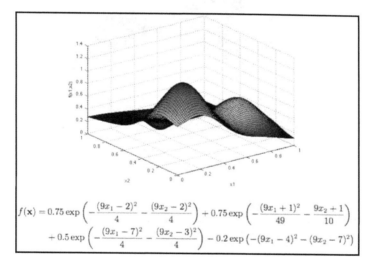

$$f(\mathbf{x}) = 0.75 \exp\left(-\frac{(9x_1 - 2)^2}{4} - \frac{(9x_2 - 2)^2}{4}\right) + 0.75 \exp\left(-\frac{(9x_1 + 1)^2}{49} - \frac{9x_2 + 1}{10}\right)$$
$$+ 0.5 \exp\left(-\frac{(9x_1 - 7)^2}{4} - \frac{(9x_2 - 3)^2}{4}\right) - 0.2 \exp\left(-(9x_1 - 4)^2 - (9x_2 - 7)^2\right)$$

Franke's function

Description

Dimensions: 2

Franke's function has two Gaussian peaks of different heights, and a smaller dip. It is used as a test function in interpolation problems.

Input domain

The function is evaluated on the xi ∈ [0, 1] square, for all i = 1, 2.

The Lim function

Here is a pictorial representation of the Lim function:

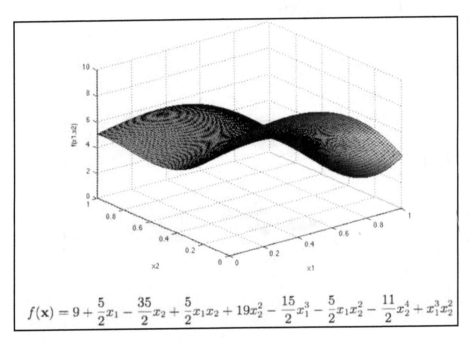

$$f(\mathbf{x}) = 9 + \frac{5}{2}x_1 - \frac{35}{2}x_2 + \frac{5}{2}x_1x_2 + 19x_2^2 - \frac{15}{2}x_1^3 - \frac{5}{2}x_1x_2^2 - \frac{11}{2}x_2^4 + x_1^3x_2^2$$

Lim Function

Description

Dimensions: 2

This function is a polynomial in two dimensions, with terms up to degree 5. It is nonlinear, and it is smooth despite being complex, which is common for computer experiment functions (Lim et al., 2002).

Input domain

The function is evaluated on the square xi ∈ [0, 1], for all i = 1, 2.

The Ackley function

Let's see the Ackley function:

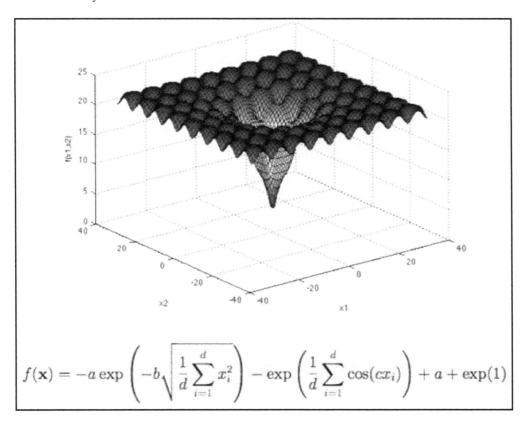

$$f(\mathbf{x}) = -a \exp\left(-b\sqrt{\frac{1}{d}\sum_{i=1}^{d} x_i^2}\right) - \exp\left(\frac{1}{d}\sum_{i=1}^{d} \cos(cx_i)\right) + a + \exp(1)$$

Ackley function

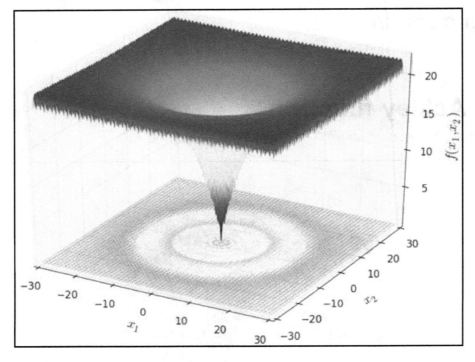

Ackley function

Description

Dimensions: d

The Ackley function is widely used to test optimization algorithms. In its two-dimensional form, as shown in the preceding plot, it is characterized by a nearly flat outer region, and a large hole at the center. The function poses a risk for optimization algorithms, particularly hill-climbing algorithms, to be trapped in one of its many local minima.

Recommended variable values are a = 20, b = 0.2, and c = 2π.

Input domain

The function is usually evaluated on the xi ∈ [-32.768, 32.768] hypercube, for all i = 1, ..., d, although it may also be restricted to a smaller domain.

Global minimum

$$f(x^*) = 0, at\ x^* = (0, \dots, 0)$$

The Bukin function N6

The Bulkin function N6 is:

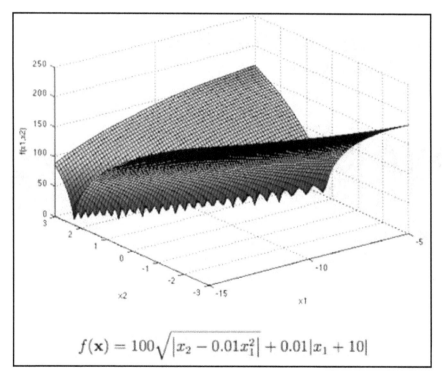

$$f(\mathbf{x}) = 100\sqrt{\left|x_2 - 0.01x_1^2\right|} + 0.01|x_1 + 10|$$

The Bulkin function N6

Description

Dimensions: 2

The sixth Bukin function has many local minima, all of which lie in a ridge.

Input domain

The function is usually evaluated on the x1 ∈ [-15, -5], x2 ∈ [-3, 3] rectangle.

Global minimum

$$f(x^*) = 0, at\ x^* = (-10, 1)$$

The Cross-In-Tray function

The Cross-In-Tray function looks like:

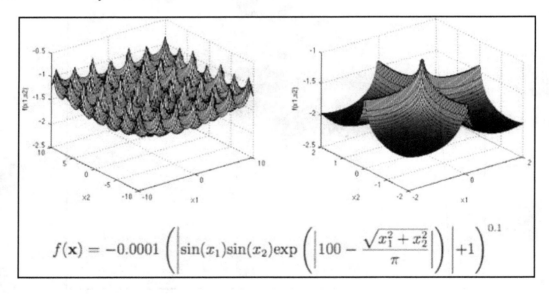

$$f(\mathbf{x}) = -0.0001 \left(\left| \sin(x_1)\sin(x_2)\exp\left(\left|100 - \frac{\sqrt{x_1^2 + x_2^2}}{\pi}\right| \right) \right| + 1 \right)^{0.1}$$

Cross-In-Tray Function

Description

Dimensions: 2

The Cross-in-Tray function has multiple global minima. It is shown here with a smaller domain in the second plot, so that its characteristic *cross* will be visible.

Input domain

The function is usually evaluated on the xi ∈ [-10, 10] square, for all i = 1, 2.

Global minima

$$f(x^*) = -2.06261, at \ x^* = (1.3491, -1.3491), (1.3491, 1.3491), (-1.3491, 1.3491)$$

$$and \ (-1.3491, -1.3491)$$

The Drop-Wave function

The Drop-Wave function is shown as:

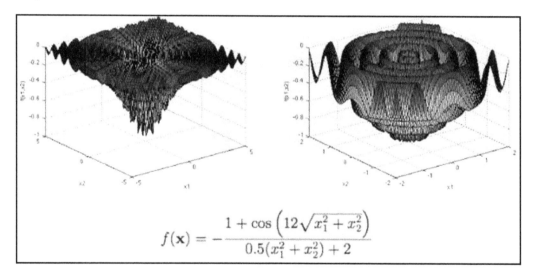

$$f(\mathbf{x}) = -\frac{1 + \cos\left(12\sqrt{x_1^2 + x_2^2}\right)}{0.5(x_1^2 + x_2^2) + 2}$$

Drop-wave Function

Description

Dimensions: 2

The Drop-Wave function is multimodal and highly complex. The preceding plot on the right shows the function on a smaller input domain, to illustrate its characteristic features.

Input domain

The function is usually evaluated on the xi ∈ [-5.12, 5.12] square, for all i = 1, 2.

Global minimum

$$f(x^*) = 0, at\ x^* = (0,0)$$

The Eggholder function

The Eggholder function pictorially represented as:

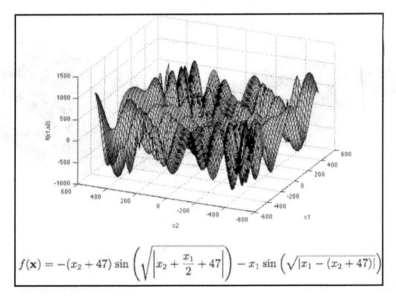

$$f(\mathbf{x}) = -(x_2 + 47)\sin\left(\sqrt{\left|x_2 + \frac{x_1}{2} + 47\right|}\right) - x_1 \sin\left(\sqrt{|x_1 - (x_2 + 47)|}\right)$$

The Eggholder function

Description

Dimensions: 2
The Eggholder function is a difficult function to optimize, because of the large number of local minima.

Input domain

The function is usually evaluated on the xi ∈ [-512, 512] square, for all i = 1, 2.

Global minimum

$$f(x^*) = -959.6407, at\ x^* = (512, 404.2319)$$

The Holder Table function

The Holder Table function looks just like its name:

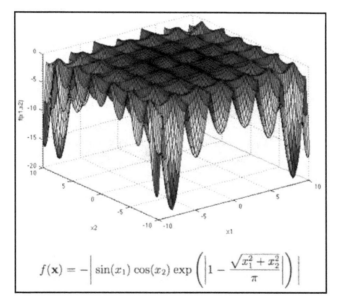

$$f(\mathbf{x}) = -\left|\ \sin(x_1)\cos(x_2)\exp\left(\left|1 - \frac{\sqrt{x_1^2 + x_2^2}}{\pi}\right|\right)\ \right|$$

Holder Table function

Description

Dimensions: 2
The Holder Table function has many local minima, with four global minima.

Input domain

The function is usually evaluated on the xi ∈ [-10, 10] square, for all i = 1, 2.

Global minimum

$f(x^*) = -19.2085, at\ x^* = (8.05502, 9.66459), (8.05502, -9.66459), (-8.05502, 9.66459)\ and\ (-8.05502, -9.66459)$

The Levy function

The Levy function is as shown here:

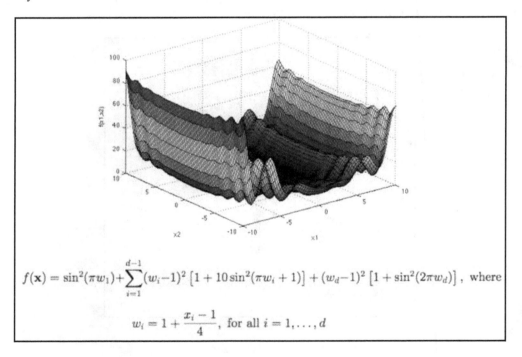

$$f(\mathbf{x}) = \sin^2(\pi w_1) + \sum_{i=1}^{d-1}(w_i-1)^2\left[1+10\sin^2(\pi w_i+1)\right] + (w_d-1)^2\left[1+\sin^2(2\pi w_d)\right],\ \text{where}$$

$$w_i = 1 + \frac{x_i - 1}{4},\ \text{for all}\ i = 1,\dots,d$$

The Levy function

Description

Dimensions: d

Input domain

The function is usually evaluated on the xi ∈ [-10, 10] hypercube, for all i = 1, ..., d.

Global minimum

$$f(x^*) = 0, at\ x^* = (1, \ldots, 1)$$

The Levy function N13

The Levy function N13 is as shown here:

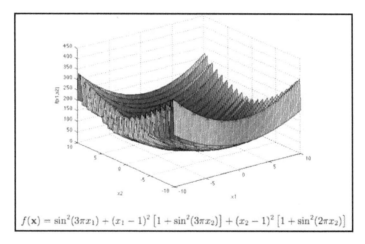

$$f(\mathbf{x}) = \sin^2(3\pi x_1) + (x_1 - 1)^2 \left[1 + \sin^2(3\pi x_2)\right] + (x_2 - 1)^2 \left[1 + \sin^2(2\pi x_2)\right]$$

The Levy function N13

Description

Dimensions: 2

Input domain

The function is usually evaluated on the xi ∈ [-10, 10] square, for all i = 1, 2.

Global minimum

$$f(x^*) = 0, at\ x^* = (1,1)$$

The Rastrigin function

The Rastrigin function is depicted as:

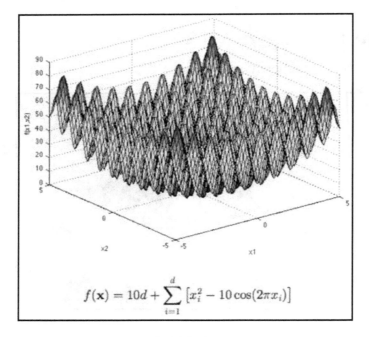

$$f(\mathbf{x}) = 10d + \sum_{i=1}^{d} \left[x_i^2 - 10\cos(2\pi x_i) \right]$$

Rastrigin Function

Description

Dimensions: d

The Rastrigin function has several local minima. It is highly multimodal, but locations of the minima are regularly distributed. It is shown in its two-dimensional form in the preceding plot.

Input domain

The function is usually evaluated on the xi ∈ [-5.12, 5.12] hypercube, for all i = 1, ..., d.

Global minimum

$$f(x^*) = 0, at\ x^* = (0, \ldots, 0)$$

The Schaffer function N.2

Here, the Schaffer function N.2 is depicted:

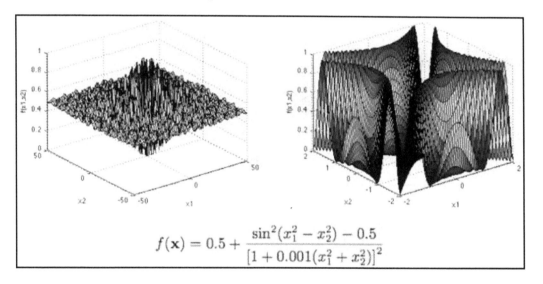

$$f(\mathbf{x}) = 0.5 + \frac{\sin^2(x_1^2 - x_2^2) - 0.5}{[1 + 0.001(x_1^2 + x_2^2)]^2}$$

The Schaffer function N.2

Description

Dimensions: 2
The second Schaffer function. It is shown on a smaller input domain in the plot on the right to show detail.

Input domain

The function is usually evaluated on the xi ∈ [-100, 100] square, for all i = 1, 2.

Global minimum

$$f(x^*) = 0, at\ x^* = (0,0)$$

The Schaffer function N.4

The Schaffer function N.4 is as:

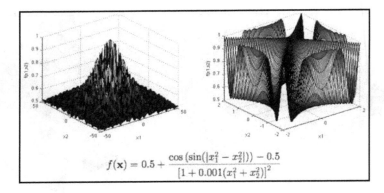

$$f(\mathbf{x}) = 0.5 + \frac{\cos\left(\sin(|x_1^2 - x_2^2|)\right) - 0.5}{\left[1 + 0.001(x_1^2 + x_2^2)\right]^2}$$

The Schaffer function N.4

Description

Dimensions: 2

The fourth Schaffer function. It is shown on a smaller input domain in the plot on the right to show detail.

Input domain

The function is usually evaluated on the xi ∈ [-100, 100] square, for all i = 1, 2.

The Shubert function

The Shubert function is pictured here:

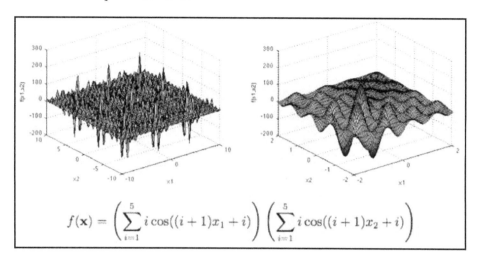

$$f(\mathbf{x}) = \left(\sum_{i=1}^{5} i \cos((i+1)x_1 + i) \right) \left(\sum_{i=1}^{5} i \cos((i+1)x_2 + i) \right)$$

Shubert function

Description

Dimensions: 2

The Shubert function has several local minima and many global minima. The plot on the right shows the function on a smaller input domain, to allow for easier viewing.

Input domain

The function is usually evaluated on the xi ∈ [-10, 10] square, for all i = 1, 2, although this may be restricted to the xi ∈ [-5.12, 5.12] square, for all i = 1, 2.

Global minimum

$$f(x^*) = -186.7309$$

The Rotated Hyper-Ellipsoid function

The following is the Rotated Hyper-Ellipsoid function

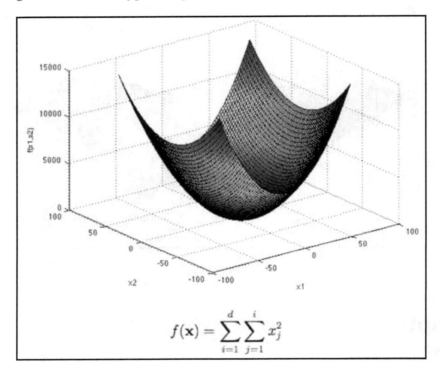

$$f(\mathbf{x}) = \sum_{i=1}^{d} \sum_{j=1}^{i} x_j^2$$

Rotated Hyper-Ellipsoid Function

Description

Dimensions: d
The Rotated Hyper-Ellipsoid function is continuous, convex, and unimodal. It is an extension of the Axis Parallel Hyper-Ellipsoid function, also referred to as the Sum Squares function. The plot shows its two-dimensional form.

Input domain

The function is usually evaluated on the xi ∈ [-65.536, 65.536] hypercube, for all i = 1, …, d.

Global minimum

$$f(x^*) = 0, at \ x^* = (0, \ldots, 0)$$

The Sum Squares function

The Sum Squares function is as shown here:

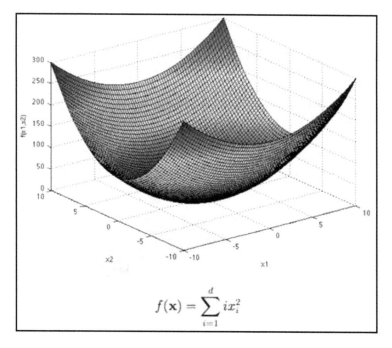

$$f(\mathbf{x}) = \sum_{i=1}^{d} i x_i^2$$

Sum Squares function

Description

Dimensions: d

The Sum Squares function, also referred to as the Axis Parallel Hyper-Ellipsoid function, has no local minimum except the global one. It is continuous, convex, and unimodal. It is shown here in its two-dimensional form.

Input domain

The function is usually evaluated on the xi ∈ [-10, 10] hypercube, for all i = 1, …, d, although this may be restricted to the xi ∈ [-5.12, 5.12] hypercube, for all i = 1, …, d.

Global minimum

$$f(x^*) = 0, at\ x^* = (0, \dots, 0)$$

The Booth function

The Booth function is depicted as:

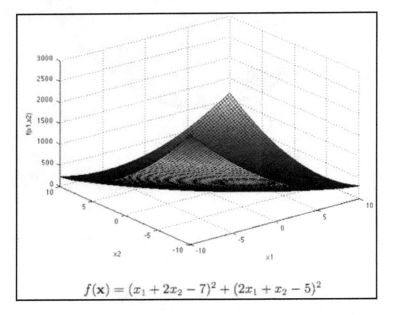

$$f(\mathbf{x}) = (x_1 + 2x_2 - 7)^2 + (2x_1 + x_2 - 5)^2$$

The Booth function

Description

Dimensions: 2

Input domain

The function is usually evaluated on the xi ∈ [-10, 10] square, for all i = 1, 2.

Global minimum

$$f(x^*) = 0, at\ x^* = (1,3)$$

The Mccormick function

The Mccormick function is show as follow:

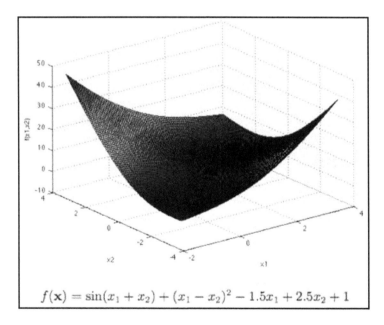

$$f(\mathbf{x}) = \sin(x_1 + x_2) + (x_1 - x_2)^2 - 1.5x_1 + 2.5x_2 + 1$$

Mccormick function

Description

Dimensions: 2

Input domain

The function is usually evaluated on the x1 ∈ [-1.5, 4], x2 ∈ [-3, 4] rectangle.

Global minimum

$$f(x^*) = -1.9133, at\ x^* = (-0.54719, -1.54719)$$

The Power Sum function

Depicted here is the Power Sum function:

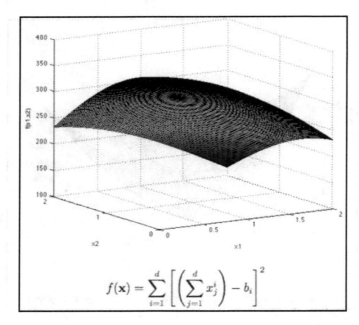

$$f(\mathbf{x}) = \sum_{i=1}^{d} \left[\left(\sum_{j=1}^{d} x_j^i \right) - b_i \right]^2$$

The Power Sum function

Description

Dimensions: d

The Power Sum function. It is shown here in its two-dimensional form. The recommended value of the b-vector, for d = 4, is: **b** = (8, 18, 44, 114).

Input domain

The function is usually evaluated on the xi ∈ [0, d] hypercube, for all i = 1, …, d.

The Three-Hump Camel function

The pictorial representation of the Three-Hump Camel function is as:

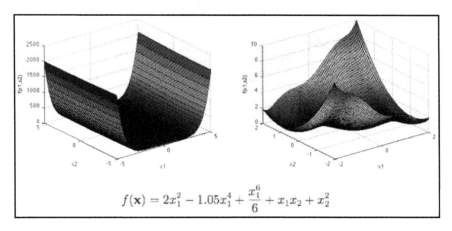

$$f(\mathbf{x}) = 2x_1^2 - 1.05x_1^4 + \frac{x_1^6}{6} + x_1x_2 + x_2^2$$

The Three Hump Camel function

Description

Dimensions: 2
The plot on the left shows the three-hump Camel function on its recommended input domain, and the plot on the right shows only a portion of this domain, to allow for easier viewing of the function's key characteristics. The function has three local minima.

Input domain

The function is usually evaluated on the square xi ∈ [-5, 5], for all i = 1, 2.

Global minimum

$$f(x^*) = 0, at\ x^* = (0,0)$$

The Easom function

Following is the Easom function:

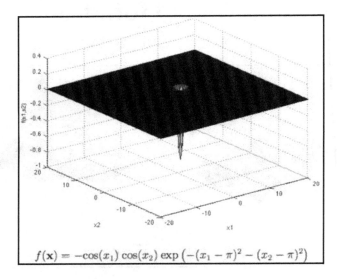

$$f(\mathbf{x}) = -\cos(x_1)\cos(x_2)\exp\left(-(x_1 - \pi)^2 - (x_2 - \pi)^2\right)$$

The Easom function

Description

Dimensions: 2

The Easom function has several local minima. It is unimodal, and the global minimum has a small area relative to the search space.

Input domain

The function is usually evaluated on the xi ∈ [-100, 100] square, for all i = 1, 2.

Global minimum

$$f(x^*) = 0, at \ x^* = (\textstyle\prod, \prod)$$

The Michalewicz function

The Michalewicz function is shown here:

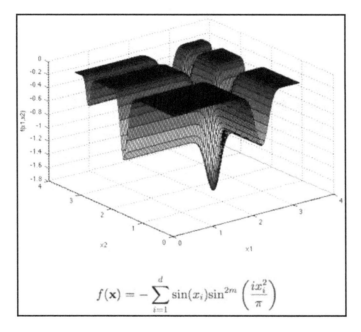

$$f(\mathbf{x}) = -\sum_{i=1}^{d} \sin(x_i)\sin^{2m}\left(\frac{ix_i^2}{\pi}\right)$$

Michalewicz function

Description

Dimensions: d
The Michalewicz function has d! local minima, and it is multimodal. The m parameter defines the steepness of the valleys and ridges; a larger m leads to a more difficult search. The recommended value of m is m = 10. The function's two-dimensional form is shown in the preceding plot.

Input domain

The function is usually evaluated on the xi ∈ [0, π] hypercube, for all i = 1, …, d.

Global minima

$$atd = 2 : f(x^*) = -1.8013, at\ x^* = (2.20, 1.57)$$
$$at\ d = 5 : f(x^*) = -4.687658$$
$$at\ d = 10 : f(x^*) = -9.66015$$

The Beale function

The Beale function is shown as follow:

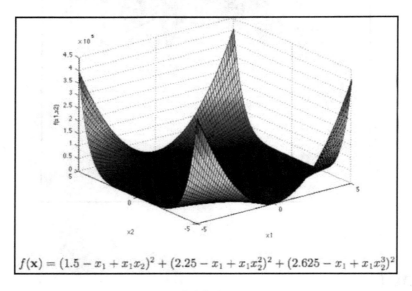

$$f(\mathbf{x}) = (1.5 - x_1 + x_1 x_2)^2 + (2.25 - x_1 + x_1 x_2^2)^2 + (2.625 - x_1 + x_1 x_2^3)^2$$

Beale function

Description

Dimensions: 2
The Beale function is multimodal, with sharp peaks at the corners of the input domain.

Input domain

The function is usually evaluated on the xi ∈ [-4.5, 4.5] square, for all i = 1, 2.

Global minimum

$$f(x^*) = 0, at\ x^* = (3, 0.5)$$

The Goldstein-Price function

The Goldstein-Price function is shown as follow:

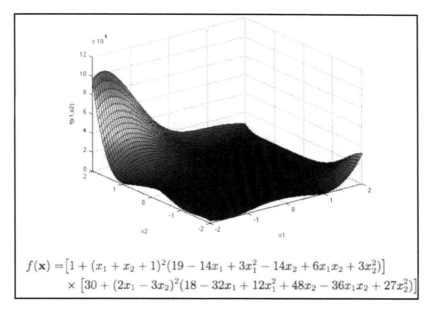

$$f(\mathbf{x}) = \left[1 + (x_1 + x_2 + 1)^2(19 - 14x_1 + 3x_1^2 - 14x_2 + 6x_1x_2 + 3x_2^2)\right]$$
$$\times \left[30 + (2x_1 - 3x_2)^2(18 - 32x_1 + 12x_1^2 + 48x_2 - 36x_1x_2 + 27x_2^2)\right]$$

Goldstein-Price function

Description

Dimensions: 2
The Goldstein-Price function has several local minima.

Input domain

The function is usually evaluated on the xi ∈ [-2, 2] square, for all i = 1, 2.

Global minimum

$$f(x^*) = 3, at\ x^* = (0, -1)$$

The Perm function

The Perm function is depicted as:

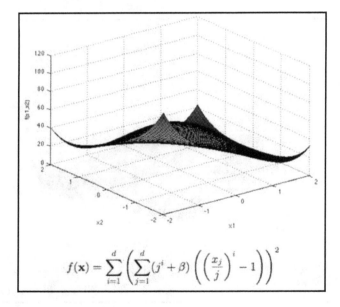

$$f(\mathbf{x}) = \sum_{i=1}^{d}\left(\sum_{j=1}^{d}(j^i + \beta)\left(\left(\frac{x_j}{j}\right)^i - 1\right)\right)^2$$

The Perm function

Description

Dimensions: d
The Perm d, β function.

Input domain

The function is usually evaluated on the xi ∈ [-d, d] hypercube, for all i = 1, …, d.

Global minimum

$$f(x^*) = 0, at\ x^* = (1, 2, \ldots, d)$$

The Griewank function

The Griewank function is shown as follow:

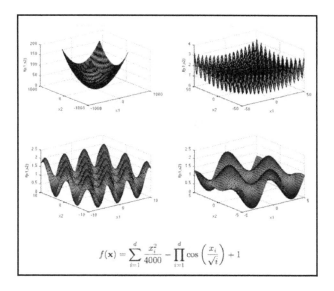

$$f(\mathbf{x}) = \sum_{i=1}^{d} \frac{x_i^2}{4000} - \prod_{i=1}^{d} \cos\left(\frac{x_i}{\sqrt{i}}\right) + 1$$

Griewank function

Description

Dimensions: d

The Griewank function has many widespread local minima, which are regularly distributed. The complexity is shown in the zoomed-in plots.

Input domain

The function is usually evaluated on the xi ∈ [-600, 600] hypercube, for all i = 1, ..., d.

Global minimum

$$f(x^*) = 0, at\ x^* = (0, \dots, 0)$$

The Bohachevsky function

The Bohachevsky function is depicted here:

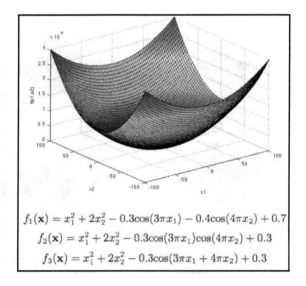

$$f_1(\mathbf{x}) = x_1^2 + 2x_2^2 - 0.3\cos(3\pi x_1) - 0.4\cos(4\pi x_2) + 0.7$$
$$f_2(\mathbf{x}) = x_1^2 + 2x_2^2 - 0.3\cos(3\pi x_1)\cos(4\pi x_2) + 0.3$$
$$f_3(\mathbf{x}) = x_1^2 + 2x_2^2 - 0.3\cos(3\pi x_1 + 4\pi x_2) + 0.3$$

Bohachevsky function

Description

Dimensions: 2

The Bohachevsky functions all have the same similar bowl shape. The one shown in the preceding image is the first function.

Input domain

The functions are usually evaluated on the xi ∈ [-100, 100] square, for all i = 1, 2.

Global minimum

$$f_j(x^*) = 0, at \ x^* = (0,0), for \ all \ j = 1,2,3$$

The Sphere function

The pictorial representation of pictorial function is:

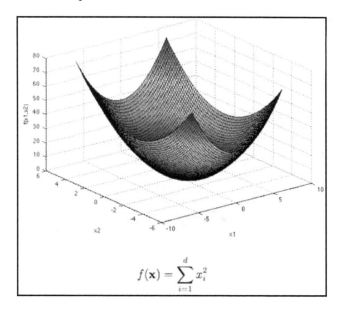

$$f(\mathbf{x}) = \sum_{i=1}^{d} x_i^2$$

The sphere function

Description

Dimensions: d

The sphere function has d local minima except for the global one. It is continuous, convex, and unimodal. The plot shows its two-dimensional form.

Input domain

The function is usually evaluated on the xi ∈ [-5.12, 5.12] hypercube, for all i = 1, …, d.

Global minimum

$$f(x^*) = 0, at\ x^* = (0, \ldots, 0)$$

$$f(x) = \frac{1}{899}\left(\sum_{i=1}^{6} 2^i - 1745\right)$$

The Rosenbrock function

The Rosenbrock function is shown as follow:

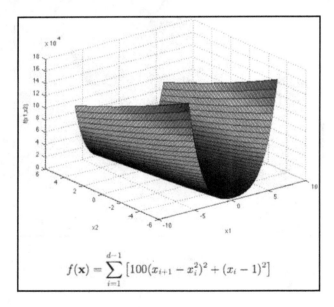

$$f(\mathbf{x}) = \sum_{i=1}^{d-1}\left[100(x_{i+1} - x_i^2)^2 + (x_i - 1)^2\right]$$

Rosenbrock function

Description

Dimensions: d

The Rosenbrock function, also referred to as the Valley or Banana function, is a popular test problem for gradient-based optimization algorithms. It is shown in the preceding plot in its two-dimensional form.

The function is unimodal, and the global minimum lies in a narrow, parabolic valley. However, even though this valley is easy to find, convergence to the minimum is difficult (Picheny et al., 2012).

Input domain

The function is usually evaluated on the $x_i \in$ [-5, 10] hypercube, for all i = 1, ..., d, although it may be restricted to the $x_i \in$ [-2.048, 2.048] hypercube, for all i = 1, ..., d.

Global minimum

$$f(x^*) = 0, at\ x^* = (1, \ldots, 1)$$

The Styblinski-Tang function

The Styblinski-Tang function is depicted as follow:

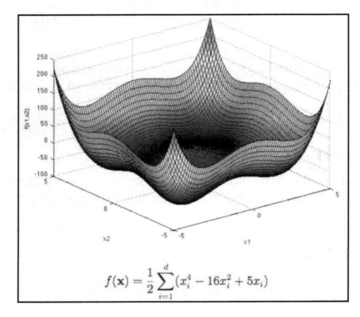

$$f(\mathbf{x}) = \frac{1}{2}\sum_{i=1}^{d}(x_i^4 - 16x_i^2 + 5x_i)$$

Styblinski-Tang function

Description

Dimensions: d

The Styblinski-Tang function is shown here in its two-dimensional form.

Input domain

The function is usually evaluated on the xi ∈ [-5, 5] hypercube, for all i = 1, ..., d.

Global minimum

$$f(x^*) = -39.16599d, \, at \, x^* = (-2.903534, \ldots, -2.903534)$$

Summary

In this chapter, we have shown you individual optimization functions, as well as their visual representations, global and local minima, and mathematical variants.

Keep reading

[1] Surjanovic, S. & Bingham, D. (2013). Virtual Library of Simulation Experiments: Test Functions and Datasets. Retrieved June 26, 2018, from `http://www.sfu.ca/~ssurjano`. Reprinted with permission

Adorio, E. P., & Diliman, U. P. MVF - Multivariate Test Functions Library in C for Unconstrained Global Optimization (2005). Retrieved June 2013, from `http://www.geocities.ws/eadorio/mvf.pdf`.

Molga, M., & Smutnicki, C. Test functions for optimization needs (2005). Retrieved June 2013, from `http://www.zsd.ict.pwr.wroc.pl/files/docs/functions.pdf`.

Back, T. (1996). *Evolutionary algorithms in theory and practice: evolution strategies, evolutionary programming, genetic algorithms*. Oxford University Press on Demand.

Other Books You May Enjoy

If you enjoyed this book, you may be interested in these other books by Packt:

C# Machine Learning Projects
Yoon Hyup Hwang

ISBN: 9781788996402

- Set up the C# environment for machine learning with required packages
- Build classification models for spam email filtering
- Get to grips with feature engineering using NLP techniques for Twitter sentiment analysis
- Forecast foreign exchange rates using continuous and time-series data
- Make a recommendation model for music genre recommendation
- Familiarize yourself with munging image data and Neural Network models for handwritten-digit recognition
- Use Principal Component Analysis (PCA) for cyber attack detection
- One-Class Support Vector Machine for credit card fraud detection

Hands-On Machine Learning with C#
Matt R. Cole

ISBN: 9781788994941

- Learn to parameterize a probabilistic problem
- Use Naive Bayes to visually plot and analyze data
- Plot a text-based representation of a decision tree using nuML
- Use the Accord.NET machine learning framework for associative rule-based learning
- Develop machine learning algorithms utilizing fuzzy logic
- Explore support vector machines for image recognition
- Understand dynamic time warping for sequence recognition

Leave a review - let other readers know what you think

Please share your thoughts on this book with others by leaving a review on the site that you bought it from. If you purchased the book from Amazon, please leave us an honest review on this book's Amazon page. This is vital so that other potential readers can see and use your unbiased opinion to make purchasing decisions, we can understand what our customers think about our products, and our authors can see your feedback on the title that they have worked with Packt to create. It will only take a few minutes of your time, but is valuable to other potential customers, our authors, and Packt. Thank you!

Index

neurons 9, 16, 35
nodes 9

O

observations 56
optimization functions
  adding 177
  maximization 177
  minimization 177
  new functions, adding 178, 179, 181, 182
  purpose of functions 177
optimization problem
  parallelizing 198
optimization
  about 62
  constraints 187
  fitness function 186
  meta-optimization 190
  methods 193
  parallel methods 198
  parameter tuning 198
  problems 186
optimizer
  selecting 193
overfitting 57

P

parallelism
  code, executing 198, 200
  using 198
particle 143
Particle Swarm Optimization (PSO)
  about 122, 196
  executing 152
  fitness 126
  original 127
  parameter effects 128
  position 126
  search strategy 127
  search strategy, pseudo-code 127
  types 123, 125, 126
  used, for replacing back propagation 129, 131, 133
  velocity 126
  working 196

Pattern Search (PS)
  working 194
PBEST 124
perceptrons
  about 16, 18
  uses 18, 20
precision 62

Q

QuickNN 250

R

random forests
  about 54
  advantages 55
  disadvantages 55
  features 55
randomness
  controlling 150
rank 218
Recall 62
reinforcement learning 15
related transformation rule 218
Restricted Boltzmann Machines (RBMs) 107
results
  back results, playing 174, 176
  information tree, updating 176, 177
  plotting 174
RNN 255, 257

S

sample application 63, 64
sequence axis 235
SharpLearning
  about 56
  model, saving 56
  models, loading 61
  models, saving 56, 61
SharpNeat
  reference 25
short-term memory 14
sigmoid function 34
sparse autoencoders 106
sparsity driver 106
splitting metric 52

www.ingramcontent.com/pod-product-compliance
Lightning Source LLC
Chambersburg PA
CBHW080623060326
40690CB00021B/4790